ADAPTING VALUES:
TRACING THE LIFE OF A RUBRIC THROUGH INSTITUTIONAL ETHNOGRAPHY

PERSPECTIVES ON WRITING

Series Editors: Rich Rice, Heather MacNeill Falconer, and J. Michael Rifenburg
Consulting Editor: Susan H. McLeod | Associate Editor: Hope Walker

The Perspectives on Writing series addresses writing studies in a broad sense. Consistent with the wide ranging approaches characteristic of teaching and scholarship in writing across the curriculum, the series presents works that take divergent perspectives on working as a writer, teaching writing, administering writing programs, and studying writing in its various forms.

The WAC Clearinghouse, Colorado State University Open Press, and University Press of Colorado are collaborating so that these books will be widely available through free digital distribution and low-cost print editions. The publishers and the Series editors are committed to the principle that knowledge should freely circulate. We see the opportunities that new technologies have for further democratizing knowledge. And we see that to share the power of writing is to share the means for all to articulate their needs, interest, and learning into the great experiment of literacy.

Recent Books in the Series

Chris M. Anson and Pamela Flash (Eds.), *Writing-Enriched Curricula: Models of Faculty-Driven and Departmental Transformation* (2021)

Alexandria L. Lockett, Iris D. Ruiz, James Chase Sanchez, and Christopher Carter (Eds.), *Race, Rhetoric, and Research Methods* (2021)

Kristopher M. Lotier, *Postprocess Postmortem* (2021)

Ryan J. Dippre and Talinn Phillips (Eds.), *Approaches to Lifespan Writing Research: Generating an Actionable Coherence* (2020)

Lesley Erin Bartlett, Sandra L. Tarabochia, Andrea R. Olinger, and Margaret J. Marshall (Eds.), *Diverse Approaches to Teaching, Learning, and Writing Across the Curriculum: IWAC at 25* (2020)

Hannah J. Rule, *Situating Writing Processes* (2019)

Asao B. Inoue, *Labor-Based Grading Contracts: Building Equity and Inclusion in the Compassionate Writing Classroom* (2019)

Mark Sutton and Sally Chandler (Eds.), *The Writing Studio Sampler: Stories About Change* (2018)

Kristine L. Blair and Lee Nickoson (Eds.), *Composing Feminist Interventions: Activism, Engagement, Praxis* (2018)

Mya Poe, Asao B. Inoue, and Norbert Elliot (Eds.), *Writing Assessment, Social Justice, and the Advancement of Opportunity* (2018)

ADAPTING VALUES: TRACING THE LIFE OF A RUBRIC THROUGH INSTITUTIONAL ETHNOGRAPHY

By Jennifer Grouling

The WAC Clearinghouse
wac.colostate.edu
Fort Collins, Colorado

University Press of Colorado
upcolorado.com
Denver, Colorado

The WAC Clearinghouse, Fort Collins, Colorado 80523

University Press of Colorado, Denver, Colorado 80202

ISBN 978-1-64215-164-0 (PDF) | 978-1-64215-165-7 (ePub) | 978-1-64642-383-5 (pbk.)

DOI: 10.37514/PER-B.2022.1640

Produced in the United States of America

Library of Congress Cataloging-in-Publication Data

Names: Grouling, Jennifer, 1976– author.
Title: Adapting VALUEs : tracing the life of a rubric through institutional ethnography / by Jennifer Grouling.
Description: Fort Collins, Colorado : The WAC Clearinghouse and University Press of Colorado, [2022] | Series: Perspectives on writing | Includes bibliographical references and index.
Identifiers: LCCN 2022036539 (print) | LCCN 2022036540 (ebook) | ISBN 9781646423835 (paperback) | ISBN 9781642151640 (adobe pdf) | ISBN 9781642151657 (epub)
Subjects: LCSH: Academic writing—Study and teaching—Evaluation. | Academic writing—Research. | English language—Rhetoric—Study and teaching—Evaluation. | Writing centers—Sociological aspects. | School improvement programs. | College teachers—Attitudes. | Teacher participation in administration. | Education, Higher—Administration.
Classification: LCC P301.5.A27 G76 2022 (print) | LCC P301.5.A27 (ebook) | DDC 808/.0420711—dc23/eng/20220830
LC record available at https://lccn.loc.gov/2022036539
LC ebook record available at https://lccn.loc.gov/2022036540

Copyeditor: Hope Walker
Designer: Mike Palmquist
Cover Photos: "Road to Ethnography" and "St. Rita's" by Jennifer Grouling. Used with permission.
Series Editors: Rich Rice, Heather MacNeill Falconer, and J. Michael Rifenburg
Consulting Editor: Susan H. McLeod
Associate Editor: Hope Walker

The WAC Clearinghouse supports teachers of writing across the disciplines. Hosted by Colorado State University, it brings together scholarly journals and book series as well as resources for teachers who use writing in their courses. This book is available in digital formats for free download at wac.colostate.edu.

Founded in 1965, the University Press of Colorado is a nonprofit cooperative publishing enterprise supported, in part, by Adams State University, Colorado State University, Fort Lewis College, Metropolitan State University of Denver, University of Alaska Fairbanks, University of Colorado, University of Denver, University of Northern Colorado, University of Wyoming, Utah State University, and Western Colorado University. For more information, visit upcolorado.com.

Land Acknowledgment. The Colorado State University Land Acknowledgment can be found at https://landacknowledgment.colostate.edu.

CONTENTS

ACKNOWLEDGMENTS

First and foremost, I would like to thank my research participants, particularly Dwayne and Kristen. I deeply appreciate their openness and willingness provide me with insight into their professional lives. In addition, Kate McConnell, the Executive Director of VALUE, continues to be open to conversation about the VALUE rubrics and critique of assessment processes in higher education. Kate has provided information as requested while being respectful of my own boundaries as a researcher not working directly with or for the AAC&U.

I couldn't have completed this project without my writing group, Dan Lawson and Tim Lockridge. They have read countless drafts of the chapters herein, and the quality of the final project is due to their continued support and insightful feedback. Zachary Dwyer also helped with this project as a research assistant who helped with copyediting. I also deeply appreciate the support of my wife, Eva, who encouraged me to keep going throughout this project.

This research was supported by my university in multiple ways. I received an Aspire Junior Faculty grant to conduct the initial research that led to this project. I was granted special assigned leave in Fall 2016 to conduct site visits. In addition, I received several internal Summer Assessment grants. I am deeply thankful to have this type of institutional support, which many of my participants in this study lacked.

Finally, I would like to thank my peer reviewers, editors and the wonderful team at WAC Clearinghouse, especially Rich Rice who encouraged me from the very beginnings of this project. Their feedback and support has been invaluable.

COMMONLY USED ABBREVIATIONS

AAC&U: American Association of Colleges & Universities, formerly the Association of American College & Universities

CWPA: Council of Writing Program Administrators

DQP: Degree Qualifications Profile

ETS: Educational Testing Service

IE: Institutional Ethnography

LEAP: Liberal Education & America's Promise

OBE: outcomes-based education

SEAE: Standardized Edited American English

VALUE: Valid Assessment for Learning in Undergraduate Education

VSA: Voluntary System of Accountability

WAC: writing across the curriculum

WPA: writing program administrator

ADAPTING VALUES: TRACING THE LIFE OF A RUBRIC THROUGH INSTITUTIONAL ETHNOGRAPHY

CHAPTER 1.

A TALE OF TWO SCHOOLS

"A rubric is the record of negotiated compromises, the lingering detritus of struggles for dominance by purists and poets and pragmatists."

- Griffin, 2010

This book is and is *not* about the national VALUE (Valid Assessment for Learning in Undergraduate Education) rubric for Written Communication designed by the American Association of College and Universities (AAC&U). While I do analyze the VALUE movement, I take this national rubric as a sort of ur-text—an entry point into assessment practice between 2016–2018. In particular, this book captures a moment in time at two specific universities, contextualizing their practice within national assessment trends. Using institutional ethnography (as defined in Chapter 3), I uncover the negotiations and compromises underlying the "adapted" VALUE rubrics used at these two institutions.

Institutional ethnography (IE) as a methodology is well suited to connect individual experiences to larger institutional trends. IE examines "key processes" that "transform the local and particular into generalized forms" that are recognized across institutions (Smith, 2005, p. 186). In writing studies, we might call these "generalized forms" *genres*. Here, I follow Amy Devitt's (2004) approach to studying genre as "actual practice" (p. 68). Genres are never neutral tools or static formulas. They are repeatedly activated by human interaction and discourse. They are created by and create our "social reality" (Barwarshi, 2000, p. 349). This book is not about *best* practice in using rubrics. Rather, it is about the ways that faculty and administrators at two small institutions engage in the *actual* practice of adapting and using rubrics and how those rubrics create and reflect the social realities in which they work.

The rubric is a genre that can tell a story about pedagogy that is both local and extra-local. It is a document that represents both material conditions of local contexts and external power structures. This book attempts to tell that story, focusing on two small institutions I call Oak University and St. Rita's College. In this book, I attempt to portray the standpoints of faculty at Oak and St. Rita's, but I acknowledge that this portrayal is never neutral. I am affected by my own experiences and opinions as a writing program administrator, a researcher in writing studies, and a White woman teaching at a predominantly White institution (PWI). These experiences followed me as I visited the campuses of Oak and St. Rita's and are a part of the lens through which I received the stories told to me by my interviewees. As a researcher, I cannot separate myself from my embodied experiences visiting these campuses. In turn, this research has had a profound effect on how I approach my own relationship to my own institution and my assessment work. I cannot, ultimately, separate myself from these stories.

This introduction presents vignettes that weave together my own experiences on these campuses with the stories told to me by participants. These stories are meant to ground the reader in these two local contexts and serve as a reference point to put the data presented throughout this book in context. Each vignette has been vetted by my main informant as representative of their experiences working for this university. These stories are meant to frame the analysis that is to come. Future chapters also incorporate more perspectives from other participants to form a more complete picture of work in assessment and writing at each institution. Appendix A provides a description of all participants mentioned in the book for easy reference. For now, I invite you to read these stories as a way to become familiar with these two institutional contexts, which may vary from your own and from those typically presented in writing studies research.

OAK UNIVERSITY: "GOOD FEELINGS"

Oak University stands atop a hill overlooking an adorable small town that has the feel of New England despite being in the Midwest. The main street of the town is lined with brown placards marking historic brick and columned buildings while people eat ice cream on park benches in front of a custard shop and interact by introducing their dogs. Here, I have my choice of historic inns and bed and breakfasts at which to stay. The historic inn I choose is a beautiful stone building from 1924, and as I walk through thick ornate wood doors, I am directed to a small desk to check in with a staff member as if I am entering their private office. She nicely prints the Institutional Review Board (IRB) consent forms that I forgot for free. An ornate stairwell takes me past beveled windows to a comfortable room: one of those with the fancy waffle-pattern cotton bathrobes to wear. The inn also sports an award-winning restaurant where I dine comfortably on risotto and creme brûlée. Although my first visit to Oak was brief—I met with the chair of the writing committee, attended a writing committee meeting, and scheduled additional interviews for a later date—it felt like a bit of a vacation.

Oak itself matches the town to a tee. Located at the top of a winding drive up the hillside, Oak feels central to, if above, the town (see Figure 1.1). Its open green spaces and historic stone buildings overlook the rolling hills adorned with fall oranges and yellows. The writing committee meets in a spacious room with a conference table and interior glass windows in a building that houses many such meeting rooms. The atmosphere is friendly and laid back: faculty wear jeans, talk about their days, tease one another, and congratulate one another on their successes.

Figure 1.1: The view from the top of the hill at Oak University. Original photograph.

My second visit is one week after President Trump's election, and the effects are palpable. The sidewalks around campus represent the feeling of the nation. Messages of support, love, and fear are written everywhere. The occasional Trump supporter comments are sprinkled in among the mix, written and rewritten. "This country is not his," one reads, with the "not" crossed out and the "is" underlined. Dialogs in chalk: "Love Trumps Hate" crossed out, then a question written by it: "Why did you cross this out? Does love offend you?" (see Figure 1.2).

I can't help but think that this writing represents the campus just as much as any artifacts collected and evaluated by the AAC&U VALUE rubric. Oak is a place of "good feelings," as one interviewee tells me, a place where everyone outwardly gets along, and yet, like the two sides of the political spectrum represented in chalk, not everyone feels included or agrees. It is in this context in 2016 that I first met Kristen, my main informant at Oak, and her colleagues on the writing committee.

Figure 1.2: Chalk writing at Oak after the 2016 Trump election. Original photograph.

KRISTEN AND THE NEW WRITING PROGRAM

Everyone likes Kristen. She's a dynamic and thoughtful person who runs a committee meeting well. A history professor by training, she is now the director of the writing program at Oak.

Actually, she's not.

She's the chair of the writing committee. But having become more familiar with the discipline of writing studies and, understanding what a writing program administrator (WPA) does, Kristen knows that what she does should carry the title of director. She told the provost this when she took the position, and although it hasn't been written down anywhere official, Kristen identifies herself as the director and others do, too.

When Kristen first started teaching at this small liberal arts college in 2008, there were a handful of disconnected first-year seminars courses. At this time, Ben, a computer scientist, was in charge of these courses as a part of his position as the dean of first-year students. The writing courses had not been evaluated in over 20 years, and Ben decided it was high time to work on them. He began with a task force to build a new first-year writing program. They began by defining the goals for the program and worked to add "meat to the goals" in terms of the actual courses and operation of the program. Ben recalls doing a lot of reading about teaching writing and even attending a WPA conference as he took the lead on forming the new writing program. Barbara, the writing center director, played a key role in helping those in different disciplines learn about best practices in teaching writing. Kristen joined in and fondly remembers the semester when six faculty members sat around designing the new program.

Around the same time that the writing program was being formed, the university signed on as one of a group of small liberal arts schools in a consortium with the AAC&U to use the new VALUE rubrics. In their 2010 accreditation review, Oak was criticized for not assessing their general education core curriculum. Philip, the associate provost, talked to his colleagues at other schools and was intrigued by the popular turn toward using the VALUE rubrics. He was on board with the push away from testing (Oak previously used the CLA+ test) and was eager for more nuanced assessment data. Philip funded multiple faculty members, including Kristen and Ben from the writing committee, to go to a training session on the rubrics led by the AAC&U and then VALUE Executive Director Terry Rhodes.

However, after a few years of working with the AAC&U rubrics, Philip was disappointed at low rates of inter-rater reliability and the push toward the use of the rubrics to compare institutions rather than gather meaningful local data. He doesn't need "busy work," he says. But the grant money is good, really good. So, he continues to work with the assessment coordinator on campus to gather student artifacts for the AAC&U's national scoring and testing. However, he backs off on being involved in how the writing program chooses to assess their program. He doesn't want to interfere with the legitimacy or agency of the new program, and he doesn't have enough confidence that the VALUE rubrics are worth it.

By 2014, the new writing program is officially underway with Ben as the "director." Kristen takes her sabbatical but knows she's slated to take over the program when she returns. She remembers that when they were first forming the program, she was relieved that the assessment piece would be saved for "someone else." But now that it turns out it's her, she dives in, full of enthusiasm to make it the best assessment she can. She works from a rubric that Ben drafted, and at the writing committee meeting I joined in Fall 2016, Kristen presented her revised version of Ben's rubric and handed out an artifact. Although she remembers her AAC&U training as "overwhelming," she wants to replicate the experience she had of being thrown into assessment in order to jumpstart the conversation with the committee. Having never done any kind of assessment outside her own classroom, the AAC&U training was essential to Kristen's understanding of assessment and rubrics. Through the process of our interview,

Kristen realizes that there is very little left of the AAC&U Written Communication rubric in the rubric she ultimately uses for the first writing assessment in Summer 2018, and yet, the original rubric was so foundational to her thinking about assessment that she sees the Oak writing program rubric as adapted from the VALUE rubric.

Although Kristen was frustrated that the university did not hire an expert in composition to direct the program, she is grateful that her colleague and friend Barbara shares her knowledge of the field. Kristen is what we might call a "convert" to writing studies, and she is adamant about spreading the word of writing across campus. For those that won't accept the program and don't want to adopt best practices, she says she'll "wait them out," and when they retire, she'll come knocking on the door of their replacement to let them know about writing at Oak.

Meanwhile, Barbara resents that the writing center director is not more directly involved with the writing committee and worries that the syllabi for the new courses are actually just regurgitated versions of what was done before the new writing program ever existed. But Oak, she explained, is a small, collegial school, a place where you pick your battles carefully.

ST. RITA'S COLLEGE: "THE SHAMBLES OF COLLEGIALITY"

The contrast in the embodied experience between Oak and St. Rita's was immediately apparent as I drove the very next day into the small factory town(s)—one runs into the next—surrounding St. Rita's College. The exit for St. Rita's is in the region where I've often heard others joke about how you don't even get off the highway for gas, a joke that further separates the populations living here from the "average" American.

The street signs point to factory entrances, and if you miss a turn, you have to drive miles until the next street breaks up the industrial landscape. My hotel is also a casino, filled with sterile, uninspiring halls of slot-machines. Checking in, I hear about a fellow customer's plans for her birthday celebration here, and I'm reminded that while this isn't my idea of a vacation, it is for some. There are restaurants in this establishment as well, mostly sports bars with pub food.

This is a town that houses a college, not a college town.

St. Rita's occupies a single, old British Petroleum Company (BP) executive building. A large metal cross greets you as you pull into the parking lot reminding you of the Catholic orientation of the institution. I'm personally reminded that this school is similar to, yet even smaller than, the Catholic high school I attended. Maybe that's why it seems nostalgic to me. The halls lack lockers, but otherwise it reminds me of high school. The science floor is painted in a bright forest green with a design reminiscent of a Rainforest Cafe (Figure 1.3). The cafeteria is a single room with vending machines and other limited offerings.

Figure 1.3: The Science Floor at St. Rita's. Original photograph.

While waiting for an interview, my main informant, Dwayne, shows me the secret seventh floor of the building. The elevator doesn't go there, but the right key takes you up a stairwell to an abandoned floor filled with artifacts of institutional history. An old secretary desk still dons 1970s carpet samples in bright orange and fire engine red. There's a small set of windows with a view of the nearby city, but Dwayne tells me with a grin: "that's not what the BP executives wanted to see."

As we turn the corner, the room leads to a 1970s shag carpet bar surrounded by glass windows and doors that lead out to a balcony that opens up on what the faculty refer to as the "Empire": the miles and miles of factories (Figure 1.4). You can almost imagine old White men smoking their cigars, drinking their whiskey and admiring their wealth. Wealth that comes on the backs of the working-class citizens that St. Rita's now serves.

Here, standing in this top floor, I feel I have a far richer understanding of St. Rita's than their rubrics could ever give me. Everything about this floor feels symbolic. There are good faculty members here, but they are overshadowed by the detritus of a failing system and what Dwayne calls "the shambles of colle-giality." I only visit St. Rita's once, but that embodied experience lingers as I continue to interview Dwayne for the next two years, hearing more about his frustrations and sometimes his small bits of hope at making change in this institution that seems forever stuck in a bygone era.

Figure 1.4: Shag carpet bar overlooking "the Empire." Original photograph.

DWAYNE AND NEW GOALS FOR GENERAL EDUCATION

Dwayne is tired. Burnt-out to be specific. He's worked at St. Rita's College for 10 years trying to improve writing instruction, general education, and assessment, and he's mentally and emotionally exhausted. Dwayne is a creative writer, but his graduate school experience gave him a strong composition background with some well-known members of the field. He even did some WPA work at his previous institution. When he was hired at St. Rita's he thought the school cared about that background in composition, but he found that few actually do. At first, he worked closely with a composition colleague, Jessica, but she didn't fare well in the hostile environment at St. Rita's and quickly moved on. She's still a light he draws on but an external one.

Only three months into his job at St. Rita's, the dean decided that junior faculty should revise general education, and Dwayne quickly became involved. "Hungry" for nationally recognized practice, Dwayne turned to the VALUE rubrics. He liked the way that they represented higher education, its goals, and its values. Dwayne and his colleagues decided that the general education curriculum should be structured around the VALUE rubrics with a clear sequence of courses that teach the skills represented in the rubrics. The plan was quickly approved. But as Dwayne lamented, he didn't know at the time that "some institutions kill ideas by approving them." The rubrics became a part of a handbook. They were on paper. Dwayne wrote an optimistic piece for the AAC&U about their use at his very small Catholic college that the AAC&U ate up as proof of their success. For Dwayne, the piece secured his tenure bid.

But real life at St. Rita's was much different than it looked on paper.

St. Rita's is an open-access school designed with a mission to bring credentials to improve the lives of factory workers in the surrounding community. The population of students has changed over the years from the factory workers themselves to their children, many first-generation, working-class students— some White, some Latinx, some Black. Dr. Z (as Dwayne and others refer to him) is a long-standing English professor and chair of the humanities, and he jokes (?) that St. Rita's is now where parents send their troubled teens for discipline in the form of education. It's a school where it is easy to get admitted but hard to graduate. By Dwayne's complex calculations, that graduation rate is an appalling 25 percent. This number is lower than that officially reported by IPEDs, but Dwayne believes it is more accurate. He attributes this problem, in part, to the overburdensome general education curriculum and many hidden, remedial requirements.

Writing at St. Rita's consists of a two-course sequence, but many students must pass remedial courses before even moving on to the "regular" sequence. These "kids," as everyone I talked to at St. Rita's calls them, just can't get up to speed quickly enough. Their writing curriculum is based on knowledge of grammar and vocabulary, and they sit at computers using grammar drill programs until they can pass at a high enough rate to take the first regular composition course. Dwayne would like writing instruction to be more rhetorically based. But Dr. Z believes these students are not ready for rhetoric and even seems to believe that rhetoric as a whole is a scam perpetrated by academics like Dwayne and Jessica.

Jessica attempted to introduce the Council of Writing Program Administrator (CWPA) Outcomes at St. Rita's, but Dr. Z would have none of it. Dwayne recalled that he would have taken "anything that worked" but that Jessica really wanted to use the CWPA outcomes, which so enraged Dr. Z that he said he wanted to fight Dwayne. To this day, no one really knows if this threat was meant to be metaphorical or not. The experience still haunts Dwayne, who recalled, "I mean, he may have, you know, he may have been kidding, right? But no one thought he was kidding."

The compromise was a portfolio to be scored at the end of the first composition course. To appease Dr. Z, that portfolio included a timed five-paragraph essay. Each portfolio is scored on a rubric by a faculty member who was not that student's direct instructor. The rubric includes two separate categories for grammar and style. After looking at the results, Dwayne reported that students who fail on one of these rubric categories almost always fail on the other. And yet, the categories not only remain, they also seep into the discussion of writing in the general education committee, a committee that Dr. Z is on as a part of his role as humanities department chair.

After Jessica left St. Rita's, Dwayne shifted his focus to the general education curriculum as a whole over the first-year writing portfolio. While general education was previously bookended by standardized testing (the CAP test), Dwayne again looks to the AAC&U for alternatives. In particular, he attended a state conference held by both the AAC&U and the Lumina Foundation around the time the Degree Qualification Profile (DQP) was released in 2014. At this conference, he learned about signature assignments that are incorporated across courses in order to evaluate student proficiency over time. He sees this as the sort of scaffolded approach that could really benefit St. Rita's students. Although the AAC&U's notion of a signature assignment often involves "real world" application, Dwayne tests the bounds of his institution only as far as he thinks they will stretch. The CAP test is replaced by a series of timed five-paragraph essays—a sophomore and junior essay now build on the freshman requirement and are scored by the same rubric that Dr. Z had already approved for the freshman writing portfolio. Other assessments are based more directly on the VALUE rubrics, such as oral communication, but the testing philosophy remains. In fact, the dry run of the oral communication assessment involved students presenting in front of a faculty panel decked out in regalia as some sort of "fun" ceremonial rite of passage. As this proved time-consuming and difficult to schedule, the presentations are now recorded to be viewed and assessed later.

This overall approach to assessment with timed writing and recorded presentations is well-liked by St. Rita's financial supporters, including a well-known grant provider and pharmaceutical company in the state. And Dr. Z seems to accept it. It also helps satisfy accreditors who were concerned that assessment only bookended the general education curriculum with no assessment in the middle. Again, the plan is approved, but it doesn't solve the underlying structural issues. Students still take up to 74 hours of core classes because of remedial course work, and they often have to retake the writing tests and courses to move forward.

But Dwayne is persistent. When I met him in 2016, Dwayne was again returning to the idea of using the VALUE rubrics to guide general education along with some new colleagues in English (Jeremy) and math (Andrea). This renewed drive was made possible in part by a change to the way that general education committee operated, and in part by a state-wide push to limit credit hours in general education. General education committee meetings at St. Rita's used to be led by a chair but open and attended by mostly English and humanities faculty. Jeremy and Andrea first sought out a more representative committee, including voting members from different disciplines. This group, albeit with varied individual understandings of the work, sought to pare down the number of core credits from an official 54 credits to 38, using the VALUE rubrics to guide new general education outcomes and curricula mapping to see which outcomes would be addressed in which courses. It was during this process that I attended a general education meeting in Fall 2016 where writing outcomes based on the VALUE rubric were being discussed. In this case, the outcomes proved to be accepted with little hassle, although St. Rita's added one for grammar and style that came from the first-year writing rubric rather than the VALUE rubric.

But things quickly went downhill after that meeting. When reading outcomes came up, Dr. Z declared that all courses should require three hard-copy books. The scientists in the room attempted to explain that they taught current journal articles in their fields rather than classic books, but Dr. Z called them "fucking ignoramuses" and stormed out of the room. Not only did he resign from the committee, but he also was asked to step down as department chair. Dwayne, being the only other tenured member of the small department, stepped into the role. While general education went forward, Dwayne struggled with supporting his non-tenured English colleagues—in one case discovering and dealing with a case of academic fraud and in another case attempting to further the career of a female colleague, Heather, who he felt had great promise but who was not taken seriously by Dr. Z. Meanwhile, St. Rita's sister institution closed permanently causing increased anxiety about the financial feasibility of their own small school. In fact, some of Dwayne's colleagues in other areas were assigned to teach speech communication courses because they could not fill enough classes in their own disciplines.

Despite these challenges, Dwayne succeeded in making changes to writing at the level of general education, moving the second semester first-year composition course to the second year. At the time of our final interview in April 2018, Dwayne and Heather were teaching the first sections of this course—which in practice was the same as the original second-semester class but taught at a level where Dwayne feels students are able to better learn the information. The new course is also the first of a two-part general education capstone, followed by a theology capstone fitting of the Catholic college context. Heather and Dwayne were set to use a new rubric to evaluate student work in this course, one that more closely fits with the AAC&U's VALUE rubric and supports a more rhetorically based curriculum. Rather than a five-paragraph essay, this assignment asked students to adapt an academic essay for a public audience.

Although he was burnt out when I talked to him in 2018, Dwayne was excited by these changes. He also had in mind a metacognitive assignment for his students to help them assess their own progress and reflect on where they stand in relation to the rubric. But years of bullying and institutional challenges wore on Dwayne, and he sent out applications for new positions. He ended his employment with St. Rita's that spring, and while I attempted to follow up several times with Heather, the project stalled, perhaps a sign of her own lack of status in the department and the institutional difficulties therein.

Meanwhile, the official graduation rate for Black students at St. Rita's remains an alarming 14 percent (IPEDS).

THE ROLE OF NARRATIVE IN RESEARCH

Ethnographies produce a type of knowledge grounded in experiences and stories. But those stories are not just those of the research and her participants. Research, like pedagogy, is a negotiation: between researcher and participants as well as between author and reader. The stories belonging to the reader and the connection made by the reader are the key to generalization of this type of research (Newkirk, 1992, p. 130). While the research itself may lead to change, the responsibility for that change lies not only with the researcher, but with those who read and are affected by the research (Talbot, 2020, p. 695). Therefore, I invite you to read this book with empathy and a sense of your own positionally. Where are you in these stories? Who are you? How does your own institutional positioning affect you and your relationship to writing and assessment? And how can you, in turn, affect change within your institution? I invite you to read this book not as an outside observer of others' lives but as an active participant in the creation of knowledge that expands beyond any one story.

CHAPTER 2.

WHAT IS OLD IS NEW AGAIN: A HISTORY OF WRITING ASSESSMENT, SYSTEMIC MANAGEMENT, AND THE NEOLIBERAL UNIVERSITY

At the 2016 Assessment Institute—a conference targeted more toward assessment professionals than writing program administrators—there is a lot of buzz about rubrics. To my surprise, rubrics are being hailed as the wave of the future. An attendee, half-jokingly, calls them "the next high impact practice." In essence, they appear to be the be the new, shiny thing—a surprise to me, who first learned about rubrics as a senior in AP English in 1994.

While this project engages with the "life" of one specific rubric—the American Association of Colleges & Universities (AAC&U)'s Valid Assessment of Learning in Undergraduate Education (VALUE) rubric for Written Communication—I begin by asking: what is this particular moment in the history of higher education assessment? Why are rubrics popular now? Where have we come from and how did we get here? Most of this book is focused on capturing moments at specific universities, as seen in the introduction. In this chapter, I aim to establish the context for those stories by exploring how rubrics exist within the larger *institutional* conversation.

Here, I mean institution in terms of higher education at large. Dorothy Smith (2005) explained that institutions are local settings but also larger entities that influence local practice. Local institutions "participate in relations that standardize their operations and generalize them across particular local instances" (p. 206). This complex set of relations and organizational structures produces the "institution" as a larger concept that organizes behaviors across local contexts. In other words, while each of our universities is its own institution, they all—to at least some extent—participate in the power structure of the *institution* of higher education. Higher education as an institution organizes and rules our local practice, and this is becoming increasingly true as we look at national assessment.

National trends in higher education (such as the need to compare universities, assign transfer credit, and design common outcomes) impact our everyday practice in our core curriculum and general education committees, assessment groups, and even in the running of our writing programs. In order to engage in critical and meaningful practice, writing program administrators (WPAs) as well as others involved in assessment need to aware of the trickle-down effect of institutional rhetoric, forwarded by large national higher education groups—what Linda Alder-Kassner (2017) called the Educational Intelligence Complex (EIC). These groups have their own agendas that may or may not match our local practice, and they often operate in the background; traces of their influence are lost in a sort of top to bottom game of telephone. For example, rubrics created for national assessment may find their way to the classroom, adopted by faculty who got them from other faculty members or from administrators who at some point—a moment lost and forgotten—got them from some workshop they went to led by a representative from an organization such as the AAC&U. This is often how the EIC operates: a wizard behind the curtain, pulling strings we don't even know that we are attached to.

This chapter seeks to trace some of what has led to our current moment within in institutional history where the scales are tipping in favor of rubrics over testing. This moment is complex. In some ways, it is attractive. Its promise of turning toward student outcomes and away from the technocratic Spellings Commission sounds encouraging. Yet as Chris Gallagher (2016) found, the moment can quickly sour as tools composition scholars have traditionally supported (such as e-portfolios) are being co-opted by a "neoliberal agenda whose endgame . . . is competency-based education" (p. 22). The focus can quickly turn from learning in individual courses to certifying competencies via rubrics. The rhetoric of austerity and neoliberalism is also a part of our current moment, and it makes this a fraught time for writing scholars and administrators. In this moment, it is particularly important that we pay attention to institutional power relations.

Historically, writing scales and rubrics have functioned within these systems of power as a tool for efficiency and social control. Previous scholars have acknowledged the racist nature of large-scale writing assessments (Elliott, 2005; Inoue, 2015). That is not to say that rubrics are always used in this manner or that they cannot do some good in the world. However, more must be done to link our current assessment system to the racist past of American education and to link our classroom practice to large-scale, institutional initiatives. Tracing the origins of any genre can demonstrate cultural shifts and reveal the ideological underpinnings of a form (Devitt, 2004, p. 92). The precursor to the modern rubric, the writing scale emerged in the early 1900s, a time when a whole new repertoire of managerial genres emerged to standardize and systematize daily work (Devitt, 2004). As Smith (2005) explained, the growth of industry and corporations led to a disconnect between workers and supervisors: "instead of being ruled directly by individuals whom we've known . . . we are ruled by people who are at work in corporations, government, professional settings and organizations, universities, public schools, hospitals and clinics, and so on and so on" (p. 18). Thus, texts became key to enforcing institutional control as individuals became removed from daily interactions with individual supervisors.

So, too, in the age of austerity and accountability endemic to the 2010s, teachers have seen an increase in reports to administrators and forms have emerged to measure and compare students across classrooms. No matter how much we work with our students and our fellow teachers to develop good rubrics for classroom use, we cannot fully separate them from an institutional system that is tied to problematic ideologies. Throughout this book, I focus on the rubric as a text that is such an "instrument of ruling" (Rankin, 2017b, p. 2). This chapter grounds that focus in historical and current political ideologies. I then introduce the AAC&U's two signature movements as relative to this project: Liberal Education and America's Promise (LEAP) and Valid Assessment of Learning in Undergraduate Education (VALUE). By placing these movements within the larger history of education and assessment, we see how they co-construct the current moment that calls for a shift toward rubrics and away from testing while still operating within the confines of neoliberalism.

UNBALANCED: SCALES OF RACIAL EXCLUSION

The early 1900s represented a shift toward efficiency and standardization across sectors: business, industry, and education. Scholars, such as Joseph Mayer Rice brought back European (particularly German) methods of incorporating science into the study of education (Elliot, 2005). It is no surprise that early talk of evaluating writing on a scale appears in a book by Rice (1914) entitled *Scientific Management in Education*. Rice's article (originally published in 1903) explained his method of scoring composition themes by placing them in one of five piles: "Excellent, Good, Fair, Poor, and Failure" (Hudelson, 1923, p. 164). The idea of using such a system came from a desire to standardize, and thus make more efficient, the evaluation of writing. In fact, Rice (1914) bragged that by using his method he was able to score "60–70 composition themes per hour" (p. 182). These early writing scales were the antecedent to current rubrics.

The drive for efficiency wasn't only about faster grading of classroom themes; however, it was about social control. This early focus on scientific management led to a push for writing ability to be tested scientifically, which brought with is a distrust in the reliability of classroom instructors. Educational scientists questioned the "lack of agreement among teachers as to the merit of their pupils' writing" and proposed scales as a solution (Hudelson, 1923, p. 163). Milo B.

Hillegas is often credited with the first writing scale developed in 1912, the "Scale for the Measurement of Quality in English Composition" (Behizadeh & Engelhard Jr., 2011, p. 194). Hillegas was the student of another key figure in early writing assessment: Edward Thorndike. Thorndike, who worked with Hillegas on their writing scale, was a proponent of eugenics who saw education as a means to weed out the intelligent population from the "dull normals" and "subnormals" and thus make society more efficient (Russell, 2002, p. 139). He sought a method for determining which individuals fell in which category and because an early (1904) study established a link between intelligence and "abilities in English," evaluating writing was important to Thorndike's goal (Elliott, 2005, p. 35).

The 10-point Hillegas scale or Thorndike-Hillegas scale (they revised it together) reads less like a modern rubric and more like a set of benchmarks, examples of writing at various levels. In the first stage of developing the scale, Hillegas gathered actual student work, but this work did not represent the full range he wanted on the scale, so he also added artificial samples. On the high end was writing from Jane Austen and the Brontës—surely no found student writing could match this. On the low end of the scale was nearly incomprehensible prose that Hillegas made up. Hillegas had 100 readers (only 73 of whom were reliable enough to make his final cut—perhaps not Austen fans?) arrange the samples from worst to best. He also had teachers and published authors judge the samples. The final set of 27 artifacts were arranged on a scale (Elliott, 2005). Teachers were then instructed to use this scale to compare their own students' work to the samples and thus grade more reliably.

Teachers themselves valued writing scales (and currently value rubrics) for making their grading more "fair." However, such measures have also been used to keep teachers in check and compare them to others. The drive for national comparison, fueled by a distrust of teachers, started with an overall drive for efficiency in education during the early 20th century. Hillegas heralded the scale for making comparisons across institutions and creating a national standard (Turley & Gallagher, 2008, p. 88). In particular, early writing scales were used at the secondary level to evaluate teachers. Principals evaluated teachers on whether or not their students improved on the Hillegas scale (Turley & Gallagher, 2008, p. 88). Similarly, today's rubrics are heralded for their ability to standardize the work of teachers and compare students to national benchmarks, but they also are a means of ruling teachers and exercising control over classrooms.

The Hillegas scale came under fire for many of the same reasons rubrics do today. Educational administrator Franklin W. Johnson (1913) complained that the scale was vastly inadequate for evaluating the content of student writing or the originality of thought. He saw it "like using a yardstick to determine the weight of material in the physical laboratory" (p. 48). Simply put, the tool was not valid for measuring writing. Even Thorndike turned on the scale, saying it was only good for identifying errors in *evaluating* writing, not errors in the writing itself (Elliot, 2005, p. xiv).

Nevertheless, the quest for the perfect writing scale continued. The 1920s saw the development of analytic-point scales to complement general scales and allow for the quality of different elements of writing to be scored independently of one another (Hudelson, 1923, p. 168). Still, Johnson (1913) warned that such scales would not improve student writing ability and anyone who expected them to do so would be disappointed (p. 163). But of course, improvement was never the sole goal. Rather, writing scales were meant to sort, compare, and exclude. The "link" between literacy and intelligence that Hillegas and Thorndike reinforced had real social consequences that continued long after their original writing scale. For example, when it came to the military, literacy tests had real life and death consequences. The Thorndike Reading Scale and accompanying literacy tests were used to test soldiers drafted for WWI and indicate the inferiority of the "negro draft" (Elliot, 2005, p. 70). In WWII, verbal analogies from the SAT were used in The Qualifying Test for Civilians to determine who might be trained as officers rather than placed in front-line combat (p. 118). Finally, in 1951, President Truman approved the Selective Service Qualifying Test that used similar questions on verbal relations as well as reading comprehension to determine who might defer the draft and go to college (p. 325). Thus, the consequence of Thorndike and his colleagues' efforts in the assessment of literacy extended far beyond the college classroom.

AMERICA'S LEGACY: ETS, TESTING, AND THE MODERN RUBRIC

Trends during these early periods are important because they show that educational measurement theorists *have always* constructed writing assessments separate from the teaching of writing (Behizadeh & Engelhard Jr., 2011). Although Hillegas intended his scale for classroom use, he still saw it as a means for keeping teachers in check across institutions. However, it is testing that Norbert Elliot (2005) called "America's unique contribution to education" (p. 4). And writing scales became essential to scoring any tests that involved writing essays.

First used in 1926, the SAT became a touchstone for the advancement of writing assessment. The emergence of the SAT and the College Board solidified the already underlying connection between writing scales and testing. It also led to the creation of the modern writing rubric and often used norming procedures.

Carl Campbell Brigham, chairman of the College Board in the 1920s and hailed creator of the SAT, was also well-known eugenicist. Like, Thorndike, Campbell Brigham's interest in writing assessment was connected to his racism. He used the "proven" connection between literacy and intelligence as evidence of lower intelligence in immigrants and African Americans (Elliot, 2005).

From this problematic history arose procedures for scoring essays that led to current practice. In order to develop reliability among essay scorers, Campbell Brigham used a process where scorers gathered around a table to read essays, each essay was scored twice, and difficult essays were sent to a special group of readers (Elliot, 2005). As resources became tight, Brigham was careful to only select readers that were consistent in their scoring. He also kept adjusting the number of points on the rating scale, which were at one point as high as 35. Even on the 10-point scale, he found that readers only regularly used four of the point values, and he ended up becoming frustrated with a numerical score at all (Elliot, 2005). The idea of using two-raters for an essay as well as the idea of a limited number of ratings (4–5) stuck.

When the Educational Testing Service (ETS) was created in 1947, reliability in essay testing was one of their top priorities. In fact, ETS became one of the primary sponsors of research on writing assessment throughout the 1940s, 1950s, and 1960s (O'Neill, Moore & Huot, 2009). For their first 20-some years, ETS struggled to find a satisfactory method of scoring essay exams. However, in the 1960s their research led to what we might recognize as the first modern writing rubric. In 1961, an ETS-funded study by Diederich, French and Carlton narrowed writing assessment to five main categories: "ideas, form, flavor/style, mechanics and wording" (O'Neill, Moore & Huot, 2009, p. 22). These categories became the basis for an analytic trait "rubric," known as there Diederich scale, in which each category was scored separately since readers had difficulty agreeing on overall quality of the essays (p. 22). While modern rubrics have become more nuanced, these categories are likely not unfamiliar to current scholars or practitioners. Thesis, organization, style, and grammar remain some of the most common rubric categories (Dryer, 2013).

Diedrich was major force in shifting to what Yancey (1999) dubbed the "second wave" of writing assessment, which focused on direct assessment through holistically scored essays rather than indirect assessment through objective tests. As Diederich said in 1974: "whenever we want to find out whether people can swim, we have them jump in the pool and swim" (as cited in Behizadeh & Engelhard Jr., 2011, p. 202). Unlike his predecessors, Diederich was also concerned with inequity. In particular, he was concerned that southern students failed the Selective Service College Qualifying Test that allowed them to defer military service at a far higher rate than those from northern colleges (Elliot, 2005).

Much of his life's work was spent in trying to assess direct samples of writing fairly. Diederich saw writing scales as means to create a common vocabulary and in doing so, ensure reliable and fair assessment (Haswell, 2014). While current writing assessment scholars recognize that "even features that seem generic . . . that are often found on rubrics and scoring guidelines should be defined by the specific situation" (Adler-Kassner & O'Neill, 2010, p. 64), for Diedrich, disagreement among readers was as a matter of individual taste rather than social circumstance (Broad, 2003). In the interest of saving teachers time and confident that common vocabulary could lead to reliable essay assessment, Diedrich advocated for employing external graders trained to score essays with high levels of reliability. It is no surprise that this effort was supported by the Ford Foundation whose name is often thought of as synonymous with scientific management and efficiency (Elliott, 2005). Diedrich's example is important to our current context because it shows how direct assessment and a drive for efficiency have historically co-existed.

In 1966, a breakthrough occurred in essay scoring that furthered both the goals of direct assessment and the drive for efficiency. Godshalk, Swineford, and Coffman designed the basis for modern holistic scoring, including the process of norming to train readers and monitor their progress (O'Neill, Moore & Huot, 2009). Each paper had four readings on a three-point (high, average, low) scale. A key addition to their process was norming the group of readers using sample papers, which were discussed as a group in order to reach consensus (Elliot, 2005). The results were strong, above .7, but the process was cut from four readers to two due to cost. Their 1966 work "The Measurement of Writing Ability—A Significant Breakthrough" they claimed that their process certified the essay as a means to assess writing ability (Elliot, 2005, p. 164).

It would be at least another decade until holistic scoring and direct assessment were dominant, but the framework for it had been laid by educational measurement specialists. Direct assessment became the national trend in the late 1970s and 1980s, and it is not a coincidence that its popularity corresponds to the rise of outcomes-based assessment in the 1980s. Outcomes originally seemed like a promising way to assess courses and curricula—one that took into account actual student work, but the history of exclusion and America's preoccupation with testing was never fully left in the past. In order to assess outcomes, raters needed measurements, and thus the writing scale gained dominance in writing assessment. By the early 1980s, it could be assumed that any process of scoring essays would involve the use of a writing scale (Dryer, 2013). While it replaced multiple choice testing, this process was still designed to be used outside of the classroom context, for trained external raters to score essays in a way that ensured reliability and acted as a check on individual teachers.

AN EDUCATIONAL INTELLIGENCE COMPLEX "TROJAN HORSE": OUTCOMES BECOME STANDARDS

Two words dominate assessment in the 1980s & 1990s: outcomes and standards. As a field, composition has distinguished the two, but in some circles, they have always been connected. So, too, have we seen outcomes conflated with competencies. Such inconsistencies in language can be disturbing for those who study writing. Chris Gallagher (2016) described a talk from an official at an accrediting agency where the guest switched almost seamlessly from a position on "authentic assessment" that those in our field would support to "validating competencies," which raises our alarm. This "Trojan Horse," as Gallagher (2016) called it, is not necessarily nefarious. But it is a way of using language that is often different from the way we see it used by writing scholars. Diving into the history of outcomes-based assessment provides us background for understanding the current discussion on outcomes, competencies, and national-scale rubrics.

William Spady was instrumental in beginning the outcomes-based educational (OBE) movement. With co-author Kit Marshall, Spady defined an outcome as "a successful demonstration of learning that occurs at the culminating point of a set of learning experiences" (1991, p. 70). Spady and Marshall's vision for "transformational OBE" was that educators would have a "guiding vision of the graduate" that would guide the development of curriculum (p. 70). In a retrospective interview, Spady lamented the loss of his transformational vision for OBE. He called current OBE: "a curriculum-driven system with what people claim to be 'outcomes' sprinkled over the top" (Killen, 2016). This "traditional" approach, Spady explained is not outcomes *based* at all. Rather, it simply adds outcomes to existing curriculum in order to meet accountability mandates (Spady & Marshall, 1991, p. 69). Part of the difference between Spady's dream and the current reality is that Spady wanted outcomes-based *education* rather the outcomes-based *assessment*.

This distinction can be explained in terms of writing scholars' own views on the role of outcomes. The Council of Writing Program Administrator (CWPA) Outcomes Statement was initially developed to guide curriculum development, not to assess it. Harrington et. al's (2005) edited collection *The Outcomes Book* is a retrospective on the WPA Outcomes Statement that draws important distinctions between outcomes, which guide curriculum, and standards, which are used to assess it. The authors of this collection agree that outcomes form the basis for designing curriculum while standards provide a check on whether or not that curriculum has been successful (Yancey, 2005). White (2005) explained that "outcomes do not require agreement on a single best way to achieve those outcomes" or agreement on the level to which they should be achieved (p. 5). The WPA Outcomes were meant to give guidance to teachers and programs, not to standardize writing curriculum (Wiley, 2005, p. 27). Nor were the WPA Outcomes developed with a rubric or even any particular type of assessment in mind. In fact, when the Council of Writing Program Administrators (CWPA) developed the WPA Outcomes in 1999, they did so to strategically *avoid* composition from being targeted by the growing movement for standards in higher education. Patricia Ericsson (2005) remembered: "Developing the Outcomes Statement was an offensive, proactive move" against first-year composition being defined by those outside the field (p. 115).

Despite this initial focus on outcomes as a guide for curriculum rather than as a means of assessment, I would wager that many of those in writing studies have at least seen, if not created, a rubric based on the WPA Outcomes. Outcomes are now about results to be reported rather than goals to define curriculum. Outcomes assessment serves the needs of reporting by "providing nice, clean numbers for university administrators' spreadsheets" (Gallagher, 2012, p. 46). Shifts in accreditation are certainly one reason for this change. While Linda Adler-Kassner and Peggy O'Neill explained in 2010 that accrediting agencies looked to institutions to set their own standards (p. 28), by 2012, Adler-Kassner noted that accreditors were under attack for this. She explained that government and public agencies were repeatedly criticizing accreditors for "allowing institutions to set their own learning standards and develop their own assessments; the lack of consistent outcomes across institutions; and the lack of comparable data" (Adler-Kassner, 2012, p. 123).

Similarly, we see a shift in a second retrospective collection about the WPA Outcomes (2013) where Paul Anderson et al. noted that many institutions were using writing outcomes for assessment to an external body, such as a state mandate. Outcomes are now inherently tied to assessment, and that assessment often comes in the form of rubrics that are designed for large-scale assessments. Theoretically, the assessment loop would then lead back to curricular development. What we learn from assessment would be used to shape curriculum and thus both assessment and curriculum would be guided by outcomes—something known in assessment circles as "closing the loop." Too often, however, the focus is on reporting and accountability rather than on teaching and learning. This focus comes from a larger focus on management and quality assurance that parallels the development of outcomes-based assessment and accountability.

ACADEMIC MANAGEMENT: THE RISE OF QUALITY ASSURANCE, NEOLIBERALISM, AND RUBRICS

As we've seen, writing scales are not new, nor is comparison between teachers or among schools. At the broader institutional level, the focus on efficiency dates back to the early 20th century when Frederick Taylor applied scientific management to make industry less wasteful, and others applied this efficiency approach to education (Wiley, 2005, p. 26). A drive for quality and efficiency also permeates writing assessment from its origins. The elusive factor of "quality" is in the very title of the Hillegas scale for "the Measurement of *Quality* in English Composition." Similarly, the question of "quality programs" and their assessment permeates WPA discourse from the beginnings of the CWPA in 1977 (Strickland, 2011). Early meetings of the Conference on College Composition and Communication (CCCCs) took this approach by focusing on systematizing first-year writing through workshops that allowed for more efficient, more accurate reading of student themes (Strickland, 2011).

What changed in the later portion of the 20th century is *who* is responsible for quality and efficiency. While early scales had a policing effect on society, early educational scientists also created writing scales so that *teachers* could more efficiently score student work. Yet in our current neoliberal landscape, *society* has become the evaluators. It is now the burden of the public to hold higher education accountable—to evaluate teachers and universities on how quickly they graduate students and how well they compare to their peers. With options like the College Scorecard and the Voluntary System of Accountability (VSA)'s College Portraits,[1] which allow students to compare universities based on factors such as cost, graduation and employment rates, potential students are tasked with finding the "best fit" for them based on the ratio of cost to value. We have made it the responsibility of the "savvy student" to choose well in order to make the most of their student loans and ensure the highest rate of return when graduating (Seal, 2018).

This push toward privatization and individual choice is a key tenant of neoliberalism and part of an overall narrative that individualized instruction is the most cost-effective and efficient means to graduation (Seal, 2018). In the introduction to their edited collection *Composition in the Age of Austerity*, Tony Scott and Nancy Welch (2016) defined neoliberalism as a change toward making public services private, or when they remain public, applying "market logics" to them. While terms like "corporate university" convey a similar market logic, applying the term neoliberalism to the academy links changes to education with overall economic changes in democratic society (Seal, 2018). Neoliberalism has

---

1   Since this research was conducted, VSA has become VSA Analytics. Their service now seems more geared toward providing these statistics to college and universities themselves. However, it appears that many universities place these facts on their websites in the hopes of using them to attract students. As of this writing in February 2022, I found many universities with links to their College Portraits stats that now come up with an error. This shift is itself testament to how such ideas circulate. At this point, College Scorecard is still available.

led to what Scott and Welch (2016) called "audit culture" where "everything must be assessed against institutional benchmarks and comparator/competitor schools are measured for its value added" (p. 12). Agents of neoliberalism shift the focus from solving economic challenges with wide-scale economic solutions to individual accountability and determining the best value for the money. As Scott and Welch (2016) concluded, it's not about cost-saving, but cost-shifting: from publicly funded universities to student debt. In such an economy, assessment serves not only to certify student success and choices but to hold universities accountable—to compare them so that students can make the best decisions with their money. Andrew Seal (2018) noted that this neoliberal society has taught students to look at their course schedule "like a bond trader looking over a portfolio" to maximize their investments.

This neoliberal shift to apply market logic to education happened gradually, starting in the 1980s. In the 1980s, "'quality' became a buzzword in management" (Strickland, 2011, p. 113). Beginning with *A Nation at Risk* (1983), a report by the U.S. National Commission on Excellence in Education, "alarmist reports" about the decline in educational quality captured the attention of both government officials and the general public (McClellan, 2016). So, too, these reports have worked to tie individual success to the success of the United States as a nation. At lower levels of education, the 2002 *No Child Left Behind* Act tied "education's role as a public good" to the progress of an individual (Adler-Kassner & O'Neill, 2010, p. 24). *A Test of Leadership: Charting the Future of U.S. Higher Education* (2006), commonly referred to as the Spellings Commission because then Secretary of Education Margaret Spellings headed the commission, is known for devaluing of teacher expertise and taking a technocratic approach that insists on external management of education (Adler-Kassner & O'Neill, 2010). Obama's 2009 *Race to the Top* initiative linked education and individual economic mobility and called for means by which parents and students could compare the product—or school—that they were purchasing with other options (Adler-Kassner, 2012). The underlying thread that connects this national discourse on education is that all students, including those from unprepared and diverse backgrounds, can succeed if they make wise choices. Wanting every individual to succeed is a noble goal, but in these reports, "success" looks the same for every student, and it is never defined *by* the student. Students should be offered different paths to that success, even individualized paths, but what is considered a "quality education" is seen as universal.

The ability to compare the "quality" of schools rests on the idea that all schools should help students reach the same education outcomes and goals. Outcomes are defined by external partners—government, corporate partners, and philanthropists—and the biggest concern is if these outcomes can be accomplished efficiently. The "endgame," according to Gallagher (2016), is competency-based education, where everything is based on meeting common competencies, not on taking particular courses. Competency-based education takes outcomes-based education to one particular extreme. As Yancey (2005) explained, outcomes have to do with what students know, but don't necessarily define a particular level of proficiency. In addition, outcomes allow for individual teaching style and are used for programmatic assessment and curricular development. In contrast, competency-based education develops standards that "act as a check on the students as well as the courses" (Yancey, 2005, p. 20). Unfortunately, the words "outcomes" and "competency" (and "proficiency") have become somewhat interchangeable at this point (Mette Morcke, Dornan, Eika, 2013).

This shift from outcomes to competencies fits with a neoliberal agenda by linking education and economic order (Seal, 2018). Accountability serves as a "sleight of hand" to distract us from systemic economic and racial inequity to higher "quality" education as a solution to economic distress (Scott & Welch, 2016). As Scott and Welch (2016) aptly put it:

> The solution to the *economic* gap is not *economic* restructuring
> (i.e. restored funding) but instead *educational* restructuring
> through accountability and efficiency mandates that push
> foundational changes in curriculum, pedagogy, and—by tying
> the 'value' of a college degree to speed of its completion and
> the earning of its recipient—what a college degree signified.
> (p. 10)

We have become focused on whether or not students reach goals, not on which goals are appropriate (Adler-Kassner & O'Neill, 2010). Thus, outcomes—a seemingly solid concept for *planning* curriculum—have become competencies that are "enshrined in the bureaucratic machinery" (Gallagher, 2012, p. 45). They must be included on forms when we propose new courses; they must appear on our syllabi, and the two should always match. And of course, outcomes must *always, always* be assessed. They have become "fetishized" (Gallagher, 2016) and measuring and *reporting* how students meet outcomes has come to serve the needs of academic management, not students (Gallagher, 2012).

Like in other industries with systemic management, the need to report to distant supervisors becomes a dominant force for how assessment work is completed. Reports abstract actual experience and define what is normal or abnormal (Nichols, Griffith & McLarnon, 2017). The genre of the assessment report "commoditizes, reifies, and obscures the dynamic, messy, material, socially useful, inescapably values-driven labor of teaching and learning" (Mutnick, 2016, p. 39). Competencies serve academic management by allowing administrators to show how their university compares to others, and when students fail to gain competencies, it is teachers who need disciplined in the form of better training and increased accountability rather than better working conditions. Teachers are the "objects of regulation" in a competency-based system (Mette Morcke, Dornan & Eika, 2012, p. 855). Put in the context of management and reporting, it makes sense that the product of the academic enterprise is a competent student and that the teacher is the employee responsible for the quality of this product.

Rubrics and their claims of reliability became one method of ensuring that success looked the same for different types of students at different colleges and universities. The word "rubric" was first used in 1981 to describe the writing scales used to holistically score essays written for Advanced Placement (AP) English exam (Griffin, 2010). By 1984, national data on student writing performance was also being collected in the United States and was being scored based on the Godshalk research group method (Elliot, 2005). Applebee, Langer, and Mullins wrote a 1984 report *Writing Trends across the Decade, 1974–1984* that further solidified rubrics, particularly those focused on primary trait scoring (using a scale for one particular trait in writing) as the gold standard for reliability (Elliot, 2005, p. 197). Elliot (2005), however, explained that minoritized students as well as Title I, lower-class schools did poorly on these assessments. Thus, we come full circle. Literacy is tied, as it was from the beginning, to the success and intelligence of an individual, and minoritized groups "test" below others. And since the individual's success is tied to the nation's success, national standards are created and incentivized to raise the "quality" of education at large.

In the absence of indirect testing, rubrics serve as a neat and clean way to report on whether or not those competencies are being met—to report on the quality of education. Bob Broad (2003) noted that scoring guides and rubrics serve to *document* the evaluation of student writing. They have become a means of communication about writing—a public record—within a larger system of academic management, yet they only capture a fraction of the values at work when evaluating student writing (Broad, 2003). Outcomes-based assessment using rubrics is now seen as "common sense" within academic management, something we accept, however begrudgingly, as a part of our work as academics (Gallagher, 2012, p. 48). While many scholars have focused on either the value or the detriment of the rubric to students, teachers, and writing programs (Anson et al., 2012; Balester, 2012; Broad, 2003; Crusan, 2015; Turley & Gallagher, 2008; Wilson, 2006), what remains relatively unexplored is the role of rubrics within this larger *institutional system*. That isn't to say outcomes assessment or writing rubrics are all bad, simply that they play an *institutional* role in governing our work.

27

ENTER THE AAC&U

This book explores how one national rubric—the AAC&U's VALUE rubric for Written Communication governs the work of writing assessment nationally and particularly at two small colleges. In this section, I discuss the role of AAC&U as a key organization that has historically defined what it means to be an institution of higher education, specifically what it means to receive a "liberal education." Their current overall mission is "to advance the vitality and public standing of liberal education by making quality and equity the foundations for excellence in undergraduate education in service to democracy" (AAC&U, n.d., "About"). Their Liberal Education and America's Promise (LEAP) movement institution-alizes the AAC&U's vision for liberal education through common outcomes and rubrics. These texts then go on to be propagated by administrators and faculty in higher education, few of whom connect them back to the AAC&U and their larger mission defining liberal education.

The definition of liberal education has shifted significantly over time, but one consistent thread has been the goal to "train good citizens to lead society" (Crowley, 1998, p. 47). However, what this training looks like, who should be trained, and what benefits society has shifted significantly since the origins of the term. Liberal education is often confused with general education, but the two movements were originally distinct (Crowley, 1998). Liberal education was first associated with training gifted individuals to master traditional subjects and read the canon of "great books," while general education was concerned with providing skills to a broader base of students to succeed professionally (Crowley, 1998). David Russell (2002) described the warring of factions defin-ing higher education, where one side believed that a good citizen was a cultured citizen, and culture was synonymous with White and Western. The other fac-tion was that of social efficiency, which maintained that all students needed specific skills and qualifications to be strong citizens. Social efficiency won out and this influenced the teaching of writing as a skill that could be tested and quantified (Russell, 2002).

Since the 1940s, the AAC&U has concerned itself with defining liberal edu-cation, and they have continued to re-define that term for the 21st century. The definition of liberal education that the AAC&U now subscribes to is quite broad. It is simply an approach to education that "empowers individuals with broad knowledge and transferable skills, and a strong sense of values, ethics, and civic engagement" (AAC&U, 2006, p. 2). Rather than a "great books" approach, we now have a "great skills" approach—liberal education means teaching skills that are transferable to careers. This definition builds on the history of social effi-ciency—the quicker these great skills can be achieved the sooner a student can move into a career and benefit society. Social efficiency has also now been linked to equity. Rather than making sure the best and the brightest read the great books, we now must make sure that all students acquire these great skills—yet as I show throughout the book, these skills still come from White values. It may be a positive step to move away from historic approaches to writing assessment that linked the knowledge of White canonical texts and SEAE to intelligence, but the AAC&U's version of equity still represents a neoliberal vision. Rather that acknowledge and fight systemic, structural impediments of education, this neoliberal vision maintains that if all students simply receive similar instruction, they will all succeed. The notion that "productivity=success=equity" is prevalent in discourse about both faculty and students within higher education (Adsit & Doe, 2020, p. 90). For the AAC&U, the solution to inequity is to define success by common outcomes (LEAP), ensure success by assessing it on common rubrics (VALUE), and thus prepare every individual for citizenship and the workforce (McConnell & Rhodes, 2017). Thus, LEAP outcomes and VALUE rubrics are seen as a part of AAC&U's overall mission as an organization to foster liberal education for all students.

Liberal (or Neoliberal) Education and America's Promise(d)

LEAP stands for "Liberal Education and America's Promise," and the product of the movement is a set of national outcomes for liberal education. According to the AAC&U, the "promise" embedded in LEAP is one made to students that higher education will be worth their time and money and lead to "a better future," that no matter what school they attend, they will acquire these particular skills (AAC&U, 2007, p. 1). But so, too, are students promised to employers as ideal future employees who graduate with the training and skills they need for the workforce. The LEAP outcomes connect these two interests and define what skills society at large can expect all students to acquire in post-secondary education.

The LEAP Essential Learning Outcomes are less a set of *measurable* outcomes than a categorization of the learning that should be valued in an overall liberal education. The 2007 executive summary stressed that different types of institutions and programs would apply the outcomes differently. Furthermore, the initial LEAP Outcomes do not read the way we've come to expect outcomes to read—as measurable goals beginning with clear verbs. Rather, they include four broad categories to help students "prepare for twenty-first century challenges:"

- Knowledge of Human Cultures and the Physical and Natural World
- Intellectual and Practical Skills

- Personal and Social Responsibility
- Integrative Learning

Under each of these broad categories there are more specific bullet points. For example, under "Intellectual and Practical Skills" the AAC&U lists six bullets, including critical and creative thinking, written and oral communication, and information literacy (AAC&U, 2007, p. 3). Under this list is a line noting that these should be "practiced extensively, across the curriculum," rather than accomplished in one specific course (AAC&U, 2007, p. 3). The LEAP outcomes, as with the original outcomes-based movement, were thus meant to *inform* curriculum, not to standardize it. Nevertheless, like the outcomes-movement as a whole, the rhetoric behind LEAP has both shaped and been shaped by neoliberal views about the purpose of higher education within the economic system of capitalism and political system of U.S. democracy.

Although the AAC&U has argued that their LEAP Outcomes are not "just about the economy" but about all areas of life, including "environmental, civic, cultural, imaginative, ethical" spheres, the outcomes were based on a survey of employers, not students or teachers (AAC&U, 2007, p. 17). The LEAP National Leadership Council, which consisted of heavy hitters from corporate settings[2] as well as colleges, formed the outcomes from a 2006 survey of employers about what they felt graduates of higher education needed (AAC&U, 2007). The council's report aimed to shift the focus away from the conversion about access, affordability, and accountability and toward the consensus of what a college graduate should "know and be able to do" (AAC&U, 2007, p. 1). To do so, LEAP relies on a narrative of consensus among educators and employers.

By including teachers in this consensus, the AAC&U seeks to separate their LEAP Outcomes from other contemporary reform initiatives, particularly the Spelling Commission Report. Although the development of LEAP's Essential Learning Outcomes began several years before the Spellings Report was released, the AAC&U officially released the LEAP outcomes later that same year, 2007, and offered them as a counter narrative to the distrust of teachers conveyed by the Spellings Commission. Rather, the AAC&U asserted that teachers should be central to educational reform (AAC&U, 2007). Nevertheless, the argument presented by the AAC&U is that teacher expertise is valuable not for what it represents within the classroom but for how it helps graduates meet the needs of

---

2   The council favored representation from Ivy League schools but did include strong community college representation. On the employer side it had a leaning toward legal professions. The group was ethnically and racially diverse as well, including strong Black, Hispanic, Asian, and Middle Eastern leadership. The group had a democratic bent, including several of those who worked for the Clinton administration, as well as those who have fought for racial and gender representation in higher education.

future employers. As is common in neoliberalism, individual success, whether defined economically or otherwise, is tied to the success of the institution and society at large.

When the LEAP council calls for "a new compact, between educators and American society" that puts "the future of democracy at the center" of education (AAC&U, 2007, p. 5, p. 9), make no mistake that it is a part of the larger narrative that Adler-Kassner (2017) called the Education Intelligence Complex (EIC)'s story of "The Problem with American Education and How to Fix It" (p. 320). The rhetoric of the AAC&U and the LEAP movement may resist some of the "technocratic narrative" of Spellings (Adler-Kassner & O'Neill, 2010, p. 85), but ultimately their approach still exists within this larger national frame. As we turn to examine the VALUE rubrics more closely, it is important to remember that alternative assessment does not automatically counter the agenda of neoliberalism, nor does it tackle the systemic issues inherent to having a national standard in the first place. A different method for "how to fix it" (rubrics instead of testing) does not resist the narrative that the structure of higher education needs fixing or that external stakeholders are the ones to develop the solutions.

DEFINING THE **VALUE** OF OUTCOMES THROUGH RUBRICS

The LEAP Outcomes were designed to be adapted by individual schools, and originally, there was no means to measure how well each school incorporated the outcomes or how well each student achieved them. However, the Spellings Commission refocused the national conversation on *measuring* the outcomes, and outcomes education as a whole moved toward accountability and assessment (Gallagher, 2016). The AAC&U looked to answer the Spelling Commission's call for accountability with an alternative to testing by developing the Valid Assessment of Learning in Undergraduate Education (VALUE) initiative in 2009 (McConnell et al., 2019; Rhodes, 2010). Then Vice President for Quality Curriculum and Assessment at the AAC&U, Terrel (Terry) Rhodes wondered: could an alternative means be used to represent the work of higher education, one that captured more of the "rich and varied dimensions" of individual institutions? (Rhodes, 2010, p. 1).

The VALUE rubrics held the promise of a different way to quantify the success of higher education. AAC&U President Geary Schneider (2015) presented the VALUE rubrics as a "more specific" means of accountability that accounts for the complexity of learning in higher education (p. vii). The goal of the VALUE rubrics was to develop an accountability measure that says something "significant about learning"—to "respect the complexity" of higher education and "embrace multiple essential learning outcomes" (Schneider, 2015, p. vii).

Sullivan (2015) added that metrics about access, completion, and earnings of graduates do not say anything significant about learning with the implication that the AAC&U's new VALUE initiative does. Whether or not the VALUE rubrics have met these goals—whether any rubric can—is debatable, however, a *belief* that they could is the reason that the AAC&U turned its attention to the creation of the VALUE rubrics.

Resisting the "technocratic" narrative of the Spellings Commission also fits with the role AAC&U sees for itself as a steward of liberal education. Adler-Kassner (2008) explained that technocrats and stewards are two historically competing views of liberal education. Stewards focus on "the cultivation of critical intelligence by means of inductive, nurturing education" while technocrats see the need for that intelligence to be managed from above (Adler-Kassner, 2008, p. 44). Although the word steward is not prominent in the current AAC&U literature, it seems telling that it comes up in the AAC&U's description of their role in relationship to the VALUE rubrics. They see themselves as "the intellectual and logistical *steward* [emphasis added] of the VALUE rubrics" (McConnell et al., 2019, p. 2). Since the role of steward is tied to fostering individual intelligence rather than managing education externally, the AAC&U continually stresses that their rubrics were designed to be adapted to local use.

From the beginning, the rubrics were meant to be "meaningful for local purposes" and "local pedagogical needs" (McConnell et al., 2019, p. 2). Rhodes and Finley (2013) rejected the language of standardization:

> Precisely because they are not standardized, the VALUE
> rubrics can be readily adapted to accommodate the language
> used to frame learning goals on individual campuses and to
> reflect different institutional missions and program variations.
> (p. 3)

Rhodes (2012) called the VALUE rubrics "meta-rubrics," rubrics to be adapted and used by multiple institutions. In 2009, the AAC&U released 15 of these meta-rubrics, including one for Written Communication. The notion of meta-rubrics to be adapted by local institutions is in keeping with AAC&U's philosophy as a steward—a guide in higher education, not a technocratic manager.

Yet, over time the role of the AAC&U has shifted to be more managerial, and the VALUE rubrics have become more standardized. As of 2019, the VALUE Institute now offers an external service for evaluation where institutions may send samples of student work to be scored by external raters (AAC&U, 2017). Thus, the AAC&U seems to be walking a well-worn path in the history of assessment. As seen historically, the use of writing scales shifted from classroom consistency to external reliability, as Diedrich and others trained external graders for higher levels of agreement (Elliot, 2005). So, too, have the VALUE rubrics evolved beyond a local, adaptable tool. They have come to play a significant role in creating *standard* tools that are used across institutions to assess and compare student (and therefore university) performance.

Whether or not the AAC&U's motivation was originally (or is currently) to manage higher education, building *national* outcomes and rubrics has a normalizing effect. Such texts shape practice, "mediating idiosyncrasies and variability in local settings" (LaFrance, 2019, p. 43). Inoue (2015) explained that writing assessment is an ecology where "individual actions by students or a teacher or rubric" do not work in isolation. Rather, they "may be instigators" within a larger ecology "that determines what possible outcomes, effects, changes, or products" (p. 120). This chapter has laid the historical foundations that form the current assessment ecology in which organizations, individuals, and texts interact.

A central question of this book is *how* rubrics normalize our discourse about writing and what power we have over this as administrators and teachers in higher education. In order to answer this question, I follow the stories of Kristen and Dwayne and their colleagues at Oak and St. Rita's as they interact with, and sometimes adapt, the VALUE rubric for Written Communication. In addition, I continue to engage with the discourse and texts of the AAC&U about the VALUE rubrics and their role in higher education. As I explain in Chapter 3, institutional ethnography provides a methodology for connecting the everyday experiences of individuals to larger power structures that is useful for understanding how rubrics function on the institutional level. Institutional ethnography examines "how individuals take up texts and coordinate their actions, so they produce *the particular institution's standard sequences*, its decision, policies, and outcomes" (Turner, 2006, p. 140). When Kristen and Dwayne decide to "take up" the VALUE rubric for Written Communication, they knowingly or unknowingly operate within the larger, historical forces of the writing assessment ecology.

CHAPTER 3.

MAPPING ASSESSMENT POWER WITH INSTITUTIONAL ETHNOGRAPHY

As established in Chapter 2, writing assessment functions within the larger neoliberal economy of accountability in the current university. Composition-ists have argued that good writing assessment is local (Huot, 2002), and yet, we cannot deny the function that assessment plays in maintaining the institution of higher education nationally. Historically, studies of writing assessment have focused on either large-scale or local assessment, and we have thus far lacked strong methodologies for connecting these large-scale institutional practices with local, individual perspectives. Also common is the move to acknowledge or criticize larger institutional movements but counter them immediately with local alternatives. For example, Chris Anson et al.'s (2012) piece "Big Rubrics and Weird Genres" began by discounting the utility of the AAC&U VALUE rubrics for assessment due to the failure of generic rubrics across disciplines and then moved immediately to providing examples of "best practice" for dis-ciplinary assessment. While such examples are valuable for WPAs, not all have the luxury of using other means of assessment if administrators farther up the chain dictate practice. This fixation on best, rather than actual practice, is not unique to studies of assessment. LaFrance (2019) noted that an overall weakness in the research of the field has been that work on program design and management tends to "standardize, generalize, and even erase identities, expertise, and labor contributed by diverse participants" (p. 7). Those who compose articles on writing program design and assessment, for example, are likely to be tenured or tenure-track members of the field of rhetoric and com-position, yet there are many who conduct writing assessment who come from other disciplinary backgrounds or are assessment professionals, rather than writing instructors or administrators.

I have my own skepticism regarding large-scale, national assessment in both theory and practice, and Chapter 2 outlines many reasons why such assessment contributes to a history of accountability, austerity, and even racism. Yet, this book is not focused on alternatives but rather on everyday, real-world practice of individuals at institutions that align themselves with the larger national move-ment of the AAC&U's VALUE assessment. That alignment may be purposeful, imposed, or even unknown by the individuals participating in the use and adaptations of the rubrics. The shift from outlining best practice in our field to looking at actual practice, requires a different approach to research, one I outline in this chapter.

Institutional ethnography, or IE for short, was established by Dorothy Smith in sociology and popularized in writing studies by Michelle LaFrance. IE provides researchers a means to study "local actualities as . . . manifest in, around, and through writing" (LaFrance, 2019, p. 12). It puts these local practices in the context of larger, institutional systems of power. Within the landscape of neoliberal austerity, it is imperative that we "uncover how what we do is coordinated by the ideological and political discourses that imbue our lives and our work" and institutional ethnography gives us a methodology for doing so (LaFrance, 2019, p. 16). Although IE has not yet been used to look specifically at writing assessment, LaFrance (2019) saw that potential when she noted that rubrics are "institutional circuits" used to bring cohesion to a writing program and align faculty work (p. 43). IE is well suited for drawing connections between individual faculty members' use of rubrics and larger, national movements that use rubric-based assessment.

IE offers a robust vocabulary for understanding the role that institutions and institutional texts play in the everyday work of individuals (LaFrance & Nicolas, 2012; LaFrance, 2019). By studying local writing assessment practice using the methodology and vocabulary of institutional ethnography, I seek to uncover how large-scale national trends, specifically the AAC&U's VALUE movement, are interpreted, used, and resisted in everyday, local practice. In this chapter, I outline the details of how IE is used to connect local practice and institutional power and describe my own methods of using IE to study the use of the AAC&U VALUE rubrics. I define what is meant by both institution and ethnography in the IE lens. I explicate key vocabulary that I will use throughout the book: problematic, ruling relations, standpoint, and boss texts. I then detail the methods of my own study and analysis, noting that while methods within IE vary widely, a common vocabulary and epistemological approach guides the collection, analysis, and presentation of data.

DEFINING INSTITUTIONS AND INSTITUTIONAL DISCOURSE

What does IE mean by institution or institutional? For Smith (2005), institutions appear in local settings, but also participate in standard operations across locations. They are "complexes of relations and hierarchical organization" (Smith,

2005, p. 206). Universities are one example. Universities exist as local institutions and as a part of the institution of higher education as a whole. However, "the university" is very different depending on whose standpoint it is viewed from (LaFrance, 2019). Writing programs and other campus communities come "into being in the moments in which people negotiate the everyday toward some highly individualized end" (p. 24).

Institutions are also held together by texts, some of which span across individual, local institutions. These texts, and their local interpretation, define "the university" as an institution. For example, LaFrance (2019) explained that statements by national organizations, such as the CWPA Outcomes Statement, are used to guide work on multiple campuses. They, therefore, define writing for individuals who may encounter them from a variety of standpoints: WPAs, teachers, students, upper administrators, and even the public. Texts like these are often key to the relationship between individuals and institutions and connect local and translocal practice (Smith, 2005). IE provides researchers a means to tie together these two different meanings of "institution"—the local, embodied practice of the institution and the institution of higher education—and allows us to explore how the two are co-constitutive. Institutional ethnographers look for texts that are replicated across settings (Smith & Turner, 2014). Such texts create what Smith and Turner (2014) labeled "institutional circuits" or "sequences of text-coordinated action" that span locations but authorize local and individual action (p. 10). Similarly, Campbell (2006) used the term institutional discourse to define shared ways of knowing across professional or managerial communities that govern institutional relations and allow for action within institutions.

Although IE looks specifically for the way that institutional discourse reinforces institutional power, it also stresses the role of individuals and the agency they have within systems. LaFrance (2019) noted that institutional discourses are "powerful and coercive" but individual, everyday activities as equally powerful (p. 115). This statement is key to the way institutional ethnographers view the institution, and why institutional ethnography does not focus solely on the study of texts. Smith and Turner (2014) explained that even when texts span institutions, the institutional ethnographer is interested in "'occurrences' at the moment of reading" (p. 9). It is in these occurrences that individual power can also be seen. One of the most important and powerful tenants of institutional ethnography is that these texts and the talk surrounding them are, in fact, "acts *of* the institution" (Turner, 2006, p. 140). Although institutional norms "speak to, for, and over individuals," ultimately for IE, individuals are the institution and can thus resist and change these norms (LaFrance, 2019, p. 18).

DEFINING ETHNOGRAPHY IN IE

It is bears repeating that: "An *institutional ethnography* is not simply an ethnography of or an ethnography that has been constructed within an institution" (Tummons, 2017, p. 150). Nor is IE a specific set of methods. In fact, unlike other forms of ethnography, IE can be conducted without conducting any sort of observation (Rankin, 2017b). Rather it is a particular *approach* to multiple types of data. Jonathan Tummons (2017) called it a "framework for inquiry," a way of thinking, and a "philosophy as well as methodology" (pp. 153–154). Similarly, Janet Rankin (2017b) called IE an "epistemological shift," noting that this precludes it being combined with other methodologies (p. 1). LaFrance (2019) clearly defined how IE functions as a methodology within writing studies to focus on the social context of writing and the way networks of texts influence people. IE can be used with a variety of specific methods, including observations, interviews, surveys, or textual analysis (such as archival work), but it always works toward the goal uncovering the influence of institutional power on everyday practice.

One distinct feature of IE that fits particularly well with writing studies is a focus on texts and institutional discourse. Rather than focusing on any and all experiences in a specific setting, IE looks specifically for "replicable forms of social action that actual situated textual activities produce" (Turner, 2006, p. 140). Textual analysis is not a means of triangulation, as it might be more traditional ethnography. Rather, IE combines a focus on textual analysis and human interaction specifically to see how human interactions are textually mediated (Tummons, 2017). In addition, IE often combines data from different locations rather than an exclusive look at one setting. In so doing, institutional ethnographers aim to map how practices are textually coordinated across settings (McCoy, 2014).

The ultimate goal of IE seems to vary somewhat among those who employ the methodology; however, some common motivations link together different approaches. As with other forms of ethnography, detailed descriptions are an agreed upon feature of IE. For Campbell (2006), the institutional ethnographer aims to develop a description of institutional relations as they play out in individual experiences. Smith (2005) referred to this detailed description as creating a "map" of institutional complexes. Throughout the literature on IE, it is clear that these descriptions of individual experience are meant to relate to a bigger, institutional picture—one that connects social relationship and texts. Another common theme is the "uncovering" or exposing of power relationships that are often not apparent to individuals. LaFrance and Nicolas (2012) defined the goal of IE to: "uncover *how things happen*—what practices constitute the institution as we think of it, how discourse may be understood to compel and shape those practices" (p. 131). This focus on *how* things happen over *what* is happening is a key difference between IE and traditional ethnography (LaFrance, 2019). Description is still key to IE, but it is for the purpose of connecting sites of practice and showing how institutional power interacts with local relationships rather than to describe what is happening at one specific site.

For Rankin (2017b) the major shift that distinguishes IE from other ethnography is that IE seeks to generate knowledge about the ways that individuals are "being organized against their own interests" (p. 1). Thus, IE often has a liberatory, social justice tint to it—it ultimately functions from the assumption that if we can uncover the ways that institutions affect individual experience, we can then work to change and improve our institutions. As with all forms of critical ethnography, IE views "personal experience *as uniquely responsive to* the social organization of institutions" (LaFrance & Nicolas, 2012, p. 134). By situating texts in the local settings where they are written and used, IE has consequences for actual practice.

Although some institutional ethnographers, including Smith (2005), see IE as addressing larger issues of power that are generalizable across multiple settings, the institutional ethnographer is not solely responsible for generalizing from the data. Rather, the knowledge produced by IE is seen as a collaboration between the research and participant. Even before IE, Newkirk (1992) acknowledged the role of the reader and their interpretive process in creating knowledge from ethnography. IE extends ethnography's focus on "the relationships between inhabitants and between the environment and its inhabitants" (MacNealy, 1998, p. 215) beyond the "boundaries of any one informant's experiences" to identify social relations and power structures that replicate across inhabitants and environments (Campbell & Gregor, 2004, p. 90). Those boundaries also extend beyond the researcher's experience and written account to connections readers make to their own local relationships and power structures.

KEY VOCABULARY IN IE

In addition to defining institutions and ethnography, IE comes with a set of vocabulary that is useful for understanding institutional power and everyday practice. One of the great ironies of IE is that as researchers, we are ourselves agents of institutional power, and that power is reflected in our own vocabulary and jargon. Although Naomi Nichols, Alison Griffith, and Mitchell McLarnon (2017) noted that the researcher should "resist the use of social science categories to group and name people's experiences" (p. 112), IE itself uses a specific set of vocabulary. In the section, I explain four key concepts in IE: the problematic, ruling relations, standpoint, and boss texts.

PROBLEMATIC

The process of conducting an institutional ethnography starts with a "problematic." The problematic in IE draws on Althusser's problematic as an ideological context for work and is broader than starting with a research question. Rather, the problematic is "a territory to be discovered, not a question that is concluded in its answer" (Smith, 2005, p. 41). The researcher may start with a work process or issue that they have observed in their own life; however, it is key for an institutional ethnographer to expand beyond their own institutional context (Campbell & Gregor, 2004; Smith, 2006; Turner, 2006). For example, Griffith (2006) used her own experiences as single mother as a starting point to examine how the term "single parent family" is used in educational research to gain funding for inner-city schools and how this use relates to real experiences of single parents. The problematic, for Griffith, was the way this term defined families within both local institutions and schools and within the larger institution of education.

As the researcher expands their research, the problematic also changes and expands. According to Rankin (2017b), while the research may begin with a problematic, that problematic should be further developed from the institutional ethnographer's analysis, which connects smaller problematics to the larger research arc. LaFrance (2019) also noted the way the problematic influences data analysis, as the researcher looks for overlap between everyday lived experiences gathered in the data and the problematic. Rather than define everything that is happening in the site of study, the researcher looks for relevance to the problematic and develops the study accordingly. It "becomes the basis for how the inquiry is conducted" (Campbell & Gregor, 2004, p. 48).

RULING RELATIONS

The term "ruling relations" is key to understanding the perspective on institutional power and texts offered by IE. Smith (2005) defined ruling relations as the "extraordinary yet ordinary complex of relations that are textually mediated, that connect us across space and time and organize our everyday lives—the corporations, government bureaucracies, academic and professional discourses, mass media, and the complicit relations that interconnect them" (p. 10). The role of texts in maintaining ruling relationships is crucial; they are the "principle instruments of ruling" (Rankin, 2017b, p. 2). Smith (2005) explained that as capitalism evolved, workers no longer knew their managers and were thus ruled not by individuals but by texts. Thus, ruling relations are specific to the arena of systemic management in which work became coordinated through texts. Writing scholar JoAnne Yates (1989) tied the evolution of systemic management in the 1870s to the expansion of genres in business communication—specifically genres such as forms, manuals, and memos. These texts evolved as genres because they fit a particular rhetorical need that emerged during this time period. Ruling relations are not created by a single text, but rather it is the *"replicability of texts"* that allows for ruling (Smith, 2005, p. 166). Again, the concept of genre applies here, specifically administrative genres that are replicated over time and eventually become "how it is done" across different settings (LaFrance, 2019; Miller, 2017; Smith, 2005).

Thus, ruling relations operate in the background and are often invisible to the subject. These texts define our roles, our subject positions, regardless of our own embodied experiences, and those experiences are displaced by "the textual real" (Smith, 2005, p. 28). For example, institutional ethnographer George Smith (2014) demonstrated how legal code defined gay sex acts as "indecent acts" and thus tied the subjectivity of queerness to the subjectivity of criminal (p. 39). Thus, ruling relations function through genres to define individuals within systems of power. It is how ruling relations function in all spheres, including higher education.

Although not using IE, Donna Strickland (2011) described early work in composition as aimed to systematize the first-year course and standardize teacher practice. The WPA role—or standpoint—came into being as a means to control the "disordered masses" of composition teachers and even the most activist WPAs cannot be entirely separated from that position (Strickland, 2011). As a part of the move toward academic management, common texts—such as common rubrics—have defined what it means to be a "teaching subject" who needs to be managed by a WPA. In addition to being textual, ruling relations are often tied to "economic relations" that are "operationalized within and beyond an institution" (Russell, 2017, p. xiv). From their position within the institution, WPAs must deal with the economic concerns of the university, such as hiring adjunct faculty to fill a last-minute vacancy. As a field, writing studies has theorized this labor, but IE provides us with a new vocabulary and ability to expose ruling relations and may "reduce the frustration we feel about living and working in societies such as ours where things seem to get decided behind our backs, or at least outside of our control" (Campbell, 2006, p. 105).

STANDPOINT

When analyzing subjectivity and subjects, IE often draws on the concept of standpoint. Standpoints are "shared identities" (LaFrance, 2019, p. 5). Standpoint is the role that an individual occupies within a larger institutional structure. Researchers often decide to approach individuals who occupy a particular standpoint and draw connections among individuals that occupy that same role. For example, a researcher looking at the medical field might choose to focus on either the standpoint of the patients or the standpoint of the nurses (Rankin, 2017b). While each individual patient will have their own perspective on their treatment, they occupy a similar standpoint in relationship to the medical institution. Standpoint is a complimentary concept to ruling relations: "Where ruling relations enable institutional ethnographers to trace broad social patterns, 'standpoint' helps the ethnographer to uncover disjunctions, divergences, and distinctions experienced by individuals within those groups" (LaFrance, 2019, p. 35). As used by feminist theorists in the 1970–1980s, standpoint theory works against positivist notions of research that obscure ruling relations and call for universality (LaFrance, 2019; Smith, 2005). Rather, the post-positivist approach of standpoint theory acknowledges that individual social realities are never neutral and that individuals are always partially defined in relationship to their role within an institution (LaFrance, 2019). An institution looks different and operates differently, depending on one's standpoint.

By turning to the concept of standpoint, institutional ethnographers can avoid defaulting to standpoint of ruling (Rankin, 2017b). The researcher becomes aware of the multiple standpoints participants occupy in relationship to institutions and ruling relations. In so doing, they can uncover social networks and ruling relationships that are otherwise obscured and contextualize an individual's social reality within the institutional setting (LaFrance, 2019). For example, in LaFrance's (2019) chapter about writing assignments in a writing intensive course, she separated out the standpoint of teaching assistants (TAs) working with the course from the standpoint of the primary instructors. In so doing, she was better able to explicate how these roles and power differentials affected individuals' interactions with course assignments and documents.

Standpoint comes into play for institutional ethnographers both as they plan their research and as they analyze their data. Smith (2005) advised starting research by identifying "a standpoint in an institutional order that provides the guiding perspective from which that order will be explored" (p. 32). During data analysis, the researcher should also seek to understand the standpoint of each participant (Reid, 2017). Finally, standpoint should be considered as the researcher reports on their research. Marie Campbell and Frances Gregor (2004) argued that part of the responsibility of an institutional ethnographer was to write texts "that express the standpoint of people and to help make them available to those who will use the work's subversive capacity in their own struggles" (p. 128). Of course, one of the critiques of standpoint theory and institutional ethnography is that the researcher can never fully remove their own standpoint in order to focus on the standpoint of the participants: "research produces rather than preserves the presence of the subject" (Walby, 2007, p. 1009). In addition, standpoints are always limited, and thus when research is presented through standpoint, our understanding is always partial (LaFrance, 2019).

BOSS TEXTS & INSTITUTIONAL CIRCUITS

Texts often form a key part of the work of IE. In particular, researchers look to examine "boss texts" that span across institutional settings. LaFrance (2019) defined boss texts as: "texts that transmit ruling relations between sites—carrying rhetorical influences, granting agency and authority, casting representations of people and their work, and sanctioning activities" (p. 42). She explained that texts such as websites, textbooks, syllabi, rubrics, and even classroom management software "can dramatically order conceptions of writing" (p. 43). Another example LaFrance (2019) gave was "employment texts," and her book detailed the way that job descriptions and annual review processes for writing center directors either value or diminish their work.

Those in writing studies may be familiar with the concept of institutional and administrative genres, concepts that overlap with the notion of boss texts. Carolyn Miller (2017) defined "institutional genres" as genres with strong conventions that come from a long historical tradition, such as the research article or presidential inaugural. Similarly, Miller (2017) defined "administrative genres" as genres dictated by those in power to serve the needs of the institution, such as forms and reports that with preset guidelines. While IE's notion of institutional discourse might include both institutional and administrative genres, it is nearly impossible to trace structures of power inherent in institutional genres through IE since they are more historically embedded in institutional systems. However, administrative genres may be viewed as they are being developed, written, or enacted.

Boss texts are part of an institutional circuit, making everyday practice actionable and authorized by the institution (Smith & Turner, 2014). They are linked to accountability and standardize practice across settings (LaFrance, 2019). Working within a genre lens rather than an IE methodology, Leslie Seawright's (2017) study of the police report fits well with this definition. The report closes a circuit of textual interactions and serves as the official account of what is often a complex series events, representing those events from an institutional rather than individual perspective. The genre of the report ultimately serves to "perform the police as an organization" (Smith, 2014, p. 34). The police becomes synonymous with the *institution* of the police rather than the standpoint of the officer on the scene. Seawright (2017) explained that the police report ultimately obscures the experiences of individuals in an attempt to gain cultural capital for the police. Thus, Seawright's explanation of the way genre works in this instance fills well with IE's terminology of boss texts and institutional circuits.

However, using the IE terminology of boss text, rather than the term administrative genres, focuses our attention on how these texts enact ruling relations. They are, in many cases, a stand-in for an absent boss. Such institutional texts often use passive voice and nominalization in order to obscure the actual agent behind the work (Grace, Zurawski & Sinding, 2014). For example, rather than a supervisor reviewing a teacher's grades, the text of a programmatic rubric fulfills that "boss" function by standardizing how and what a teacher should grade. Just as an individual police officer was rendered *the police* through the process of reporting, we see individual faculty members become synonymous with the institution of higher education through the boss texts that guide their work.

Institutional ethnographers seek to interrupt this circuit of texts and return to the moments where boss texts are created and responded to. Dorothy Smith and Susan Marie Turner (2014) referred to this moment as the "text-reader conversation" (p. 12). Unlike some methods of analysis (such as actor-network theory), IE does not grant texts agency but rather sees individuals as agents who "activate" texts (Smith & Turner, 2014, p. 9). Thus, observation and interviews with individuals are key to IE rather than focusing on textual analysis.

THE IE PROCESS

The process of conducting an institutional ethnography varies from researcher to researcher as well as by each individual study. While I define certain stages to the process of IE and my own study, it should be noted that these stages are often recursive. It is the flexibility of research process and the valuing of participants' perspectives rather than the researcher's that maintains IE's specific ontological approach (Rankin, 2017b). For example, gathering texts might be done as an initial stage but new texts might be gathered as they are created or come up in interviews. Likewise, defining the problematic sets the study in motion, but also keeps it flowing as the researcher continually returns to and re-defines it. Research methods in IE are always evolving to the benefit of the study. IE resists the positivist approach that rigid set up ensures quality research; rather, rigor comes from continually returning to the problematic to draw connections between individuals and social structures (LaFrance, 2019). IE also finds its rigor in the map of social relations that is developed as the final product of the ethnography (DeVault & McCoy, 2006). For example, the selection of interviewees may be open-ended, and new participants may emerge as the study evolves, but those interviews must ultimately inform the researcher's understanding of the problematic.

1. Defining the Problematic

According to Marjorie DeVault and Liza McCoy (2006), the first stage in IE is to "identify an experience" from which the problematic is drawn. This experience is often drawn from the researcher's own practice. For Susan Marie Turner (2006), that practice often centers on a process that uses a particular text. My problematic stems from such a process: university-wide writing assessment completed using the AAC&U VALUE rubrics. In 2014, my institution began a university-wide assessment of their upper-level core curriculum classes, some of which were designated "writing intensive." As we do not have a writing across the curriculum (WAC) program, this assessment was led by the assistant provost for institutional research. He led a small committee in adapting the AAC&U's VALUE rubrics for written communication and critical thinking and then trained a group of faculty raters to assess artifacts from across campus. This was the first time I had heard of the VALUE rubrics and, believing that best writing assessment is local, I was curious and concerned about the use of a national rubric to score artifacts at my own institution.

Defining the problematic also involves identifying the standpoint or standpoints at play. For example, LaFrance (2019) defined the practice of constructing writing assignments in a course that involved teaching assistants (TAs) and faculty members collaborating in a hierarchical setting as the problematic for one of her institutional ethnographies. For LaFrance, the standpoint of TAs and the standpoint of faculty members were central to researching her problematic, which rested on how the interaction between these two standpoints formed a perception of writing within the university. Knowing that the assessment using the VALUE rubric at my institution was not administered or conducted by experts in writing studies, I was curious how understanding of the rubric would vary according to disciplinary standpoint. Thus, my initial research at my institution involved observing the norming sessions using the rubric and interviewing faculty from across campus about their scoring experience. Indeed, I found differing understandings of the rubric based on different perspectives about writing.

This local research served as a sort of pilot study that defined my research and the problematic. I was concerned with taking a national rubric for writing into a local context and modifying it, and I was particularly concerned about how doing so influenced non-compositionists. However, to truly define my concerns as a *problematic* in IE terms, I needed to see if other institutions were taking similar action and if these actions raised similar concerns. This step involves expanding to different work sites to see how similar work practices are carried out in other settings and how institutional power connects these processes across sites (Smith, 2005; Smith, 2006). After two summers of research at my home institution, I decided to expand my study to other colleges and universities.

2. Gathering Texts

In writing studies, stage two of an institutional ethnography is often focused on gathering of public documents about the site that has been identified for research. The researcher locates official documents before going into the site and interviewing local informants about the use of the documents (LaFrance, 2019). These documents may be policy documents rather than local texts (Rankin, 2017a). For my study, stage two involved the gathering of and analyzing AAC&U documents about the VALUE movement. In addition, I conducted a national survey about the use of the VALUE Written Communication rubric to gather local versions of the rubric and information about their use. The first grounded me in national policy (or at least national suggestion) about best practices in assessment. The second allowed for insight into actual practice and gave me a set of modified rubrics to analyze.

I should note that I initially saw this part of the study as gathering background information or "getting up to speed," not as a part of the institutional ethnography. In other research methods, it might be viewed as such. However, LaFrance's (2019) book, which was released after my data was collected, clarified for me the importance of gathering these institutional texts as a key part of process of the institutional ethnographer. Without a deep familiarity with the way the AAC&U frames their VALUEs rubrics, I would not be able to analyze the way the larger institution of higher education interacts with local institutional practice. In addition, DeVault and McCoy (2006) framed the second stage of institutional ethnography in terms of following action over time as it is organized in a set of documents. Although I would later do this with my specific institutional settings, it was also important to trace how the VALUE rubrics were organized and enacted over the course of many years by the AAC&U in their own literature and studies. Document collection, however, was not one static stage of my research—particularly as the AAC&U continues to release new studies and data about the VALUE rubrics, and the rhetoric of those resources continues to shift. Even after local data collection ceased in 2018, I continued to attend multiple presentations and webinars held by the AAC&U about the VALUE rubrics and read new materials they released. These materials are featured prominently in Chapter 4 but also appear throughout the book.

3. Identifying Sites of Study & Standpoints

Identifying standpoints is also ongoing throughout the research process. I initially identified the standpoint of non-writing specialists as key to my study; however, at the time, I had not fully embraced IE, and thus my initial attempt to identify participants was more positivist in nature. I separated my survey participants into schools based on Carnegie classification, and then identified where the VALUE rubric was used: in a first-year writing program, a WAC program, a university-wide assessment, or another setting. I thought that this would offer me a range of standpoints, but ultimately, this type of positionally was not useful. I found that these classifications—the classifications of the institution of higher education—conflicted with the lived experiences I found at the two institutions I selected for further study. Thus, it was almost serendipitous that I ended up with two institutions that represented vastly different standpoints within higher education.

The two schools that I identified for further research are referred to by the pseudonyms St. Rita's and Oak University. I selected St. Rita's as a representative "MA college" with "postbaccalaureate programs," as it is listed on the Carnegie classification website. However, this extremely small school, with a student body of less than 1000, is confined to one building, and the master's degree programs had no bearing on my study or the use of the VALUE rubrics. Likewise, defining the type of program was not fully relevant to the two small institutions I selected. At St. Rita's, the general education committee was looking at the VALUE rubrics, but a version was also used to assess portfolios from first-year writing classes. At Oak, the writing program covered both first-year writing classes and writing across the curriculum. However, the rubrics had also been used for general education and some Oak faculty had attended the national AAC&U training.

Thus, my understanding of and selection of standpoints evolved throughout my data collection. Rather than the positionally of the institution, I began to look at the positionally of my participants, non-writing specialists. Much has been written about the use of rubrics within our field, and our scholars in writing assessment already have a voice in this conversation. Drawing from my own experience where a local assessment professional rather than a composition specialist conducted university-wide writing assessment using the VALUE rubrics, I wanted to know more about the standpoint with which non-writing assessment and non-writing studies faculty approached such processes. The two schools I selected were both small, and neither had an area of rhetoric and composition faculty. Although Oak University has a writing center professional, their writing program administrator, Kristen, came from the discipline of history, and their new writing program was established under the leadership of a computer scientist, Ben. At St. Rita's, the general education assessment process was being led by a faculty member in English, Dwayne, who specialized in creative writing, but who had some training in composition and was thus drawn to improve writing instruction. However, he held no official title related to writing.

These two main informants—Kristen and Dwayne—thus provided a standpoint not often depicted in writing studies. In addition, I sought a variety of standpoints within the two institutions I visited. I interviewed faculty from across the curriculum as well as a provost or associate provost at each institution. By interviewing a member of the upper administration, I was able to see how larger institutional initiatives, such as grant funding from the AAC&U, influenced assessment decisions on campus. Together these perspectives helped me define my problematic and explore how writing and writing assessment is defined from these multiple standpoints within these institutions.

4. Observations, Interviews & Hidden Documents

The next stage of IE is collecting personal accounts and gathering non-public documents (LaFrance, 2019). Turner (2014) stressed that institutional ethnographers should examine the "traces of [a text's] production" but also show the way these texts are read and how those readings influence decision making. The core of my institutional ethnography comes from the data gathered from observations, interviews, and textual resources gathered at St. Rita's and Oak between 2016–2018. I observed meetings where the rubrics were discussed and norming sessions where raters were trained to read the rubrics. At Oak, I observed several writing committee meetings as well as a norming session for assessors. At St. Rita's, I observed a general education committee's members discussing goals and the VALUE Written Communication rubric. These moments "activated" the text of the rubric and defined how it was used in the real practice of assessment at these universities.

Kevin Walby (2007) also suggested interviewing those who "bring the text(s) into institutional processes" (p. 1013). Interviews in IE are often not as structured as they might be in other methodologies, but they are more than just "talking to people" (DeVault & McCoy, 2006). Site visits and observations may lead to less formal interviews and interview questions emerge organically from the research process (Campbell & Gregor, 2004; DeVault & McCoy, 2006). I began by setting up interviews with members of the committees I observed, but I also allowed my research visits to develop organically. At St. Rita's, I found participants saying things like, "you should talk to so-and-so, let me see if they're in their office." Although Oak was more spread out, I noted others who were mentioned in interviews or suggested to me as potential participants and contacted them for an interview. Thus, my interview pool expanded as my research developed.

Interviews in IE often involve referring back to specific texts. DeVault and McCoy (2006) instructed the institutional ethnographer to question interviewees about boss texts and to also collect any additional texts as mentioned in interviews. For example, they reference Ellen Pence's study, where she asked social workers how they would change a reporting form they used if they could. Similarly, when I interviewed writing committee members, I asked them about the rubric they were using, including their understanding of the terms used and any changes they would make to their rubric. These interviews were somewhat structured because I focused primarily on the text of the rubric and the process of revising the rubric and/or assessing artifacts that the participants were involved with. However, I did allow these interviews to digress into multiple tangents as led by participants, and this data revealed particularly relevant information about how participants' backgrounds and relationships influenced their work with the rubric. As I continued regular interviews over the course of two years with my main informants, these interviews, in particular, became less formal. Although these interviews still focused on assessment and rubrics, the less formal nature of the ongoing relationship with my key informants also allowed for factors such as institutional politics and faculty relations—and their impact on the work of assessment—to emerge as key factors in my study.

Finally, as they conduct and transcribe interviews, institutional ethnographers listen for information about other texts that may relate to the problematic (Walby, 2007). These texts may be official local documents or may be less official texts used by individual interviewees. Kristen at Oak diligently gave me copies of reports, meeting minutes, and rubric drafts. However, I was sometimes handed texts within an interview, such as a rubric used in class by a particular faculty member, and these "hidden texts" served as another data point in uncovering the ways that ruling relations affect perceptions of writing and writing assessment on campus. For example, Patrice at St. Rita's handed me a rubric that she was given years ago by English faculty that she still used to assess writing in her classroom. While participants were not always able to locate texts that they referenced or did not always follow through, these local "hidden" texts added to my understanding of ruling relations at these schools.

5. THE DIALOG OF ANALYSIS

Analysis in IE is seen as a form of dialog that emerges between the researcher and their notes/interview transcripts (Smith, 2005). Institutional ethnographers also put data from one institution in conversation with data from other institutions, thus creating a dialog across scenes. Rather than applying formal coding, the researcher might approach their data with a new set of questions that allows them to draw connections between participant stories (DeVault & McCoy, 2006;

Smith, 2005). For example, Campbell (2006) suggested approaching interview transcripts with questions such as: "What is the work that these informants are describing or alluding to?" and "How is the work articulated to institutional work processes and institutional order?" (p. 111). LaFrance (2019) stressed the importance of the connections the researcher makes between lived experiences and institutional discourse, and the need to look for "overlap of competing values and ideals" (pp. 39–40). In short, the institutional ethnographer looks for "recurring events or recurring use of words" across institutional contexts in order to define "how things happen *here*, in the same way they happen *over there*" (Campbell & Gregor, 2004, p. 69).

Often, institutional ethnographers refer to analysis as a process of mapping, which leads some researchers to form textual or visual maps demonstrating power relationships between institutions and individuals. For example, Debra Talbot (2017) created visual maps to show how each teacher she interviewed connected to ruling relations. Even if there is no creation of a physical map, the researcher engages in a "kind of analytical mapping that locates individuals and their experiences within a complex institutional field" (Campbell, 2006, p. 113). Mapping can also refer to a more narrative form. Walby (2007) described a process of "ghostwriting" where the interviews were transformed into narrative accounts that were then shared with the participants. Rankin (2017a), too, wrote chunks of narrative representing the experiences of different participants. While maps look different for each institutional ethnography, the process of linking individuals to ruling relations is key to the work of analysis in IE.

I used multiple techniques when analyzing my data, and as is typical for institutional ethnography, this process was ongoing rather than one final stage of the research. During my site visits, I took extensive notes as well as some photographs. Afterwards, I wrote brief narrative accounts of my visit, particularly centering on the embodied experience I gathered from being physically present at the sites. I transcribed all interviews and meeting recordings myself and wrote memos with my initial thoughts after I completed each transcription. Working across these experiences, I drafted the narratives seen in the introduction to this book, which I shared with my two key informants who agreed that they represented their experiences.

When analyzing interview and observation transcripts, I drew on James Reid's (2017) concept of a "listening guide." Reid (2019) analyzed transcripts for four institutional factors: relations of ruling, reflexivity, textually mediated relationships, and cultural/social context (p. 37). Although I used different terminology, I also read my interviews and meeting transcripts for multiple levels of interaction between individuals and institutions. I separated out larger institutional influences (organizations, grants, etc.), disciplinary influences, local influences (from the particular school), classroom teaching, and personal/external influences (family, individual interests). I also marked statements about writing and about assessment in which the participant made broad statements that seemed absent of these influences. As a researcher, I do not see these instances as void of institutional influences; however, I found it important to see what statements about writing the participants expressed as being universal rather than disciplinary or personal. For example, when I asked some participants what good writing looked like to them, they responded with statements that seemed generalized—it is *clear, concise*—but as we know from previous research such terms mean different things to members of different disciplines (Zawacki & Gentemann, 2009).

When identifying large-scale institutional influences, I particularly looked for factors that spanned local settings. The AAC&U VALUE Written Communication rubric was clearly one of the major influences I looked for in my study. However, participants also referred to other large-scale institutional factors, such as accreditation, grant funding, and testing. I paid attention to any references to these wide-spread influences on higher education as a whole. I also looked for more specific "institutional *language*" in transcripts, such as places where participants reference position titles or policies (Rankin, 2017b, p. 4). Talbot (2017) looked for teachers using language from policy documents. Similarly, I "listened" when participants used specific language from the VALUE rubrics, such as using terms like "benchmark," or titles of other VALUE rubrics such as "Civic Engagement." I also looked for institutional language that reflects practices in higher education as a whole, words such as "proficiency" or "standards." Also included in the category of institutional influences were references to training sessions held by the AAC&U that my participants attended. Mapping these large-scale institutional influences helped me see how the AAC&U and other organizations, policies, and financial considerations influence writing assessment and how that assessment represents institutions of higher education.

I marked local institutional influences separately from large-scale institutional influences. These local influences ranged from specific factors of institutional setting, such as student population to individual faculty relationships. Although committees are a common structure in academia as a whole, I marked references to specific local committees and times that interviewees referenced their role on these committees as local influences. In particular, I focused on the faculty relationships on these committees. Some of these instances involved specific local stories, but others were about the interaction among faculty in the meetings I observed. One of the stark differences between Oak and St. Rita's was the element of faculty relationships as well as the very different populations of students they serve. These local influences help show how larger cross-institutional initiatives play out very differently due to multiple local factors.

Another way to examine the relationship between large-scale influences in higher education and local institutional context was to look for moments where participants referenced larger disciplinary structures. Often (but not always) when participants spoke of a disciplinary community (chemistry, English, etc.), they spoke as teachers with individual classrooms rather than as members of a larger institution. For example, they rarely mention disciplinary organizations or journals. These moments contrast with moments when participants make generalizations about writing that they view as universal, such as referring to the "standard academic essay" as if one form transcended disciplines and classrooms. This tension between disciplinary language and generalizations about good writing is common when assessing writing across the curriculum (Zawacki & Gentemann, 2009). Common rubrics can reinforce these bad ideas about writing as a general form. Although both institutions I visited had committees with representation from around campus, I found that acknowledging disciplinary difference was more common at Oak than St. Rita's where faculty were more likely to talk about writing and teaching as general enterprises. In part, this may be due to the size of St. Rita's. Faculty there routinely taught in what I might consider a variety of disciplines. Patrice, for example, taught government along with sociology—disciplines that would likely be separate at a larger institution. Also, in the category of disciplinary influences, I included references to the discipline of writing studies or composition. Although neither of my main participants had a Ph.D. in the field, both interacted with the discipline in different ways. In addition, other faculty had experiences, often during their graduate studies, with composition as a field of study, and these experiences influenced their views on teaching and assessing writing.

Finally, there were a range of external and/or personal influences that proved to be an important part of understanding the relationships between these individual participants and their institutional settings. These influences connect individuals with larger societal structures, particularly racialized social structures. In particular, two participants shared a good deal about their own personal background and how that influenced their relationship to their profession in academia. Dr. Gerald Z, a key participant at St. Rita's, continually discussed his "blue collar" upbringing as the son of a cop, an identity that complicates his relationship with academia as a whole as well as with his first-generation students. Brad, an art history professor at Oak, also talked about his working-class upbringing, but he shared how his own participation in a study abroad program expanded his empathy for international students and upended his views on education. These two interviews, compared in Chapter 7, brought unexpected individual circumstances to the study that provided significant insight into how *individuals* operate within—but also in opposition to—the institutional structures of higher education.

Although much of my analysis focuses on these rich interviews and observations, the texts of the AAC&U as well as local texts also inform this study. The VALUE rubric for Written Communication and the "adaptations" the participants made to the rubric to create local versions were the focus of the interviews and observations. Early in my study, I imagined tracing the language changes between the VALUE Written Communication rubric and local writing rubrics over time, but as I will explain throughout the book, this type of analysis was not possible with the data gathered. Rather than ask "how" the rubrics were adapted, I often asked what adaptation meant to my participants and how the rubrics informed their views on writing and writing assessment. Like Walby (2007), I listened for references to all texts that influenced participants views on writing and assessment. In so doing, I aimed to map the limits of the influence of the VALUE rubrics in relationship to other texts that influenced writing assessment on these campuses. Following DeVault and McCoy (2006), my analysis of these texts is always in relationship to the interviews, which explore how the participants use and interact with these documents as assessors, curriculum planners, and instructors.

ANALYSIS CHAPTER OVERVIEWS

In what follows, I use the lens of institutional ethnography to discuss the AAC&U Written Communication VALUE rubric as part of an institutional circuit that includes many texts working together to define writing and writing assessment at colleges and universities. Drawing on Campbell's (2006) goals for institutional ethnography as a methodology, I seek to "develop a detailed, descriptive analysis" (p. 123) of the way that this a national rubric for writing shapes and organizes the work of those who teach and assess writing at Oak and St. Rita's. Chapters 4 and 5 work together to define the VALUE rubric for Written Communication as a boss text and to uncover the ruling relations behind the rubric. Boss texts have authority because they define "ideals of accountability, professionalism, and disciplinarily" (LaFrance, 2019, p. 80). The VALUE rubrics have redefined accountability in higher education in terms of rubrics, particularly when accounting for "soft skills" such as writing. Over time, the VALUE rubrics have also emerged as a means of national comparison, a tool for accreditation that proves schools are meeting national "ideals of accountability." Chapter 4 explains how the VALUE rubrics, in conjunction with larger governing forces in higher education such as grant funding and accreditation, defines what it means to be an institution of higher education. I describe how administrators and faculty and Oak and St. Rita's strategically adopt the rubrics as means of legitimizing their institutions and writing programs.

A second way that the VALUE Written Communication rubric functions as a boss text is in defining what it means to assess writing not through the original rubric, but through the rubric adaptation and assessment process designed by the AAC&U. Although the exact text changes, these alternations do not erase the influence of ruling relations. As Smith and Turner (2014) explained, replicability of texts does not imply that they are read or used the same way in each setting, yet the text is significant because it is recognized and replicated across settings. From the beginning of my research, I discovered that even when I could not directly trace the language of a locally-used rubric to the original VALUE Written Communication rubric, participants viewed the rubric as an adaptation. The very fact that they were using a *rubric* to assess writing came from their experiences with the AAC&U. In Chapter 5, I look at what "adaptation" means at both a national level and also to participants at Oak and St. Rita's. I examine how the dynamics of the writing committee at Oak and the general education committee at St. Rita's influence the final "adaptation" of the rubric for use in particular ways at these institutions.

Originally, I considered classroom use of the VALUE Written Communication rubric as a part of my problematic. However, the majority of my research participants did not use the rubric in the classroom. Nevertheless, their standpoint as classroom teachers influenced the way they viewed rubrics. Chapter 6 discusses the rubric as a genre of power both in and out of the classroom. In this chapter, I examine how faculty evaluated writing in their classroom and how they developed classroom rubrics. I also explore how the genre of the rubric becomes as stand-in for all classroom practice when used for large-scale assessment. Specifically, committee members at Oak and St. Rita's were seen as representatives of their departments and classrooms and thus worked to make sure large-scale assessment efforts accounted for their specific pedagogical practices. When looking at programmatic and national practice, which is often done in the absence of an assignment prompt, the student artifact is viewed as representative of classroom practice and the rubric is separated from other classroom genres.

Finally, Chapter 7 directly addresses the way that societal factors, specifically American individualism and a White racial habitus affect assessment and views of faculty members at St. Rita's and Oak. Drawing on the work of Bourdieu as well as Bonilla-Silva, Asao Inoue (2015) explained the way that "race as *habitus* structures and is structured into our lives," including our "expectations for writing" and the way that we assess it (p. 43). The idea of a racial habitus means thinking about race as continually being constructed through the body, through language, and through differences in opportunities and experience in the world. The racial makeup of the student body varied significantly between Oak and St. Rita's. Oak is a primarily White institution, while St. Rita's has a mix of White, Black, and Hispanic students. Yet, the faculty at both schools often adopt a colorblind rhetoric where the default for a prepared college student is White. This White racial habitus is coded within the rubrics these faculty members use and create, particularly in the dimensions for sentence-level "errors." While many faculty members in my study represent a sort of colorblind racism, I delve further into the way that two faculty members in particular discussed race, language, and their own experiences as White men. These two interviews also show us how White men exercise and/or abdicate their own individual power within the White racialized structures of academia.

Together these chapters present a nuanced and complex view of how rubrics, specifically those developed at the national level interact with local institutional and individual power dynamics. My conclusion addresses how the context in which rubrics are used is set at the national level, the university level, and the classroom level. I work to offer suggestions for how we think about these institutional levels in relationship to each other and to our own individual practices within teaching and administration. The rubric is a genre of power, a boss text, that is part of an ecology of assessment. Institutional ethnography helps articulate how that power is enacted and embodied in the everyday working lives of those who teach and assess writing at post-secondary institutions.

CHAPTER 4.

DEFINING THE VALUE RUBRICS AS BOSS TEXTS

The language of institutional ethnography helps define the role that rubrics play within the larger institution of higher education. This chapter defines the rubrics as boss texts that function as a part of the institutional circuit of accountability within higher education. As explained in Chapter 3, boss texts as a concept is similar to that of the administrative genre. Boss texts *transmit ruling relations between sites"* (LaFrance, 2019, p. 42). They "regulate—often standardize—practice, mediating idiosyncrasies and variability in local settings" (LaFrance, 2019, p. 43). By following common genre conventions, boss texts represent the work of the individual as actionable at the institutional level. Thus, they complete a circuit that represents actual lived work of individuals in a way that is accepted by institutions. People engage in institutional circuits by "building from an actual situation, a textual representation that will fit an institutionally authoritative text" (Griffith & Smith, 2014, p. 12). One specific type of institutional circuit that is particularly relevant to assessment work is the "accountability circuit," which is used to separate work into components to measure that work (p. 14). A rubric clearly fits this definition by separating the complex work of writing into clear, measurable components.

In fact, LaFrance (2019) called rubrics "the quintessential institutional circuit" (p. 43). At the classroom level, rubrics are used to define "good writing" to students, who work to produce writing in line with the rubric, and to teachers, who then assess that work according to the rubric. Work that the student puts into drafting, researching, or other parts of the writing and learning process ultimately must be represented in a way that aligns with the rubric. That rubric holds both teachers and students accountable to the same definitions of success. It makes the work of the individual student actionable in the form of a grade—the common currency across education as an institution. At a programmatic level, rubrics often serve as an institutional representation of the teaching and learning achieved within a writing program. They smooth out the idiosyncratic nature of instruction in a way that shows the classes across the program meet the same goals and learning outcomes (LaFrance, 2019). They close the institutional circuit by making the work of the writing program actionable—whether that action is changing curriculum or (more likely) simply reporting on current practice in order justify and continue that practice. In this way, all rubrics function as a part of accountability circuits.

Thus, all rubrics can be viewed as boss texts. Even in cases where the teacher designs their own rubric and the student can directly interact with that teacher; even when that student is consulted in the rubric development, teachers and students draw on prior genre knowledge to create the rubric. Key terminology that is repeated over time, across locations, is a sign that ruling relations are at work (LaFrance, 2019). For example, an individual teacher may use the category "Style and Mechanics" on their rubrics, simply because it is a common category that they have seen on rubrics over time. Dylan Dryer's (2013) corpus study of rubrics showed that these categories are common across institutions and teachers. Yet, it is unlikely that teachers using these categories recognize their origins in Diederich, French, and Carlton's 1961 ETS rubric. Organizations, such as ETS—or the AAC&U—thus function as the "bosses" that define our conception of good writing over time and across locations. However, those creating the rubrics may follow these conventions without knowledge of this larger institutional circuit they operate within. A professor may create their rubric based on one they saw in a book or received from a colleague; a group of students will draw on genre knowledge from other rubrics they have been scored on in the past. The use of these repeated conventions is simply how genres and boss texts work, but such workings are often not acknowledged or explicitly considered by those interacting with the texts.

The difference between the VALUE rubrics and classroom rubrics is that the VALUE rubrics are boss texts *by design*. The AAC&U sought to create meta-rubrics that would be used across institutions. Although they did expect that individual institutions would adapt and localize these rubrics, the rubrics also grew from the LEAP Outcomes, which are viewed as shared outcomes across various higher education stakeholders, as discussed in Chapter 2. Whether or not the VALUE rubrics are tweaked for local practice, they are still meant to connect local practice to national practice. This initiative has been wildly popular. As of 2018, the AAC&U reported that the rubrics had been downloaded over 70,000 times by members representing over 5,895 unique institutions and organizations (McConnell et al., 2019, p. 1). These national rubrics close an even larger institutional circuit. Rather than make the work of teaching and learning within one classroom or program actionable, they represent the work of higher education as a whole. They smooth out differences between institutional contexts in favor of representing an overview of commonly achieved outcomes and levels of proficiency. That overview is then viewed as actionable to organizations hoping to improve higher education at the national level.

The years of my study (2016-2018) represent a key time in which the AAC&U's VALUE rubrics "moved from the periphery of student outcomes assessment discussion to the center of conversations about the quality of student learning within and across institutions" (McConnell et al., 2019, p. 1). As high-lighted in this chapter, the increasing popularity of the VALUE rubrics solidi-fied their position as boss texts and furthered the power of both the AAC&U and its funders over higher education. This chapter explains the VALUE rubrics themselves: their creation, their purpose, their form, and their use. Using doc-uments from the AAC&U about the VALUE rubrics and connected initiatives, this chapter maps how these particular rubrics act as boss texts at the end of an accountability circuit in higher education. I then demonstrate how this rela-tionship plays out at Oak and St. Rita's. In particular, I explain how these two small schools sought out the VALUE rubrics specifically for their status as boss texts. They strategically make use of the rubrics as a part of a package of texts that defines them as an institution of higher learning, worthy of accreditation. While not every individual at these schools is aware of the origins of the rubrics or their role in higher education, those in administrative positions do recognize the authoritative power imbedded in these texts and seek them out not because they agree they are valuable instruments of learning but *because* they legitimize their institutions.

THE VALUE RUBRIC DESIGN

To further understand the way the VALUE rubrics work as boss texts that define assessment in higher education, it is important to understand how they were developed, their intended use, and the way that this purpose has shifted over time. In 2007, the U.S. Department of Education funded the AAC&U to develop 15 VALUE rubrics based on the LEAP Outcomes (McConnell et al., 2019).[3] Each rubric contains a definition of the outcome it is meant to score, framing language that adds to this context, and a glossary of terms. For example, the framing lan-guage for the Written Communication rubric grounds it in disciplinary knowledge and cites statements by our national organizations: NCTE, CWPA, and CCCC. The glossary defines language, such as "disciplinary conventions" and "genre," that may not be known across fields (AAC&U, 2009b). This page is separate from the actual scale of the rubric, which has a set of dimensions along the left-hand side and performance levels at the top (Figure 4.1 and Appendix C).

Each rubric contains four performance levels, one capstone level (4), two milestone levels (3 & 2), and one benchmark level (1). The levels are always presented in this order with the highest first as a philosophical move toward an "assets-based—versus deficit-focused" view of learning (McConnell & Rhodes, 2017, p. 26).

---

3   A 16th rubric was added later.

CRITICAL THINKING VALUE RUBRIC

for more information, please contact value@aacu.org

Learning Outcome

Definition

Performance Levels

Performance Descriptors

Dimensions

Definition

Critical thinking is a habit of mind characterized by the comprehensive exploration of issues, ideas, artifacts, and events before accepting or formulating an opinion or conclusion.

Evaluators are encouraged to assign a zero to any work sample or collection of work that does not meet benchmark (cell one) level performance.

Levels (4,3,2,1,0)	Capstone 4	Milestones 3	Milestones 2	Benchmark 1
Explanation of issues	Issue/problem to be considered critically is stated clearly and described comprehensively, delivering all relevant information necessary for full understanding.	Issue/problem to be considered critically is stated, described, and clarified so that understanding is not seriously impeded by omissions.	Issue/problem to be considered critically is stated but description leaves some terms undefined, ambiguities unexplored, boundaries undetermined, and/or backgrounds unknown.	Issue/problem to be considered critically is stated without clarification or description.
Evidence *Selecting and using information to investigate a point of view or conclusion*	Information is taken from source(s) with enough interpretation/evaluation to develop a comprehensive analysis or synthesis. Viewpoints of experts are questioned thoroughly.	Information is taken from source(s) with enough interpretation/evaluation to develop a coherent analysis or synthesis. Viewpoints of experts are subject to questioning.	Information is taken from source(s) with some interpretation/evaluation, but not enough to develop a coherent analysis or synthesis. Viewpoints of experts are taken as mostly fact, with little questioning.	Information is taken from source(s) without any interpretation/evaluation. Viewpoints of experts are taken as fact, without question.
Influence of context and assumptions	Thoroughly (systematically and methodically) analyzes own and others' assumptions and carefully evaluates the relevance of contexts when presenting a position.	Identifies own and others' assumptions and several relevant contexts when presenting a position.	Questions some assumptions. Identifies several relevant contexts when presenting a position. May be more aware of others' assumptions than one's own (or vice versa).	Shows an emerging awareness of present assumptions (sometimes labels assertions as assumptions). Begins to identify some contexts when presenting a position.
Student's position (perspective, thesis/hypothesis)	Specific position (perspective, thesis/hypothesis) is imaginative, taking into account the complexities of an issue. Limits of position (perspective, thesis/hypothesis) are acknowledged. Others' points of view are synthesized within position (perspective, thesis/hypothesis).	Specific position (perspective, thesis/hypothesis) takes into account the complexities of an issue. Others' points of view are acknowledged within position (perspective, thesis/hypothesis).	Specific position (perspective, thesis/hypothesis) acknowledges different sides of an issue.	Specific position (perspective, thesis/hypothesis) is stated, but is simplistic and obvious.
Conclusions and related outcomes (implications and consequences)	Conclusions and related outcomes (consequences and implications) are logical and reflect student's informed evaluation and ability to place evidence and perspectives discussed in priority order.	Conclusion is logically tied to a range of information, including opposing viewpoints; related outcomes (consequences and implications) are identified clearly.	Conclusion is logically tied to information (because information is chosen to fit the desired conclusion); some related outcomes (consequences and implications) are identified clearly.	Conclusion is inconsistently tied to some of the information discussed; related outcomes (consequences and implications) are oversimplified.

Figure 4.1: Parts of the VALUE rubric, used with permission.

In addition, the move signals an alignment with backwards design and outcomes-focused education by stressing the end goal of college-level achievement. These levels represent a progression through learning but were not meant to represent specific years in school, grades, or college readiness standards (Rhodes, 2010). Nor are the levels meant to be equidistant. As John Hathcoat explained in a 2019 webinar, the rubrics do not provide schools with interval data, but they do have order (Rhodes, et al., 2019). In other words, a project that scores a four is better than a three but not necessarily as much better as a three is from a two. Thus, scores should be reported for each section of the rubric rather than combined for an overall score (McConnell & Rhodes, 2017; Rhodes et al., 2019). In addition to these four scores, the AAC&U makes use of a zero score that indicates that dimension is not present in the artifact being scored or that the performance does not reach the benchmark level (Rhodes & McConnell, 2021).

Unlike the LEAP outcomes that were developed primarily from a survey of employers, the VALUE rubrics were based almost entirely on the work of faculty experts. Including faculty and disciplinary experts in this process was a valuable move against the rhetoric of accountability movements that have typically been rooted in corporate rather than faculty interests. However, including faculty only goes so far. According to Lil Brannon (2016), national organizations tout the fact that faculty are *being granted* the opportunity for a voice" but this actually "displaces educators from the center of education" simply through the fact that someone *else* is doing the granting (p. 226). Nevertheless, with the creation of the VALUE rubrics, the AAC&U made an effort to connect their LEAP outcomes to actual practice within higher education. Teams of instructors analyzed rubrics that were already being used at institutions across the country with the goal of coming up with wording that allowed the rubrics to be used across multiple disciplines and institutions (McConnell et al., 2019). The Written Communication rubric author-team included heavy hitters from our field: Linda Alder-Kassner, Terri Flateby, Susanmarie Harrington, Jean Mach, Noreen O'Connor, and Carol Rutz (K. McConnell, personal communication, October 25, 2021). However, the VALUE rubrics bear little trace of the specific individuals who authored them. Rather, they are credited to the AAC&U as an organization and "faculty teams" are referred to only in vague terms when explaining the rubric-creation process.

Such erasure of individual agents is a feature of boss texts. Just as an official police report turns an individual police officer into a generic "police officer" agent (Smith, 2005), ascribing authorship for the VALUE rubrics to generic "faculty teams" erases the identity of the specific faculty who authored the rubrics. The *particular* expertise of the authors is erased. So, too, are other identity markers, such as racial identity. Attribution to a generic faculty team assumes a racial neutrality that is impossible to achieve (Inoue, 2021b). These erasures reinforce the narrative that faculty are one hegemonic group that has reached consensus on the goals of higher education. Yet, scholars within writing studies have shown that such consensus is neither achievable nor desirable (Adler-Kassner & O'Neill, 2010; Anson et al., 2012; Broch Colombini & McBride, 2012). Consensus is neither liberatory nor democratic but a tool of systemic management (Strickland, 2011; Gallagher, 2012). The "voice" given to individuals is erased and subsumed within the work of the institution. The organization becomes the absent boss—a surrogate author of texts produced by individuals whose identity is obscured. This is reflected in our citation practices—the AAC&U is listed as the "author" of the VALUE rubrics. Yet, ruling relations rely on the narrative that consensus is both possible and positive.

WHO FUNDS THE FUNDERS? RULING RELATIONS AND ADVOCACY PHILANTHROPY

Boss texts cause ruling relations to remain invisible to the user of the texts (Rankin, 2017a). On one end of the spectrum, the specific faculty teams who wrote the VALUE rubrics are invisible to the end users of the rubrics. On the other end, only crediting the AAC&U also erases the involvement of mega-foundations and philanthropists for whom the AAC&U serves as an intermediary. Here, too, the involvement of specific individuals is erased, thus obscuring the connections across multiple organizations and foundations that "rule" higher education. When looking at the ruling relations behind the VALUE rubrics, we must look beyond the AAC&U to the "company they keep" (Alder-Kassner, 2012). The VALUE rubrics are tied to other boss texts in higher education, such as the Lumina Foundation's Degree Qualification Profile (DQP) and systems of accountability, such as accreditation and the Voluntary System of Accountability (VSA), now VSA Analytics. Together these organizations and their documents "rule" higher education by defining for multiple universities what it means to be an institutional of higher education, what outcomes students should achieve for a degree, and the performance level to which they should hold their students.

The philanthropic foundations behind these initiatives also play a significant role in funding colleges and universities in austere times. Adler-Kassner (2017) referred to this web of foundations and organizations operating behind the scenes of higher education as the Education Intelligence Complex (EIC). These foundations seek to influence education on the policy level through broad-scale reform in what is commonly known as "advocacy philanthropy" (Adler-Kasser, 2012; Hall & Thomas, 2012). By involving themselves directly with state government and accrediting bodies, these mega-foundations have focused on education at the national rather than the local level. Throughout the 2000s, mega-foundations increasingly began to work with intermediaries, such as the AAC&U, to carry out their agendas rather than providing funds directly to individual institutions (Hall & Thomas, 2012). As an intermediary, the AAC&U gains funds from multiple external sources. The Bill and Melinda Gates Foundation and the Lumina Foundation, who have increasingly become involved in student success initiatives, have also become more involved with the AAC&U. Initially, the VALUE rubric design was funded by the State Farm Companies Foundation and the U.S. Department of Education's Fund for the Improvement of Post-Secondary Education (Schneider, 2015). The refinement of the rubrics in 2016–17 was funded by the Gates Foundation, the Spencer Foundation, and the Sherman Fairchild Foundation (McConnell et al., 2019).

In 2017, Lumina provided a large grant to fund the VALUE Institute where universities can send in student work to be scored by external raters and receive a report in return (AAC&U, 2017). The AAC&U's connection with Lumina explains why the AAC&U's LEAP Outcomes and VALUE rubrics have now been framed as in congruence with the 2014 Degree Qualifications Profile (DQP). The goal of the DQP was to define what graduates should be proficient in when they finish their degrees (Adelman et al., 2014). In the introduction to the DQP, President and CEO Jamie P. Merisotis (2014) listed Lumina's sole purpose as increasing "college attainment" but he links that attainment to quality. By defining a set of proficiencies for each degree level (Associate's, Bachelor's, Master's), Merisotis believes that we can make college "what our global economy and democratic society increasingly demand" (p. 2). After the release of the DQP, the language of "outcomes" in AAC&U publications shifted to "outcomes and proficiencies," and the two terms became interchangeable in the literature (Grouling, 2017). Furthermore, the AAC&U began to frame the VALUE rubrics as designed to assess the DQP proficiencies, despite the fact that the VALUE rubrics were created five years before the DQP was released.

This overlap between the AAC&U and Lumina is not merely a matter of funding. Of the four authors listed for the DQP, two have particularly strong ties to the AAC&U: their President Carol Geary Schneider, and Paul Gaston, Distinguished Fellow in the AAC&U Office of Quality, Curriculum, and Assessment. The other two, Cliff Adelman and Peter Ewell, have since written plans for other AAC&U initiatives. Although less involved in the VALUE rubrics, George D. Kuh is another such individual who has been highly involved in the AAC&U. In addition, he is also the founding director of the National Institution for Learning Outcomes Assessment (NILOA). This overlap in individual leadership between these organizations and mega-foundations is important when mapping ruling relations.

Nevertheless, like the authors of the specific rubrics, these individuals are erased through boss texts and ruling relations. Gates may be a household name, but the names listed above are not. As Cassie Hall and Scott Thomas (2012) explained, mega-foundations are "concentrating power away from practice" (p. 30), and in so doing, they cause frustration among those who ultimately use the texts. For example, faculty members may wonder why they are being asked to use a particular rubric that doesn't align with their notions of best practice, unaware that the rubric is attached to grant funding the university needs or that using the rubric can help the university keep accreditation. Furthermore, the obfuscation of ruling relations allows foundations to create an accountability circuit while existing outside of it. These elite individuals are neither elected nor appointed; they simply have the funds or position to make their voices heard (Hall & Thomas, 2012, p. 31). They use institutional power to hold *others* accountability to their visions.

For example, the Voluntary System of Accountability (VSA), a system designed to compare universities based on performance, was originally funded by Lumina. The now defunct VSA College Portrait website was launched in 2008 in order to allow state officials and policy makers as well as the general public to compare institutions and their reports on student learning outcomes (VSA Analytics, n.d., "About"). The AAC&U originally resisted the mission of the VSA. For example, Joan Hawthorne's (2008) piece in the AAC&U's *Liberal Education*, questioned the very idea that comparing how institutions meet outcomes in general education would provide meaningful data, and Terry Rhodes (2012) critiqued the use of tests by the VSA as the primary means of measuring student learning. Yet, by 2012, the same year that Rhodes declared the VALUE rubrics would be used to measure student progress toward the DQP, the VSA and the AAC&U began working together. One potentially positive result of this collaboration was that the VSA moved away from a testing approach to measure success toward one that used rubrics. They provided trainings on using the VALUE rubrics to score student work and then reported on their success (VSA, 2012). However, the original purpose of the rubrics also shifted with these changes. The AAC&U had been clear that the performance levels of the rubrics were not meant to correspond to the year of schooling (Rhodes, 2010), yet the VSA considers the "Capstone" level on the rubric to represent what graduating seniors should be able to do (VSA, 2012). Thus, the AAC&U gradually moved away from their mission of adapting their rubrics for specific context toward a managerial mission of accountability. Whether these changes are directly the result of advocacy philanthropy or not, this shift fits with the larger documented shift in the goals of mega-foundations toward supporting data systems that establish metrics to hold higher education accountable (Hall & Thomas, 2012).

It also solidifies the use of the VALUE rubrics as boss texts that "regulate—and often standardize—practice" (LaFrance, 2019, p. 43).

DRAWING LEGITIMACY FROM BOSS TEXTS

The AAC&U often cites the number of schools that use their rubric as evidence that the VALUE rubrics are working. For example, Kate McConnell et al. (2019) argued that the sharing of the VALUE rubrics among colleagues equated to validity. But as is often the case with boss texts, individuals do not use them because they believe in them but rather because of their status as boss texts. This sort of institutional power is sought after by colleges and universities to verify their position in the larger institution of higher education. Throughout my interviews at Oak and St. Rita's, it became clear that regardless of participants' individual feelings about the rubric, administrators and experienced faculty see the VALUE rubrics as an important way to tie their work to higher education as a whole and thus legitimize their institution. In turn, those in the writing program at Oak see the VALUE rubric as a way to legitimize their new program within their university. None of these participants loved the VALUE Written Communication rubric in its original form, though some were harsher critics than others. Rather, they sought the legitimization that comes from its status as a boss text.

Oak: Being Good Participants

As a part of a conglomerate of small colleges, Oak was targeted by the AAC&U who sought small liberal arts schools to test their rubrics and provided generous funding to do so. Multiple participants mentioned that Oak's most recent accreditation review listed general education assessment as a place for improvement. Thus, when the AAC&U approached administrators at Oak with grant funding and a means to satisfy their accreditors, they jumped on board. Philip, the associate provost, was skeptical of the rubrics, but he was willing to commit to the AAC&U deal, which involved providing artifacts and data to the AAC&U and sending faculty to score national artifacts. The payoff for him was the training on rubrics, the connection to other small schools seeking assessment methods, and—of course—the money. Oak became one of the AAC&U's test schools and began to use the rubrics in core assessment, particularly the rubrics for Quantitative Reasoning, Oral Communication, and Written Communication.

Once administrators become involved in such grant initiatives, they commit their faculty to certain external exceptions. As Philip explained, a certain number of faculty had to be trained by the AAC&U and then commit to the scoring of artifacts collected on the national level. Jon, a political science professor, was a part of the general education committee using the VALUE rubrics, and he participated in the AAC&U training. The training actually turned him against using the rubrics, and he expressed a hope that Oak would move back to testing instead. However, he recognized the need for Oak to be "good participants in the AAC&U process." For Jon, "the AAC&U deal was really good about providing political cover to academia." He noted the political value of being connected to the AAC&U and using their initiatives, which he hoped could "get state legislatures off our back." Thus, Jon followed along with using the VALUE rubrics not because he agreed with the outcomes they assess or the levels of proficiency but because he acknowledged their value as boss texts that bring an external legitimacy to the assessment process at Oak.

The first two chairs of the writing committee, Ben and Kristen, also participated in the AAC&U training for the VALUE rubrics. Ben had already discovered the VALUE rubric for Written Communication when he was searching for best practice while forming the new writing program. However, rather than reinforce that find, the AAC&U training left Ben feeling like the VALUE rubrics were "insufficient." However, he noted that some kind of assessment data must be presented, or the new writing program would "lose legitimacy." The VALUE rubrics served this purpose. Meanwhile, it seems that Kristen draws on the AAC&U not only to legitimize the writing program, but also her status as the "director." As mentioned in the introduction, Kristen was referred to as the director of the program but officially only held the status of writing committee chair. Kristen expressed a desire to "be an expert in [assessment] before we dive in," and lacking her own expertise, she drew significantly on her experience with the AAC&U training when planning how to approach assessment with the writing committee. She recalled the way the AAC&U training gave the new scorers artifacts and asked them to dive in, which she found overwhelming at first. Mirroring the language she used to describe this experience, she explained her plan to give the writing committee artifacts and the rubric and say, "Go." She also noted that she decided not to collect assignment prompts with the writing artifacts because in the AAC&U training she scored artifacts in the absence of assignment prompts. Kirsten sees the AAC&U as a resource she can call on when building her own assessment process. In an early interview with Kristen in 2016, she mentioned being unsure how to implement the program's assessment plan and mentioned that she might reach out to the AAC&U for guidance.

By the time the Oak writing program conducted its first full assessment in May 2018, the rubric used by the program bore little resemblance to the original VALUE rubric for Written Communication. Nevertheless, Kristen began the norming session by talking about the AAC&U and their processes. She explained to her faculty scorers how the rubric evolved from the VALUE rubric.

While some of this may have been added for my benefit and the benefit of my study, the degree to which Kristen ties her practice back to the AAC&U seems to also serve a purpose of legitimizing her process. During the norming session, she also related to struggles expressed by the raters by signaling back to her own learning process in the AAC&U training. In particular, she mentioned on multiple occasions that she had to work to change her own mindset from grading papers to assessing artifacts for large-scale assessment. Drawing on this experience helps Kristen relate to the faculty doing the scoring but also reinforces that she has been through this process and has learned the ins and outs of scoring with rubrics. Jon was a part of the 2018 assessment group, and he backed Kristen up throughout the norming session by also referring back to the AAC&U. For example, when faculty started questioning the language of the rubric, Jon said: "In the AAC&U training, the first lesson of the training is we are not going to revise the rubric today." Later when a question came up about the performance levels, Jon explained the way that the AAC&U purposefully placed the highest (capstone) level first on the rubric. He told others, "The AAC&U people wanted us to follow a very particular process for doing this." Despite his own skepticism of the VALUE rubrics and the AAC&U, Jon seems to use these moments to draw on his AAC&U training to help Kristen quash questions about the writing program's rubric and assessment process and legitimize the writing program in the eyes of the faculty raters. In addition, neither Kristen nor Jon refers to individuals they worked with through the AAC&U training but rather to the AAC&U as an entity in and of itself.

Kristen also recognized the importance of the writing program assessment in connection to larger assessment and accreditation efforts on campus. Initially the writing program had no budget of its own, so connecting with Philip and the AAC&U grant allowed the program to pay faculty to build the writing program rubric. No matter how different the final rubric ended up being, framing it as an "adaptation" of the VALUE rubric allowed for funding that would otherwise not have been available. In addition, Kristen sees the connection between her work with rubrics and the university's goal of meeting accreditation standards. After a couple of years of working on the rubric and writing program assessment process, she described a report she submitted to Oak's head of institutional research. Rather than provide any feedback on the process Kristen had worked so hard to create, the administrators at Oak were simply thankful to include Kristen's report in their materials for accreditation as proof they were doing what was asked of them. The connections between the work of the writing program and the larger grant from the AAC&U as well as accreditation efforts seem superficial, yet they are significant in legitimizing both Oak and the writing program in the eyes of external stakeholders.

St. Rita's: Getting on the Radar

While Oak was approached by the AAC&U to join their consortium and receive grant funding, St. Rita's wasn't initially on the AAC&U's radar. Dwayne recalled how the case study he published about St. Rita's and the VALUE rubrics[4] came about after he initially completed an AAC&U survey:

> I did their survey. And then they [the AAC&U] wrote, and they're like, "Oh, I didn't even know you existed," pretty much. I'm like, "Well, we do." And they're like, "Could you write up what's going on?" And I think they asked about fifty schools to do it, and they took about ten. And they took mine.

Part of Dwayne's motivation for writing the case study was simply to put his school on the AAC&U's radar—to show that they exist. In turn, by publishing Dwayne's case study, the AAC&U gets another notch in its belt to say that another type of institution is using its rubrics. It was this published case study that first made me aware of St. Rita's as well, but I found that what was happening there in practice bore little resemblance to the narrative told in the official AAC&U literature. Even Dwayne admitted that, while the piece was "not all puffering," he was far more hopeful about the impact of the rubrics at St. Rita's at the point when he wrote it.

There is a strong sense at St. Rita's that what is put on paper is not what is put in practice. Dwayne continually lamented that St. Rita's approves ideas and then ignores them. Even Gerald (Dr. Z) complimented Dwayne for bringing in the VALUE rubrics to make the college look good but noted it's only "on paper." In particular, Dwayne explained that initially he got the AAC&U VALUE rubrics added to the college's handbook in the hopes that both faculty and students would see them, and they would become "a part of the culture." But little happened in practice. A few years later, a new dean came on board and "discovered" the rubrics and "acted like nobody had even mentioned it before." This dean attempted to draw connections with the AAC&U's LEAP initiative, but again, nothing really happened. That dean left, and Dwayne became frustrated with the continual turn over in administration and the lack of turnover in ideas.

This same pattern of discovering and rediscovering the rubrics repeated in the general education committee I observed. When Dwayne first came to St. Rita's in 2009, the dean tasked him and other junior faculty members with re-writing the general education curriculum. Being inexperienced, Dwayne and the group were "hungry for things that were nationally normed, already benchmarked."

---

4   I do not cite this case study in order to maintain Dwayne's confidentiality.

The group used the VALUE rubrics to re-write course goals for general education. But, Dwayne said, "we didn't realize that some institutions kill ideas by approving them." When I observed a general education committee meeting in 2016, two junior faculty—Jeremy and Andrea—were re-writing the general education goals based on the VALUE rubrics. Andrea, the co-chair of general education, expressed a need to "be really careful" with how she and Jeremy proceeded when they were fairly new to the institution and working with those who had been there for 20 plus years. Jeremy, like Dwayne before him, saw the VALUE rubrics as a way to convince other faculty members to move forward: "We're going to pin down [the general education goals] using the AAC&U VALUE rubrics because they're normed nationally." In the committee meeting, Dwayne supported these efforts, but to me, he repeated: "But they don't know that we kill ideas by approving them."

There are many reasons that the AAC&U rubrics are difficult to fully implement at St. Rita's, and I will continue to return to this point in subsequent chapters. For the purposes of this chapter, what is important is the tension between the need for the VALUE rubrics as boss texts—they are "nationally normed"—with the fact that the rubrics simply aren't designed for a school like St. Rita's. Gerald (Dr. Z) expressed frustration that the academic world as a whole doesn't see institutions like St. Rita's. He's not alone in this frustration, and almost everyone I talked to at St. Rita's expressed the feeling that their students started well below the benchmark level on the AAC&U rubrics. In Chapter 7, I return to how this characterization of their students is problematic, yet there is a very real difference between St. Rita's and many institutions within higher education that incentivizes them to seek connections to national practice.

In a critique of the outcomes assessment movement as a whole, Michael Bennett and Jacqueline Brady (2014) explained that universal outcomes create a culture where underprivileged students have to catch up on skills rather than one that directly addresses the economic inequities that leads to their under-preparedness in the first place. They noted that the outcomes movement ends up meaning that more "working-class students at poor colleges and universities" are required to take high-stake assessments (p. 150). The students at Oak simply do their coursework, and then it is anonymously sampled for assessment purposes. In contrast, faculty at St. Rita's felt the need to know whether or not *specific* students are ready to move on in the curriculum, and thus their assessment methods are tied directly to students rather than to overall assessment of their programs. At St. Rita's, students submit portfolios at the end of first-year composition to be assessed with the rubrics, and this assessment determines whether or not they pass the class. In addition, to prove that students are progressing in general education, the committee added other checkpoints where all students are assessed directly. On paper, these checkpoints are called portfolios and thus seem in keeping with best practice and the use of the VALUE rubrics to score portfolios. In practice, the first-year portfolio is a mix of classwork and a timed essay. And sophomore and junior "portfolios" are only timed essays and a reflection letter.

Teachers in both the first-year course and upper-level courses feel a pressure to teach to these assessments. In fact, the remedial course in writing involves what Jeremy calls a "competency-based" approach where students use computer programs to drill grammar knowledge to reach certain "benchmarks." I'd wager that the compositionists who originally created the VALUE rubric would be dismayed at this practice. But for Jeremy, this program is "really drawing from the VALUE rubrics because I know the competencies we're shooting for in the portfolio, and so I've drilled down from those into what are the grammar and mechanics they need to achieve." Again, it is possible that Jeremey made this connection the VALUE rubric for my benefit, knowing that is the starting point for my study. However, Jeremy also mentioned the importance of the DQP for a model of general education. He explained that he saw the DQP as similar to the VALUE initiative in defining standards for higher education, only that VALUE added actual rubrics. Institutional ethnographers look for these references to larger institutional structures to "hear the traces of the institutions' otherwise taken-for-granted social organization" (Rankin, 2017a, p. 4). It's clear that even when the textual traces of the language of the VALUE rubric are absent, the traces of them continue in the discourse of faculty.

Another example of terminology used at St. Rita's that bears the mark of the AAC&U is the repeated reference to "signature assignments." Signature assignments are AAC&U's way to address the fact that many artifacts from the classroom simply do not fit their rubrics. While they do not seek to entirely standardize assignments, they do advocate for signature assignments that are designed specifically to demonstrate growth in key outcomes across the curriculum (AAC&U, 2015a). Dwayne attended a workshop on signature assignments held by Lumina and the AAC&U, and he has incorporated the terminology into the portfolio process at St. Rita's. In particular, he draws on the idea that signature assignments are linked to assess progress as students move through the curriculum. However, rather than referring to work being embedded in coursework at St. Rita's, the repeated timed essays are referred to as "signature assignments." This language is repeated by multiple members of the general education committee as they evaluate general education goals. They referred to the "signature assignments" as points when the goals are "tested" and "measured." When the question of changing the signature assignments came up, Dwayne welcomed this, stating: "The current model was an emergency lacking other things." He recognized that his version of signature assignments as repeated timed essays is not ideal, and yet he uses that terminology from the AAC&U to stress that St. Rita's needs to assess the same skills at multiple points in the curriculum. Meanwhile, others at St. Rita's seem to repeat the language, unaware of where it comes from or how it does not fully align with the original concept by the AAC&U.

Dwayne indicated that he was not yet proud of this process; however, it serves St. Rita's well in terms of legitimizing their institution. Four of the seven faculty members I talked to at St. Rita's mentioned their struggles with accreditation. In particular, the accreditors were concerned about the lack of data-driven decisions on campus and about the lack of assessment as anything other than an end point. "Signature assignments" scored on the same rubric allow for St. Rita's to show that they are assessing outcomes over time, across the curriculum. And drawing directly on the AAC&U's language is familiar to both accreditors and granting agencies. In addition to pleasing their accreditors, the signature assignments program was favored by the Lily Foundation—a top philanthropic foundation that provided St. Rita's with direct funding for initiatives that prepared students for the workplace.

Accreditation and legitimization are particularly important for institutions like St. Rita's. Lucinda, the vice president of academic affairs, described the history of St. Rita's as a school that certified blue collar workers in their highly industrial region and thus allowed them to move up into white collar positions. However, she acknowledged that this is no longer acceptable as a goal for an institution of higher education. Rather, she mentioned multiple times that students must have "a legitimate college degree" and that such a diploma signifies to employers that students have mastered fundamental skills. The rubrics, for Lucinda, fit with the AAC&U's promise to employers. St. Rita's students have a legitimate degree because their work is scored using national rubrics, developed and tested outside of the local setting. Similarly, Jeremy explained the importance of the VALUE rubrics for showing that students had the "minimal competency" for a degree as defined by the DQP. These boss texts—LEAP outcomes, VALUE rubrics, and the DQP—are used strategically, by name, to legitimize St. Rita's and their curriculum, even when faculty repeatedly admit they are pitched too high for their student population.

CONCLUSION

While composition scholars have referred to outcomes assessment as a "Trojan Horse" (Gallagher, 2016) and the VALUE rubrics as "fooling" us (Anson et al., 2012), the AAC&U did not create the LEAP outcomes of VALUE rubrics to trick faculty. Philip does not join the AAC&U VALUE process to directly regulate what faculty teach—in fact, he shies away from signature assignments because he does not want to encroach on faculty freedom in the classroom. Neither does Dwayne use the terminology of signature assignments to purposefully deceive the general education committee. Rather, these "tricks" are a part of the way that ruling relations and boss texts operate. LaFrance (2019) explained that "key terms and statements are generated by our national organizations to offer a sense of shared values and guide our work with student writers on fairly different campuses" (p. 117). In their role as stewards of higher education, the AAC&U hoped to do just that—to guide, not to regulate higher education. However, they cannot escape the ruling relations of mega-foundations nor can the faculty at St. Rita's and Oak escape the demands of accreditation or the conceptions of what it means to complete a degree that rule their practice.

Ruling relations bring key terms and key documents—boss texts—to multiple institutions, and over time, these terms and documents become embedded in the everyday work of these institutions. Outcomes and terms are reproduced and "become enshrined in the bureaucratic machinery" (Gallagher, 2012, p. 45). While some administrators draw on these outcomes and terms strategically, others—such as those talking of essay exams as signature assignments at St. Rita's—repeat them not knowing that they are drawing on institutional language that goes beyond their own context. Multiple ruling relations are at play and which ruling relations are obscured is dependent on standpoint. Kristen and her colleagues at Oak attended VALUE training sessions held by the AAC&U, and Dwayne went to training sessions hosted by the AAC&U and the Lumina Foundation on signature assignments. They refer directly to the terminology of the AAC&U and sometimes even to individuals on their staff. Philip goes as far as to refer to the two key VALUE staff members—Terry Rhodes and Kate McConnell—by first name only, saying he considers them "friends, in a sense." Yet, even those participants who worked directly with the AAC&U did not necessarily consider the larger connections to institutional power, such as the interaction between the AAC&U and their funders. Similarly, individual faculty members not involved in administration were more likely to see their colleagues—those involved in writing and assessment committees —as rubric-creators and be unaware of the AAC&U as an organization or the faculty teams that wrote the VALUE rubrics. Patrice, a long-time faculty member at St. Rita's, sees Dwayne as the creator of rubrics, and even when I mentioned the AAC&U rubric, she repeatedly said she'd have to ask Dwayne about it, lamenting that he hasn't given her the most recent copy of what *he* wants her to use in her classroom.

Whether participants purposefully draw on boss texts or unknowingly use them, the concepts of institutional ethnography help us connect national movements, such the VALUE rubrics to practices at individual institutions. The concept of ruling relations helps us see where ideas of "best practice" come from, how these concepts unite institutions across locations, and how they morph into everyday practice that may actually look quite different between institutions (LaFrance, 2019). In Chapter 5, I look specifically at the idea of adaptation. From the beginning of my study, I was struck by how different the "adapted" VALUE rubrics looked from the original Written Communication rubric. Through a trickle-down approach of discovering the rubrics, key practices put in place by the AAC&U in the beginning have been lost over time due to both misunderstandings of purposes of the rubric and an inability to align actual practice with those original intentions. Yet the connection with the AAC&U also constrains perceptions of assessment at Oak and St. Rita's.

CHAPTER 5.

CONSTRAINT AND CHOICE IN RUBRIC ADAPTATION

As seen in Chapter 4, drawing on national assessment practice can be a strategic choice to satisfy accreditors and funders. As boss texts, the VALUE rubrics legitimize the work done at local institutions. They also legitimize a certain process of conducting assessment. While the rubrics ultimately used at St. Rita's and Oak are quite different than the original VALUE rubric for Written Communication, both schools began with the idea that assessment meant using rubrics to assess outcomes. As explained in Chapter 2, as outcomes have become connected to rubrics, there has been emphasis on making them measurable. The LEAP outcomes seem to fit with the original philosophy that outcomes are broad, not meant to signal specific levels of achievement. However, the VALUE rubrics operationalized these outcomes and, alongside the DQP, began to dictate national practice in terms of performance levels. Outcomes is a word that is clearly charged with a complex history within education. Most participants in my study used the term "goals" to describe what their programs wanted students to achieve, yet the term outcomes was used by Philip and Dwayne, who were the most closely connected to the AAC&U. By tying their institutions to the AAC&U, matching outcomes with the rubrics became a concern for administrators at both Oak and St. Rita's. Although Gallagher (2012) noted that outcomes assessment means local institutions are only responsible "decisions regarding means, not ends" (p. 51), the means, too, are taken as a given by Oak and St. Rita's. Neither school questions the use of the rubrics as the means for assessing writing. Rather, the rubric is seen as a neutral tool, the logical progression from an outcomes-based approach to education.

But genres are always ideological (Barwarshi, 2000). The rubric—*as boss text*—reinforces institutional power and comes imbedded with views on what assessment, and writing, should look like across institutions. Genres are "both constraint and choice, both regularity and chaos" (Devitt, 2004, p. 156). This chapter examines the tension between constraint and choice when the writing committee at Oak and the general education committee at St. Rita's use the VALUE rubric as an exemplar. I begin by placing the processes at Oak and St. Rita's in national context by showing trends in rubric modification. The VALUE rubrics are often referred to as "meta-rubrics" because they are meant to be adapted to local context. Thus, the VALUE rubrics are seen as exemplars of the rubric genre for outcomes-based assessment. As with all genres, "variation is permitted to the degree that it does not negate either function or appropriateness" (Devitt, 2004, p. 149). So, what does adaptation of the VALUE rubric for Written Communication look like? How much variation is seen as allowable?

Anson et al. (2012) have argued that generic rubrics, such as VALUE, "wear the guise of local application," but in reality, only make faculty *think* they agree on generic, generalized criteria. The ideology of the rubric supposes that agreement is possible, and thus faculty spend hours of work dedicated to achieving it. Just as a "writing assignment tells a story of work," (LaFrance, 2019, p. 48), so, too, the rubric tells the story of this work toward faculty agreement and consensus, as well as where that work fails. That work is reflected in the final text of the adapted rubric, but it can never be fully captured by the text alone. It is only through conversations with the people involved in that work that understanding becomes possible. By returning to the actual text-user conversation, or the moment when the participants respond to and use the text, institutional ethnographers seek to make visible how the text coordinates their work (Smith & Turner, 2014). We are able to sort through the mess that is invisible in the final textual product to see how participants negotiate their actual work. In these "moments of negotiation," we see how individual understandings of work function within an institution (LaFrance, 2019, p. 52). This chapter shares moments from meetings and interviews at Oak and St. Rita's where participants engaged with the rubric and wrestled over how to use it in actual assessment practice. After reporting on national trends in adapting the VALUE Written Communication rubric, I examine how the rubric guided the committees at Oak and St. Rita's to consider their own local goals within the ideological framework of the rubric. The heart of an institutional ethnographer's analysis is in noticing when "the knowledge generated in the daily *doing* of work is subordinated by, or in tension with, other (abstract) knowledge that is used or *supposed* to be used to decide and to act" (Rankin, 2017b, p 7). At both Oak and St. Rita's, the process of aligning local goals with the VALUE rubric highlights the tension between what rubrics are able to capture and what goals programs are designed to meet.

NATIONAL ADAPTATION OF THE VALUE RUBRIC FOR WRITTEN COMMUNICATION

The VALUE rubrics were meant to be modified, but what does this look like nationally? Prior to visiting Oak and St. Rita's I sent a national survey to writing program administrators and assessment professionals at 289 institutions who appeared to be using a version of the Written Communication rubric. I asked specifically about the use of the rubric as well as how it was adapted. I also asked that those who adapted the rubric upload a copy of their new rubric. I received 75 survey responses, and 17 of those uploaded a rubric. However, one of these was an exact copy of the VALUE Written Communication, so I did not count it as a modification. In addition, the AAC&U's Office of Quality, Curriculum, and Assessment (OQCA) conducted multiple surveys about the VALUE rubrics, including a 2018 survey on institutional use. This web-based survey was sent to anyone who had downloaded one or more of the VALUE rubrics from the AAC&U in the past 10 years. The goal was to record how institutions were actually using the rubrics and compare the views of different stakeholders (faculty v. admin). Overall, 1,448 responses were received (McConnell et al., 2019). Both my 2016 survey and the AAC&U 2018 survey asked participants to identify how the rubrics were being used at their institutions. In this section, I compare my specific results about the Written Communication rubric with the AAC&U's overall results of their survey about all the VALUE rubrics. I then explain specifically how the AAC&U Written Communication VALUE rubric aligns with the rubrics used at Oak and St. Rita's.

Written Communication, along with Critical Thinking, is the most used VALUE rubric (McConnell et al., 2019). A full copy of the original rubric can be found in Appendix B. The specific use of the Written Communication rubric parallels how participants are using the rubrics overall. On the AAC&U survey, participants identified general education as the most prominent place the rubrics were used, with 529 responses, or 37 percent, selecting this option. The next most common use was within academic degree programs or majors (421–29 percent) with writing-intensive experiences as third at 325 participants (22 percent) (McConnell et al., 2019). In terms of other common practices, 902 institutions said they used the rubrics for faculty development, and 897 specifically said they were used for assignment redesign workshops (McConnell et al., 2019). In my survey, university-wide assessment was most common use for the Written Communication rubric, reported by 36 participants (33 percent) (Figure 5.1). The next highest use was as an example for faculty at 22 participants (20 percent), which fits with the AAC&U's finding about faculty development and workshops. The third most common use on my survey was for writing program assessment with 19 participants (18 percent). This third category seems to fit the AAC&U's finding about writing intensive courses. The modified rubrics uploaded to my survey mirror these trends. Fourteen of these rubrics were clearly designed for use with general education or program-wide assessment, while one represented assessment of writing within a particular disciplinary course on food science.

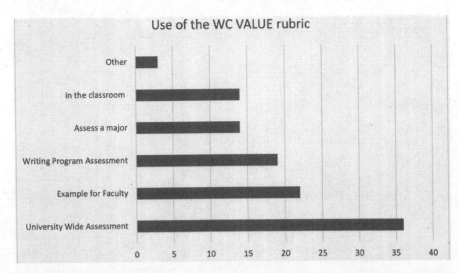

Figure 5.1: Uses for the Written Communication VALUE rubric (2016) survey results.

Both surveys also asked about how and why the rubrics were being modified by institutions. As described in Chapter 4, the original VALUE rubrics contain a front page with a definition of the outcome being assessed, a framing section, and a glossary. The rubric itself consists of four performance levels and a number of dimensions as well as specific performance descriptors to describe what is expected at each performance level for each dimension. This format is used across all original VALUE rubrics (AAC&U, n.d., "Parts"). While modified VALUE rubrics tend to maintain the general structure of dimensions on the left side, performance levels, and performance descriptors, the 16 rubrics I collected demonstrated a wide variety of layouts. Some were formatted in Microsoft Word or Excel; others were PDF files. Some neatly fit on one page, others spanned multiple pages. For example, one rubric was four pages long with 18 dimensions, including all the dimensions from the original VALUE Written Communication and many more. Another rubric was brief with only four dimensions and only included performance descriptors for the capstone and benchmark levels, leaving both milestone levels without description. Although the AAC&U explained that the original rubrics were not necessarily meant to line up with academic standing, some rubrics clearly designated which performance levels corresponded with which courses or levels in schooling. For example, one rubric specifies that the fourth level should be addressed in a senior capstone course and that levels one and two should be addressed in first-year foundations courses.

According to the AAC&U survey on all the VALUE rubrics, the details of the performance descriptors was the most commonly modified part of the rubrics, followed by the specific dimensions for assessment (McConnell et al., 2019).

However, a fair number of schools noted that they changed the names of the performance levels, which sometimes included changing the order of the performance levels so that low was first rather than high (McConnell et al., 2019). In an open-ended question, the AAC&U survey respondents commented that they sometimes combined rubrics, such as Critical Thinking, Oral, and Written Communication. My participants also mentioned changing performance descriptors and dimensions, and one combined the Written Communication rubric with other VALUE rubrics. In addition, the words used to describe the performance levels as well as the order in which they appeared was a common variation.

While the AAC&U asked what was modified, the large scale of their survey could not confirm if those answers matched the actual modified rubrics. My survey went a step farther by asking participants to upload a copy of their modified rubric. For example, the AAC&U study reported that only a small number of participants modified the glossary section of the rubric, but this does not necessary account for participants who did not use the glossary at all, or who were even unaware of its existence on the original rubrics. Of the 16 modified rubrics I collected, only one included a glossary. Nine rubrics had changed the names of the performance descriptors and three used only numbers. Some of the modifications to these levels were minor, such as adding the word "advanced" to the Milestone (3) performance level. However, many changes were in direct contrast to the goals of the AAC&U. The AAC&U stressed that the order of the performance descriptors, with Capstone on the left, was intentionally meant to present a "assets-based" rather than "deficit-focused" approach to assessment (McConnell & Rhodes, 2017). So, too, the language of "benchmark" for the entry-level performance descriptor was meant to signal a starting point not a deficit. Yet, six of the rubrics I examined changed the entry-level performance descriptor to use deficit-based language with words such as "insufficient," "unacceptable," and "poor." Three also put the negative first, against AAC&U's recommendation that capstone always be the left-most side of the rubric. Finally, two rubrics that I examined deleted one of the middle levels, moving from four performance levels to only three.

When we get into the dimensions of the rubric, we begin to see even bigger differences between the adapted rubrics and the original VALUE rubric for Written Communication. Only four of the 16 rubrics uploaded to my survey maintained the language of the original five dimensions:

- context & purpose
- content development
- genre & disciplinary conventions
- sources & evidence
- control of syntax & mechanics.

Six of the rubrics changed the dimensions so significantly that they could be considered an entirely different rubric. Others modified the dimensions less significantly (Figure 5.2). For example, one institution removed the "sources & evidence" category because they decided to score Written Communication alongside Information Literacy, and a dimension for sources was already covered in that rubric. Another school kept the original dimensions but added one for "focus, organization, and cohesion." While composition scholars might recognize organization as a part of "genre and disciplinary conventions," this addition seems to reflect a general sense that organization is missing from the original rubric. In fact, "organization" was the most added dimension and appeared on six of the modified rubrics I examined. Other commonly added dimensions are "central message" or "thesis," "development/support," and "focus." The most common deletion was "genre and disciplinary conventions," which was completely eliminated in eight of the 16 rubrics. A dimension for sentence-level or language concerns was present in all but one rubric; however, only seven kept the specific language of "syntax and mechanics," often modifying this dimension to the more generic "mechanics" and/or "style." It is somewhat concerning that "content development" was completely eliminated in a third of rubrics and was the second most missing category. This deletion seems to signal a view of writing as a skill that can be assessed separately from knowledge and ideas. It may also signal that faculty scoring papers across general education or for programmatic assessment do not feel qualified to judge content outside their own discipline, even while seeing style or organization as universal elements of writing.

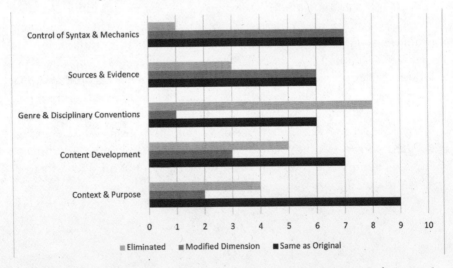

Figure 5.2. Modifications to VALUE Written Communication Rubric 2016 survey results.

Across the board, reasons for modifying the rubrics ranged from changing them to be more specific for classroom use to modifying them for different levels of learning, including graduate study (McConnell et al., 2019). Specifically, my respondents listed reasons for changing the language of the dimensions as making them "less disciplinary" or simplifying the language. When writing about the WPA Outcomes, Keith Rhodes et al. (2005) noted:

> Professional language, characterized by words like rhetoric,
> genre, and conventions (and register), is useful to people who
> have grown used to a common set of associations, including
> the historical uses of these terms. But to others, it smacks
> of snotty language people use to show that they understand
> because they are on the in—and of course people who don't
> understand are on the out. (pp. 14–15)

A tension reflected here is the desire and need to modify rubrics for use in different disciplines and university settings. After all, the rhetoric of consensus by the AAC&U presents this as a major advantage of using the VALUE rubrics. However, much of the good work done by composition specialists in creating the rubrics to fit with the core concepts of our field seems erased in pursuit of this consensus. It is telling that only *one* of the 16 modified rubrics from my survey retains the framework and glossary for the original rubric. Six do maintain a definition of written communication; however, the glossary of terms, the suggestions for the best use of the rubric, and all references to disciplinary documents produced by NCTE and CCCCs are gone. So, too, are the local teams that adapt the rubrics often erased in the texts of the rubrics themselves. Even though I collected modified rubrics, it was often unclear from the text itself *who* was doing the modification. Rather, the rubrics often included a line giving credit only to the AAC&U. This chapter continues by examining how the specific processes of adaptation at Oak and St. Rita's work to flatten disciplinary difference in order to achieve consensus and fit institutional goals with the rubric as an assessment instrument.

RUBRIC MODIFICATIONS AT OAK & ST. RITA'S

Both Oak and St. Rita's provided me with a draft of their writing rubric in 2016, although both noted they were still in the process of development. These drafts fit with these national trends for modification of the VALUE Written Communication rubric.[5] Both of the rubrics kept four performance levels but changed

---

5   Rather than include the full text of these rubrics, I choose to use pieces throughout the

what they were called and the order in which they were presented. Both have the lowest category first and both use more negative language for it. At St. Rita's it was "insufficient," and at Oak, "weak" (see Table 5.1). Both used "developing" to describe the next performance level. Then we have "sufficient" for St. Rita's and "stable" at Oak. Finally, the highest level is "exemplary" for St. Rita's and for Oak, "mature."

Table 5.1: Performance Levels on Local Rubrics

St. Rita's	Oak
Insufficient	Weak
Developing	Developing
Sufficient	Stable
Exemplary	Mature

Although these changes are not insignificant, it is the changes to the dimensions that make these rubrics significantly different from the original VALUE rubrics. Fitting with the changes seen at other institutions, neither rubric has the dimension "genre & disciplinary conventions" or "content development," two frequently changed dimensions nationally. Oak's rubric has four dimensions that seem to draw a bit on the dimensions in the original VALUE rubric:

- Argument
- Audience & Community
- Research & Sources
- Process & Style

In particular, "research & sources" seems similar to "sources & evidence." "Audience & community" makes a nod to both "disciplinary conventions" and "context and purpose," and "style" is a common substitution for the AAC&U language of "control of syntax and mechanics."

St. Rita's dimensions, too, have hints of the VALUE language but vary even more significantly than the Oak dimensions. St. Rita's five dimensions are

- Responding to assignments
- Structure and Coherence
- Evidence and Analysis
- Prose Style and Syntax
- Spelling, Word-Choice, Grammar, and Punctuation

---

study as relevant. These texts were continually shifting, particularly the rubric at Oak. Thus, pinning down one version for representation in this study seems to misrepresent the overall dynamic nature of the work.

These categories have traces of the AAC&U categories of "syntax and mechanics" and "evidence and sources" but ultimately vary significantly from the original rubric. "Responding to assignments" could be viewed as similar to "context and purpose" but clearly frames that context as only the classroom. In contrast, Kristen (chair of the writing committee) noted on multiple occasions that "audience" on the Oak rubric was meant to push faculty to think beyond the professor as the only audience for writing. Kristen drew on her training with the AAC&U for this push. She remembered being struck that assuming the professor was the audience was listed as the entry-level performance criteria on the VALUE rubric. Meanwhile, the faculty at St. Rita's disagree on whether or not their students are ready to write anything beyond the classroom and whether or not "sources" should be used in papers until they are upperclassmen. Adaptation, then, depends heavily on institutional context and faculty views of writing in the classroom.

The concept of standpoint is significant in the response to and use of the rubric. As shown in previous chapters, Oak and St. Rita's occupy a different standpoint in relationship to higher education as a whole. Oak is a top liberal arts college where there is no question that students have already learned a lot about sources and citation when they enter. St. Rita's caters specifically to "underprepared" students; faculty agree that they do not enter at the "benchmark" level of the AAC&U rubric. So, too, does standpoint within the institution matter to how the texts are viewed. Kristen is trained by the AAC&U and has a good understanding of their philosophy and their rubrics. She also works with others who have such training, including Associate Provost Philip who is able to directly speak with the main staff members of the VALUE initiative and provide them with feedback. Meanwhile, Dwayne (my main information at St. Rita's) is heralded as the VALUE expert on his campus, while admitting to me that he is actually kind of "fuzzy" on the signature assignments idea that he advocates for. A textual analysis of the rubrics at Oak and St. Rita's can tell us what the local "adaptations" of the VALUE rubric look like, what text they keep, and what is changed. But it cannot tell us *how* the process of adaptation is enacted across locations or what those words mean in practice to individuals at these institutions.

To further examine how these local contexts affect the actual rubric modification process, I draw on observations of meetings where the rubrics were discussed and interviews with participants where we talked specifically about the text of the rubric. While Oak and St. Rita's contrast significantly in both their process and the result of that process, one common constraint was the need to reconcile current institutional, program, and course goals with rubric-based assessment. Using outcomes to define what a student should know or do by the end of a course or program of study is now common practice in higher education; however, how that quest is framed and undertaken can tell us a lot about ruling relationships. Outcomes are a form of currency within higher education, another boss text. They are included on course and program proposals and are necessary to get those approved. They are then added to syllabi, as is often required by accreditation. Finally, those outcomes must be assessed in order to show that we are doing what we promised to do five, ten years ago when we (or someone else) submitted the proposal for the course we are teaching. I do believe that outcomes are important to quality education, and that such outcomes must be communicated to students. However, more often than not, the role these outcomes play *institutionally* separates them from actual practice and confines growth and change within our programs and our classrooms. At Oak, Kristen was very clear that while the committee can make all the changes they want to the rubric, they cannot change the goals of the writing program. Meanwhile, at St. Rita's, Dwayne operates in the opposite direction, using the rubric to "move from a checklist of courses to a set of goals" for general education. In both cases, the need for goals and outcomes interacts with the way faculty use and adapt the VALUE Written Communication Rubric.

OAK'S WRITING COMMITTEE AND THEIR WRITING RUBRIC

Multiple committees at Oak implemented the VALUE rubrics, including the core curriculum committee that used them wholesale for assessment purposes. However, with my particular interest in writing and rubric adaptation, my study focused on the work of the writing committee. Staring ten years before my study, Oak began looking at its writing curriculum and forming a plan for a new writing program. Their approach to teaching writing is a first-year seminar model where faculty from across the disciplines teach in the program, combining writing pedagogy with a topic of interest from their field. For example, Kristen first became involved in the program because she had taught a history course on the Titanic at a previous institution and was looking for a home for that course at Oak. Her department chair suggested she teach it as a first-year seminar. At that point, there was little oversight of first-year seminar courses, and as Kristen noted, "there were no overarching goals, no coherence of any kind" to the writing courses.

As the chair of the new writing committee, Kristen values creating that coherence through both overarching goals and assessment practices. The committee started in 2013 as a part of the new writing program and now approves courses for the W (writing) designation. They make sure that faculty proposals have a strong writing component that fit the goals of the new writing program. The committee was also tasked with developing an assessment plan for the program. In 2015, before my study began, the writing committee had developed a rubric draft after looking at the VALUE Written Communication rubric. When my study began in Fall 2016, Kristen wanted to introduce new committee members to that rubric and continue working on it before beginning actual assessment. In November 2016, the writing committee used the draft to score several sample artifacts and then offered suggestions for improving and clarifying the rubric. Kristen took these suggestions and made additional changes to the rubric. After a few rounds of this process, Kristen sought additional feedback from faculty beyond the writing committee. In May 2017, she conducted an assessment workshop in which she led six additional faculty members through a sample assessment process. This half day workshop went through the sort of norming session that is typical for assessment training. Kristen provided sample artifacts and led the committee in scoring them based on the rubric. The workshop participants shared their scores and discussed them. This workshop was both to get additional feedback on the rubric and to do a dry run of the assessment training process. After additional rubric revisions, Kristen conducted the first full assessment in May 2018. Six additional faculty members went through a norming session scoring sample artifacts with the rubric and then spent the rest of the day using the rubric to score student artifacts that Kristen had collected from first-year seminar courses as well as from graduating seniors.

In both the committee itself and the assessment workshops, Oak seeks to involve faculty from across the curriculum (see Table 5.2). The writing committee at Oak is made up of six faculty members. The chair of the committee is appointed by the provost for a three-year term. The first chair, Ben, is from computer science, and Kristen is from history. The department chair for English is an ex officio member of the committee, but this does not seem to have anything to do with disciplinary expertise. Rather, Ronnie noted that when the committee was started, the majority of first-year seminars were taught under English, so the department chair was added to the committee because decisions made would "affect staffing in the English department." Ronnie is, in fact, a medievalist who works in queer studies, not a compositionist. The other members are elected by the faculty to represent their divisions or colleges. A more complete "cast of characters" from both schools is included in Appendix A, but when I observed three meetings in the 2016-2017 school year, the committee was made up of the following members:

Table 5.2: Writing Committee Members at Oak, Fall 2016

Pseudonym	Role on Committee	Discipline
Kristen	Chair	History
Ronnie	Ex-officio	English
Amelia	Science Representative	Chemistry
Brad	Fine Arts Representative	Art History
Nina	Interdisciplinary Representative	Environmental Studies
Shirong	Humanities Representative	History

Meanwhile, Barbara, the director of the writing center, was a part of the task force that created the initial writing program but has since felt excluded. She is active in the discipline and professional organizations of composition and has experience coordinating a writing across the curriculum program at a previous institution. And yet, she "tried in five different ways to be on the committee." She worried that those appointed to the committee may "know nothing about writing." This sentiment is in direct contrast to the rhetoric of the AAC&U, which sees writing as a skill that employers and faculty of all fields can agree on. Although the committee at Oak worked to revise the rubric for local purposes, they fell in line with the value of reaching consensus about writing across disciplines. In fact, consensus among the committee members is not seen as enough, and Kristen seeks more feedback from those in other disciplines through the 2017 assessment workshop and the 2018 scoring processes.

MAKING A RUBRIC FROM GOALS

The writing program at Oak has four overarching goals. Under each of these goals, there are three-to-four specific bullet points. The four goals were directly listed on the rubric used for assessment in the program and became the four dimensions for scoring. The rubric has one page for each dimension with the full goals listed at the top, including the bullet points, and then a chart describing the levels of performance in that dimension from weak through mature. The complete rubric can be found in Appendix D.

The initial task force that created the writing program went through a lengthy process of creating these goals, and it was important to the committee that the goals directly inform their assessment process. The goals are, as Kristen stated on multiple occasions, the one thing that cannot be changed by the committee. Although other language of the performance descriptors on the rubric shifted between 2016–2018, the goals and bullet points remained at the top of each page. The language of the assessment dimensions did shift slightly, but the four assessment areas continue to match the four overarching writing program goals. In addition, as the committee ran into difficulty aligning the goals with the assessment process, they left notes to clarify the way the goals interact with the rubric. On the final 2018 rubric, argument is the only area to not contain a clarifying note.

When the writing program at Oak was first established, the task force sought common goals to unify the program. For Kristen, the goals are "basically the only thing that holds the whole program together." The initial writing task force spent a year reading materials, examining other programs and coming up with the goals for the writing program. They sought feedback from everyone they could. After this involved process, the goals of the new program went through faculty governance for approval. Kristen is not eager to repeat this process, and this constrains the language the writing committee feels like they can use on the rubric. When concerns about not being able to assess areas on the rubric come up at the writing committee meeting in Fall 2016, Kristen noted that changing the language of the goals would involve a lot of "faculty meetings." The committee agreed that more meetings should definitely be avoided. She then let subsequent committees know that the language of the goals was static and could not be adapted.

One dimension of the rubric that the 2016 writing committee struggled with was originally titled "research and sources." The committee questioned whether "evidence" and "research" are the same or whether some disciplines use evidence that isn't necessarily research. However, the goals of the program repeat the term research, specifying that students should "use research tools fluently," and "evaluate the credibility of potential research sources." Kristen felt that these particular bullet points in writing program goals "actually hamstring us a little bit." She felt that the language implies students finding their own research, but some of the papers produced in the program are based on sources the professor assigns. She noted that those sources, too, should be evaluated critically. In addition, she explained that the syllabi for first-year writing courses often "talk about evidence in some way, they just don't necessarily talk about traditional research." While the committee doesn't change the bullet points, they do change the overall title of the rubric dimension from "research and sources" to simply "evidence." In addition, they directly addressed the issue in a note underneath the program goals on the rubric:

> Note: Not all writing assignments require students to gather
> textual sources through traditional library research. We have
> framed this guiding language to try to accommodate a broad
> spectrum of assignments that require students to incorporate

some form of evidence, while acknowledging that "evidence"
may take various forms (artistic works, quantitative data,
interview transcripts, primary literature, etc.) in different
disciplines and genres.

In so doing, they address the issue of confusion during assessment; however, the
goals that specify research are still what students see on syllabi.

Another area that the committee struggled with were any goals that related
to the writing process. Kristen recalled that process was important to the faculty
when the goals were initially composed. For committee member Brad, process
is key to writing pedagogy: it is "the living core of what we do in evaluation,
in pedagogy, and in the program." The writing program goals at Oak stress the
writing process in two separate places, under the dimension called "Audience &
Community" and the one called "Process & Style." Here, the goals of the program directly call for peer review in addition to pre-writing and self-reflection.
However, these are difficult to assess programmatically, particularly when using
only one artifact and not a portfolio. Both the committee revising the rubric and
the committees using the rubric thus struggled with the fit between the rubric
and the process-oriented writing program goals.

Under the goal about audience, one bullet point specified that students "evaluate and critique other people's writing and respond to critiques of their own
writing." Kristen recalled that when the initial task force composed this goal, they
were thinking that students "should be able to do peer review." However, following
the assessment procedure that Kristen is familiar with from her AAC&U training,
she developed an assessment of *individual* artifacts across the curriculum without
any contextual documents. This procedure makes assessing the writing process an
impossible ask. Peer review is not something the committee can assess. So, they
shift the meaning of this goal away from peer critique to mean evaluating and
critiquing source material in their writing. Similarly, another bullet point under
the audience goal specified that students should "see their own writing from the
viewpoint of others." Again, this potentially signals the need for faculty to incorporate a peer review process in their classrooms. Yet, in the assessment, Kristen asks
the group to consider this goal as the writer being aware of "the viewpoint of readers." As with the "evidence" dimension, this difficulty in aligning the goals of the
program with the assessment rubric is accounted for through adding a note under
the goals on the rubric. This note acknowledges the difficulty and asks scorers to
take into account factors "like internal consistency and students' self-awareness."
However, unlike the evidence dimension, Kristen does not seem to want to actually change the goals. She still wants faculty to incorporate peer review into their
classrooms; she just does not see a way to assess it programmatically.

Finally, the dimension of "process & style" represents a tension between the need for students to engage in the writing process with wanting to include a dimension on the rubric about style, grammar, and mechanics. Ben, who led the creation of the goals, said that he hoped the category didn't seem like a "catch-all" for what wasn't captured under goals one through three. Kristen also commented that "those two things got shoved together because we wanted the process idea to be in the goals." The original goal reads: "Students should be able to understand writing as a process and to apply conventions of style and grammar." Under this, the first bullet directly mentions the process of "pre-writing, revising, drafting, and responding to feedback," while the other two focus on "control over style" and prose that is "organized, clear, and concise." An assumption built into this dimension on the rubric is that if a student engages in the writing process their style, grammar, and mechanics will improve, and that assumption is expressed by multiple faculty members. Ben noted that there is an "interplay" between process and style and that through the writing process students come "to appreciate that style." Jon explained that "if it's clean, then that suggested to me that they've been over it a few times."

However, not all assessors accept this connection between process and style as readily. In particular, it is two international faculty who question this connection. Marisella, who teaches Spanish and was involved in the 2018 assessment, recognized that strong style may not signal a robust writing process. She stated, "hopefully the polishedness of the final product indicates that there was sufficient rounds of [revision], but it might not because it could be this is just a really strong writer who doesn't need to do a lot of drafting." Shirong, from the 2016 committee, grew up in Singapore speaking both English and Chinese. He worried about international students struggling with the "process and style" portion of the rubric and noted that his colleagues may not be familiar with the way their other languages affect English language learners (ELL) as writers. He noted that when looking at writing from Chinese-speaking students he was able to see why sentence structures were different than expected based on his knowledge of the language, and thus understand the content of the paper. However, he found that non-Chinese speaking faculty felt the sentence structure interfered with meaning. While White, English-speaking faculty members assume that revision will be evident in the final paper, Shirong acknowledged that stylistic conventions have a cultural component that doesn't necessarily disappear with revision. In addition, he puts the responsibility for recognizing this on the faculty assessor, not the student, calling for additional training for faculty on how different linguistic backgrounds affect writing.

Just as the genre of the rubric erases the faculty authors, the writer's identity and the reader/assessor's identity is almost always absent from the actual assessment process. The AAC&U *does* care about the background of the writer, an issue I will return to in Chapter 7. In *On Solid Ground*, McConnell and Rhodes (2017) advocated for sampling artifacts so that racial, ethnic, and socioeconomic status is not erased and for disaggregating student data by race to look for areas of inequity. However, contextual issues, including the identity and background of the student writer, are not included as a part of the scoring process—either by the AAC&U or by Oak. Student identity is not accounted for in the dimension of "style" on the rubric, nor is the ability of the reader to understand that style. Rather the identity of those who interact with the rubric is seen as outside the context of rubric-creation or the initial assessment process.

Kristen continually reminded her scorers that the *context* for scoring is the writing program goals and the rubric itself. They should not try to figure out what level or course the project comes from. Unsaid is that they should also not try to figure out the race or linguistic background of the student. As the committee revised the 2016 rubric, the word "consistency" became a surrogate for the idea of context. For example, scorers may not know what the assignment prompt was or who the paper is written for, but they see a consistent level of jargon as an indication that the writer is aware of audience. Similarly, using sources of a consistent kind in a consistent manner signals that the writer is aware what type of research is being asked of them. The note included under the "process & style" dimension of the Oak rubric acknowledges that the raters do not have access to evidence of the writing process explicitly mentioned in the first goal but encourages raters to "*take factors like internal consistency into account when assessing the first bullet point.*"

Although consistency is a key word that repeated throughout the meetings I observed and the interviews I conducted, "internal" is also important here. It articulates a formalist view of writing. This view perpetuates a myth that factors such as linguistic background, race, gender, and other identity categories are *external* to the writing process, when we know that writing and identity are, in fact, deeply connected. The original VALUE Written Communication rubric (2009) defined "context" by a multitude of factors including the audience, the writer, the intended distribution of the text, and the social/political factors influencing the text. The scholars in writing studies who authored the rubric knew these factors to be inseparable from writing, yet the actual process of assessment makes every attempt to separate them. In 2016, Kristen hoped to collect more contextual information, particularly the assignment prompt. But by the time she trained scorers in Summer 2018, she stressed: "You score what you have in front of you, and you don't think about . . . the only context that matters is the context of the rubric." Kristen does not even attempt to list the things "you don't think about" here, although it is at this point in the training that Marisella asks about the inclusion of non-English papers in the assessment. Clearly, Marisella is thinking about it. And clearly, Kristen is, too, because she thinks about the ways English-speaking faculty would be unable to read non-English papers and therefore does not include any. These identity factors *are* considered, but their consideration is erased, silenced, by both the text of the rubric itself and the process of assessment.

INSTITUTIONAL ACTION

The erasure of these "external" considerations is something that Kristen and the writing committee enact, but it is also simply how boss texts are designed to function. Boss texts "render the messiness of daily work and experience institutionally actionable" (Peacock, 2017, p. 100). Assessment work is messy, even more so when writing is involved. While enacting the Oak writing program goals related to process in the classroom is a matter of adding peer review or pre-writing exercises, assessing those goals across the program is difficult to implement, particularly with one artifact and a rubric. The guiding language of the original VALUE Written Communication rubric signals that it is meant to be used to score writing portfolios that include contextual documents. Yet, when Ben and Kristen train with the AAC&U, they are presented with solo artifacts removed not only from the classroom context but also from the institutional context. The scorers do not know what level the student is, what course they are taking, what the assignment is, or even what type of institution the artifact comes from. When Kristen implemented the assessment at Oak, she collected 60 artifacts from first-year students, and 60 from seniors to be scored on the same rubric by raters who do not know which artifacts come from which classes or levels. The AAC&U training served as the starting point for building this process of assessment at Oak and is seen by both Ben and Kristen as a practical way to begin. There are good reasons why they draw on this, not the least of which is the funding available for the program in doing so. Kristen's ability to test the rubric comes from leftover AAC&U funding provided by Associate Provost Philip, which she can take advantage of only because she ties her local process to the national AAC&U process.

At this point, some compositionists might want to jump in and ask Kristen: why not use portfolios? As a researcher, I wondered this, and in fact, I mentioned the idea to multiple participants. Yet, from an institutional ethnography perspective, the goal of the research is to discover how local practice interacts with ruling relations, not to impose our own expertise on the participants, as we are not experts in their everyday work life (Rankin, 2017a). Rather than conclude that portfolios would "fix" the issues with assessment faced by Kristen and the team, it is important to examine their own perceptions of using them and the constraints they faced.

While my interview participants agreed that portfolios would be a way to capture the process goals—perhaps the only way—no one questioned the assessment plan in committee meetings. Kristen sees portfolios as a potential longer-term goal, as something on her "dream list." However, she doesn't seem to think it should be the first thing the writing program tries. Implementing a portfolio requires institutional support that goes beyond an agreement that portfolios are good practice. Philip was concerned with software that made portfolios difficult to implement beyond the department or course level. He noted that the institution had looked into special portfolio software, but then determined that their learning management system was already suited to portfolio development. The idea stalled, though, when the institution switched to a new learning management system. In addition to the need for technological support for portfolios, the implementation of a writing portfolio seems beyond the expertise of the writing committee. Barbara noted that other small liberal arts colleges use portfolio assessment productively in their writing programs and that she feels it would have been the best option to assess the program at Oak. Kristen, too, admired these other writing programs, particularly the well-known program run by Carol Rutz at Carlton College. Yet, she seems to see implementing a similar program as beyond her abilities. "Their system seems so great to me," she said, "but it also seems like so much work to get that up and running." As I will explore more in Chapter 6, the lack of disciplinary expertise in writing weighs on Kristen and affects what she sees as feasible when creating the assessment at Oak.

Using a rubric based on the writing program goals to score individual artifacts is seen as actionable by the writing committee. It may be difficult at times, but it seems like a doable assessment process. However, in actually implementing the process over the course of the two years I studied Oak, the purpose of the assessment shifted. As stated in 2016, the task of the writing committee is to assess the new writing program. And so, the committee labors to reconcile the use of a rubric with the goals of the writing program, adding notes to clarify goals for scorers and shifting how goals like "process" are defined. However, by 2018, Kristen recognized that this method does not actually capture the impact of the writing program directly. While Kristen can collect first-year artifacts directly from composition courses, the other writing courses are spread across the curriculum, and so it is impossible to collect them from a course that only has seniors. Therefore, she collected any senior artifacts she can get, not necessarily ones from writing program courses. She also realized she cannot rule out the possibility that senior artifacts score better because of factors other than the direct influence of the writing program. Thus, when introducing the assessment process to the 2018 scorers, she says with a bit of a chuckle: "This is not actually an assessment of the writing program; it's an assessment of student writing at Oak under the writing program." This shift also came about because Philip and others in the administration decided to stop using the VALUE rubrics for general education assessment. Kristen explained that Philip then made it clear to her that "the writing committee is now responsible for assessing writing at Oak." The writing program goals, then, become a stand-in for *all* writing done at Oak, not just within writing program courses. In 2018, Kristen compiled a report on the first assessment, and that report is included in Oak's accreditation file. The goals and the rubric are texts that make the messy work of teaching writing actionable, assessable, reportable.

ST. RITA'S GENERAL EDUCATION COMMITTEE & THE PRIMACY OF ENGLISH

At St. Rita's a writing rubric is used to evaluate first-year writing, as well as later general education courses, and to create writing goals for general education. (The rubric can be found in Appendix E.) Unlike Oak, the writing rubric is used to directly assess individual students rather than writing across the university as a whole. In terms of first-year writing, at the end of each semester English faculty use St. Rita's writing rubric to score portfolios from first-year writing classes to determine if students pass of fail. In addition, they score sophomore and junior portfolios from across campus—which consist of one timed essay and a cover letter. The purpose of this system is to pass (or hold back) students but also to show how students are progressing through the general education curriculum. Thus, the rubric that is used in this context is tied to both first-year writing and the general education curriculum as a whole. When the general education committee looked to revise their curriculum and their goals based on the VALUE rubrics, they turned to the rubric used by English faculty to score these portfolios. While Oak followed the basic AAC&U process for modification and worked hard to reach consensus among faculty from different disciplines, the faculty at St. Rita's defaulted to what is done within English and first-year writing. This is significant because unlike the other VALUE rubrics the general education committee referenced, the Written Communication rubric had already been significantly modified. To further understand this process, I observed a general education committee meeting and interviewed both English faculty who participated in scoring the portfolios and members of the general education committee.

When I observed the general education committee in Fall 2016, they were not composing a rubric or even considering revising it. Rather they were using the rubric to create new general education outcomes. As described in Chapter 4, this rubric was used to score timed essays, which are referred to as "signature assignments," collected in the first-year writing course as well as at later points in the general education curriculum. The rubric shows that by the completion of general education, writing should fall in the "3 Sufficient" performance descriptor. The process of aligning the general education goals with this rubric is interesting simply because it reverses the more common logic that rubrics are created to assess outcomes rather than outcomes being created to fit rubrics. As shown in Chapter 4, however, St. Rita's sees the rubrics as a national source for legitimacy, something they need to align their curriculum with to be taken seriously. Therefore, the discussion of the rubric dimensions was related to whether or not those dimensions should be used as general education goals.

When I attended the committee meeting, there were six proposed outcomes for written communication within general education and five dimensions of the rubric used at St. Rita's. In general, these mapped onto one another. The one exception was the addition of a general education goal about following "expectations appropriate to a specific discipline," which appears to make a nod to the VALUE Written Communication rubric dimension of "genre and disciplinary conventions." Although my participants did not directly address this point, it also seems that this addition makes sense when looking at multiple courses in general education rather than just first-year writing courses. The other goals clearly aligned with the rubric used to score the "signature assignments" collected at multiple points throughout the general education curriculum at St. Rita's (see Appendix E). The first written communication outcome for general education states that the writer will respond to the prompt, matching the "responding to assignments" dimension of the rubric. There are also outcomes that address the dimensions of "structure and coherence" and "evidence and analysis." Finally, there are two goals for sentence-level issues. One goal specifies that "the work includes some variety of sentence types," and the other that "language generally conveys meaning . . . although writing may include some errors of grammar or mechanics." Again, these match the two separate dimensions on the writing rubric.

Lucinda, a former English faculty member now in administration, noted to me that she did not support these two separate dimensions for style and mechanics but was "out-voted" when the writing rubric was created. In her role on the general education committee, she tentatively brings back up the issue of combining the two rubric categories, at least when it comes to the general education goals. This particular moment in my observation is telling of how the general education committee took English courses as the default standard for their general education goals on writing. In Chapter 6 I return to this moment to explore the relationship between the overall general education process and individual classroom practice, but here I focus on how it signals the role of English as an authority on writing within general education. When Lucinda raised her concern, the question for the general education committee became whether or not these sentence-level issues are a concern for the general education curriculum as a whole or are the specific purview of first-year writing courses. Dwayne asked: "If they're using the same type of sentence, a simple sentence, over and over and over again, is it a problem in our general education?" He pointed out that the specificity of the goal for sentence types is not in keeping with the generality seen in the VALUE rubrics. At this point in the meeting, Lucinda took the initiative to comb through documents on her laptop to find the exact course outcomes from the composition sequence.[6] My assumption, listening to the concerns brought up by the committee, was that if those goals were listed as first-year composition course goals, then the committee would conclude that they did not also need to be specified in the general education goals. However, the opposite happened.

Lucinda eventually found the outcomes and read several relevant ones out loud to the committee: These outcomes stated that students will write with a variety of sentence types, correct grammar, complete sentences, and active verbs. Dwayne then scoffed at the goals, called them "aspirational" and not a good representation of where students actually are in first-year classes. Lucinda backed away from her request to scratch the sentence variety goal from general education and instead said, "wouldn't it be great if they're reinforced in other general education courses . . . where they could get to mastery at the end." The committee agreed and Jeremy, as chair, declared that they would keep the sentence variety goal for general education. We see here that the goals of English then become the goals of general education. Rather than actually consider if features like using "active voice" are disciplinary specific, the committee assumes that what English is teaching is what everyone should teach when it comes to writing.

In part, this synecdochical relationship between English and the rest of the university when it comes to writing is not unique to St. Rita's. As we saw at Oak, the writing committee was tasked with assessing writing for all of the university, not just for their program. However, St. Rita's does not have a writing committee, a writing program, or even have an English department. Rather, the Humanities department oversees three programs, including English. Yet, Patrice, a social scientist, noted that English has the most faculty members on campus and that they "call the shots." Noting that several English faculty have moved up in administration, such as Lucinda, Patrice stated: "We're in a period now where English rules." Patrice objected to the "supremacy of English" on campus and yet she frequently calls on her English colleagues when she teaches writing, asking them for the most up to date rubrics and inquiring about what *they* want her to do in her classes.

---

6   Although several people present taught the course, none seemed to know what the goals were without searching for that information.

THE "OGRE" OF ENGLISH

While Patrice may see the English faculty as unified ruling front, the tensions among English faculty are high. In particular, Gerald, usually referred to as Dr. Z by his colleagues at St. Rita's, was the humanities chair at the beginning of my study. Dr. Z is a self-proclaimed "ogre and bloviating authoritarian" who exerts his control not only over students but over his colleagues. Through direct stories and indirect references, the English faculty seem to agree that Dr. Z is the reason for at least some of the major differences between the rubric used at St. Rita's and the original VALUE rubric. In particular, Dr. Z was adamant about the two dimensions for "prose, style and syntax" as well as one for "spelling, word-choice, grammar, and punctuation." Lucinda is not alone in questioning the need for these two separate rubric dimensions. In fact, Dr. Z appears to be of the minority opinion, yet the other faculty let him have his way. For example, Heather said she was a "fan" of the original VALUE Written Communication rubric "because the sentence stuff is smushed together." Yet, she was part-time and not consulted when the current writing rubric for St. Rita's was created. She is concerned that students "don't understand enough about the difference between prose stye and punctuation" to have to separate categories on the rubric be helpful to them. Since the students are directly scored using the rubric at St. Rita's there is the added element of creating them in a way the students will understand. Dwayne is also concerned about the way the two dimensions affect students. He explained that when he studied the first-year writing portfolio scores, he found that students who failed in one of these categories almost always failed in the other. He is concerned that students are held back in progressing through their degree by surface-level errors. But that is exactly the result Dr. Z wants. He complained that the VALUE rubric is flawed because students could "score really low at the sentence level and still pass," and "that's where all our students are fumbling the ball all the time." Dr. Z firmly believes that students need a foundation in grammar and sentence structure before progressing in writing, and he sees the rubric as a way of enforcing this kind of gatekeeping at the first-year level. While I explore his view in more depth in Chapter 7, particularly in relation to racial and institutional power, the key point here is that the way the rubric is adapted has much to do with the faculty dynamics at play on the committees doing the work.

Despite Dwayne's hope to "move closer to the VALUE rubric" and others appreciation for the national rubric, the conversation about writing and general education I observed stalled any changes to the way writing is taught or assessed at St. Rita's. At the time of this writing in 2021—three years after closing my data collection—the rubric on the St. Rita's website for scoring portfolios in general education is the same rubric I saw in 2016. While Oak faculty spent years tweaking and testing their rubric before using it, in one brief conversation, St. Rita's agreed to simply move forward as they had been doing. And regardless of large differences in their rubric and the Written Communication VALUE rubric, they framed what they were doing as using a modified VALUE rubric. Even Dr. Z agreed that this connection brought with it a sense of legitimacy for the assessment work done at St. Rita's, yet he prevents any meaningful use of the VALUE Written Communication rubric to proceed.

INSTITUTIONAL INACTION

Examining the challenges at St. Rita's can give us a different perspective on what is happening when faculty work to "adapt" the VALUE rubric and why that process does not always end in a new rubric or assessment process. In addition to the social conflicts and disciplinary dominance of English at St. Rita's, there are practical reasons for why the process did not go any further. St. Rita's is incredibly small, with a student population under 1,000, including both undergraduate and graduate programs. The AAC&U and higher education, in general, is not often aware of institutional circumstances like the ones these faculty engaged with on a daily basis. This difference is enacted in concrete ways such as the funding sources and faculty labor available for assessment work. Kristen held the 2017 summer assessment workshop in order to get more feedback on the rubric from faculty across the curriculum. She was able to do so, and pay faculty participants, because Philip had leftover money from the AAC&U grant that needed to be used. In contrast, faculty at St. Rita's are always hurting for funds. Dwayne explained to me that he disliked that St. Rita's writing portfolio was only a timed essay and a cover letter. However, the English faculty read all the portfolios in one marathon six-hour session, and neither the funds nor the time were available for them to do more. Despite Patrice complaining that English is the largest discipline on campus, there are, in fact, only four full-time English faculty members to do this work.

In addition, sampling student work for assessment rather than scoring every student essay is never considered at St. Rita's. Oak is small, but still more than twice as big as St. Rita's with an undergraduate population of about 2,000. When working with the AAC&U, Philip found that they did not have realistic expectations for the amount of work produced at a small college like Oak. He noted that the AAC&U seemed to send the same instructions to everyone, asking for 300 senior artifacts. For Philip, that is "60 percent of [the] senior class," and so he negotiates with the VALUE staff who ask him to determine what a reasonable number of artifacts is for a school his size. At St. Rita's, it is difficult to even know how many seniors there are. Nearly half of their small undergraduate population attends part-time, and many drop out before they reach their fourth year. Traditional class standing seems antithetical to real conditions at St. Rita's. However, with a total undergraduate population around 500-600, it is safe to say that 300 senior artifacts would be significantly more than the total number of seniors. This is yet another challenge for St. Rita's when attempting to fit in with national "best" practice. It is not only a matter of underprepared students who don't come to college ready to meet the first benchmark on the rubric or a matter of needing to adapt rubric language. The "universal" process designed by the AAC&U does not fit the institutional size of St. Rita's.

While no one expects consensus-building to be an easy process, proponents of it also do not always anticipate the emotional labor involved when interacting with colleagues such as Dr. Z. When Crystal Broch Colombini and Maureen McBride (2012) explained that "storming" is a natural part of the norming process, they did not anticipate the literal storming out of the room calling colleagues "ignoramuses" that Dr. Z reportedly did in a later general education meeting. Rather, the example they give of these periods of dissent is a reader objecting to how assessment artifacts were gathered (Broch Colombini & McBride, 2012). Unfortunately, Dr. Z's outbursts are not unique in academic life. Bethany Davila and Cristyn Elder (2019) conducted a survey of bullying in WPA workplaces. They classified 41 percent of their responses as examples of verbal abuse where colleagues yelled or swore at others in anger. These unhealthy dynamics directly affect the environment in which faculty work together to create and adapt rubrics. Rubric adaptation, when done by committee, relies on a certain level of collegiality and commitment that is difficult to achieve at St. Rita's. Perhaps more common than bullying, faculty bring their own agendas to the table that cannot be fully separated from their own career aspirations. John Trimbur (1989) noted that it is naive not to recognize the way knowledge production is motivated by individual career moves not simply consensus of a group of experts. Dwayne and Heather rely on a working relationship with Dr. Z as their department chair and must weigh their own careers alongside what they think is best practice in assessment. Under these conditions, it is no wonder that the faculty default to existing practice rather than fight to modify it.

CONCLUSION

While the AAC&U recognizes that their rubrics can, and often should, be modified for local practice, they advocate for a universal process in which faculty on a campus reach consensus on a modified rubric (Levi & Stevens, 2010). They also view the rubric modification process as one of *translation*: "the VALUE rubrics can and should be *translated* [emphasis added] into the language of individual campuses, disciplines, and even courses" (Rhodes, 2010, p. 21). The mission of the AAC&U in creating the VALUE rubrics was to "establish that rubrics can provide the assurance that regardless of where they teach—type of institution, part of the country, or mix of programs—faculty are indeed talking about the same outcomes and sharing the same expectations for learning" (Rhodes, 2010, p. 1). By assuming that their process can work anywhere, that there is a "level playing field" in which institutions engage with outcomes and assessment and arrive at the *same place*, the AAC&U interpolates universities and their faculty as decontextualized neoliberal subjects. Institutional ethnography returns these subjects and their discourse to their context. It "rediscover(s) discourse as an actual happening" (Smith, 2014, p. 227). After reading this chapter, it should be clear that those at Oak and those at St. Rita's, while both stating they use modified VALUE Written Communication rubrics, do *not* share the same expectations for learning, nor do they operate on a level playing field.

It could be argued that neither institution fully follows the practices laid out by the AAC&U. At Oak, the faculty clearly draw on the AAC&U's overall assessment process that Kristen and Ben learned in their AAC&U training. They work with faculty to norm; they revise the rubric repeatedly; they test it, and they reach what might even be considered a type of consensus. However, the rubric is ultimately meant to follow the goals of the writing program, not the dimensions of the original VALUE rubric. Those goals, particularly when it comes to process, are poorly captured in the genre of the rubric. The opposite happens at St. Rita's, where none of this process is present and yet the original AAC&U VALUE rubrics appear in their written materials, like the faculty handbook. Excepting the written communication outcomes, which are affected strongly by the faculty dynamics at St. Rita's, the general education outcomes replicated the dimensions of the VALUE rubrics. Yet, faculty agree those rubrics are not designed for the population of students that attends St. Rita's. Both schools interact with the VALUE Written Communication rubric as they work to define outcomes and rubrics, but neither fully implement what the AAC&U potentially had in mind when they advocated for rubric adaptation. Nor do they fully lean into their particular, local, and embodied institutional and programmatic contexts.

While so much is different about these two intuitions, I would argue that the very process of using a rubric for writing assessment links them together. In particular, rubric-based assessment leads faculty at both schools toward a common perception (or misperception) of writing. The genre of the rubric and the perception of the VALUE rubrics as exemplars of the rubric genre reinforces an assumption that writing is linear skill-based learning. It is telling that one of the most common modifications nationally to the VALUE rubrics is reversing the order of the performance descriptors. In particular, this change is rarely discussed or debated, but simply assumed. Progression is inherent in the form of the rubric, and so it makes sense to users to start at the beginning, the lowest level and work toward the higher end. When I asked participants about this change, they hadn't really considered it, noting that the lower to higher order seemed natural. Perhaps one reason why so many faculty want to change the order of the VALUE rubrics to have the weakest level on the left is that rubrics position the instructor to read with a deficit-based lens, for where the text does *not* line up with the rubric rather than for textual possibility (Wilson 2006). For Dr. Z, this order is natural not only from the point of view of skill progress but from a cultural perspective. "One thing I remember was that it made absolutely no sense," he told me referring to the order of performance levels in the original VALUE rubric, "as if you're reading Chinese!" Individuals like Dr. Z come to texts with their own cultural and ideological backgrounds that affect their reading, yet genres encourage some readings over others. A rubric is not recognizable as a rubric without performance levels, and so it impossible to read a rubric outside the ideological frame of pedagogical progress.

We also see this frame enacted when the Oak committee struggles to fit their writing process goals into a rubric. These goals signal a different type of progression—one of labor rather than skill. Whether or not the writer engages in a writing process, whether they pre-write, or respond to feedback, is never entirely discernible from one static artifact. And yet, the committee at Oak, unable to break from the frame that all the writing program goals must be measured by the rubric, must redefine process in terms that can be seen in the final product. They must believe that "internal consistency" signals process and awareness of audience in order to continue with their work and meet their charge of measuring outcomes on a rubric. Here, the genre constrains what is possible in terms of how the committee can interpret and operationalize the program's goals.

The final product of the modified rubric erases the tension between individuals and the social conditions that influence their work. For Amy Devitt (2004), genres are "a nexus between an individual's actions and a socially defined context" (p. 31). Delving into the tensions, constraints, and choices of those at Oak and St. Rita's challenges the notion that modifying a rubric is ever only a matter of local translation. Furthermore, the assumption that calibrating scorers is a means of consensus-making does not account for the many local and personal dynamics that come into play when designing and using rubrics. The AAC&U sees themselves as guiding this process of consensus-building and thus furthering democratic aims, but as shown in the example from St. Rita's, that process may be anything other than democratic.

CHAPTER 6.

FOLLOWING THE "BREADCRUMBS" FROM COMMITTEE TO CLASSROOM

The 2016 Faculty Survey of Student Engagement (FSSE) showed that 76 percent of faculty across the curriculum used rubrics to evaluate assignments. Of those, only 29 percent created their own rubrics (Zilvinskis, Nelson Laird & Graham, 2016). Turley and Gallagher (2008) warned, "If teachers are handed a rubric—from state, district, or the teacher next door—we need to consider the law of distal diminishment and be skeptical of the ability of that rubric to improve students' writing" (p. 92). There are dangers to separating any rubric from its original context or believing that it can easily be ported to a new setting. Thus, I originally saw classroom use of the VALUE rubrics as a part of the problematic guiding my study. I was concerned that faculty were finding the rubrics or being given the rubrics by administrators and then using them directly in assessing student work for grades in the classroom.

The AAC&U originally recognized the danger of using the VALUE rubrics in the classroom. Rhodes (2010) explained in the introduction to the rubrics that they were "not designed for use in assessing individual class assignments" (p. 2). This idea is reinforced by the statement at the top of all the VALUE rubrics that they are "intended for institutional-level use in evaluating and discussing student learning, not for grading" (McConnell et al., 2019, p. 6). Yet, in my 2016 survey of how the Written Communication rubric was being used, "as an example rubric for faculty" was the second most popular option, just under university-wide assessment. Similarly, in 2019 the AAC&U noted that there were many articles written about the VALUE rubrics that "described making modifications for specific grading of assignments" (p. 16). The VALUE rubrics' status as boss texts and meta-rubrics means that they are often presented as exemplar rubrics, not only for assessment professionals but also for instructors.

However, tracing the connections between the classroom and larger scale assessment efforts is not a simple matter of collecting documents and tracing their origins. Faculty often rely on others to share rubrics, but they do not always remember where they got them. Amelia, a science professor at Oak, expressed a common sentiment: "I stole it from a colleague who developed it again from a colleague, right?" Meanwhile, Dwayne, who wanted general education revisions at St. Rita's to impact pedagogy, longed for "a trail of breadcrumbs that leads back to the curricular." When talking to faculty about their rubrics, I often felt that I was being presented with an isolated breadcrumb, disconnected from its path, and I wondered how we can "close the loop," as assessment professionals often say, without much of a trail to follow. When I asked participants at Oak and St. Rita's directly if they would use the VALUE rubric in their classroom, I repeatedly heard "no." Thus, I did not focus on collecting classroom rubrics, observing classrooms, or asking students how they interpreted the rubric. However, classroom practice did frequently come up in my study. In keeping with common interviewing practice in institutional ethnography (DeVault & McCoy, 2006), when participants mentioned their classroom rubrics or offered me examples, I gathered these as a part of my data. This sometimes was a trail of breadcrumbs itself as faculty turned to a file cabinet or folder in their office and rifled through, handing me rubrics they found. I also listened to the interviews for descriptions of classroom practice, particularly when it came up in reference to work done on the committees creating rubrics and outcomes.

In this chapter, I describe what crumbs I did find—what participants at Oak and St. Rita's said about using rubrics in their classroom, including what they consider rubrics to be and how they develop them. Even when there seems to be little direct connection to the VALUE rubrics, there are multiple parallels between the way rubrics as boss texts operate in the classroom and the way they operate in large-scale assessment. Furthermore, classroom practice directly impacts the modification of and use of the rubrics at the institutional level. Even when they try not to, faculty often envision particular classroom settings and students when scoring artifacts across a program. So, too, they work to make the rubric flexible (and vague) enough to capture all possible classroom practices. At both institutions, faculty were also concerned with how the work done on their committees would change pedagogy. In some cases, faculty hoped for a change in classroom practice, fearing the committee work would have no real impact on curriculum or student learning. In other cases, they feared having to change their own assignments and assessment in the classroom. Either way, these tensions represent the frustrations faculty feel when larger ruling relations interact with their teaching.

Finally, I use rhetorical genre theory to understand what happens when we attempt to either use the same rubric across contexts or "translate" it for use in a different context. The notion of translation indicates that moving between contexts is simply a matter of tweaking language. Yet writing scholars know that context intimately affects genres. So, too, does the role of the individual person within a system of genres. Each role (or standpoint) within a system has its own genre set. Those genres gain meaning through their interaction with other genres in the system (Bazerman, 2004). For example, a student essay (part of the set of the student) directly responds to the assignment prompt (part of the set of the teacher). The two work in concert as a part of the rhetorical situation, one informing the other. Similarly, rubrics as a genre work differently in the classroom than they do in large-scale assessment. In the classroom, rubrics are a part of a classroom-based system: they work in conjunction with the assignment sheet, teacher feedback, peer review, and other classroom genres. In large-scale assessment, as Kristen reminded her raters at Oak, the only context that matters is the rubric itself. Here, the genre of the rubric stands in for all teaching while the student artifact must stand in for all student writing.

Although the VALUE Written Communication rubric was designed to be used in conjunction with assignment prompts, it is purposefully vague in order to represent multiple classroom contexts over the course of a college student's career. Furthermore, both logistical and philosophical concerns have led to the separation of the rubric and the assignment sheet in actual assessment. This practice has then reinforced the need for assignments that fit with the rubric in the first place and led to the direct intervention by the AAC&U in assignment design. While these efforts are newly underway at the time of this writing, the direct impact of large-scale rubrics on classroom assignments has long been felt in secondary education. Joanne Addison (2015) detailed how the Gates Foundation used grant funding for educators to align assignments with Common Core Standards and the rubrics that assess these standards. In addition, composition-ists have worried that generic rubrics, such as VALUE, lead to generic assignments that "violate principles of good assignment creation" (Anson et al., 2012, para 6). The relationship between large-scale assessment and classroom practice thus represents another tension between institutional power (ruling relations) and everyday local practice. By removing the rubrics from their context, from their genre sets and systems, ruling relations continue to flourish and obscure the everyday work of faculty and students.

FACULTY USE OF CLASSROOM RUBRICS

Collecting documents from faculty gave me a fresh perspective on how they viewed rubrics, including what they considered a rubric to be and what role it played in their pedagogy. In the glossary of Peggy O'Neill, Cindy Moore, and Brian Huot's (2009) *Guide to College Writing Assessment* they define a rubric as a "scoring guide" that "specifies a point scale and identifies the salient features of the text for each point" (p. 204). They note that rubrics may use checklists or paragraphs when describing each point level. This description does seem to presuppose a certain form—one that is linear in order to show a progression in quality. Defining a scale is key to making assessment criteria a "rubric" rather than a list of guiding questions or dimensions to be assessed. Similarly, in an *Assessing Writing* editorial, Martin East and Sara Cushing (2016) defined a rubric as "a guide listing specific criteria for grading or scoring academic papers, projects, or tests, an instrument that describes a specific level of performance within a scale" (p. 1). Yet, not all the documents faculty provided to me as example rubrics had a scale or described what point level equated to what grade. Just as I was surprised to learn that administrators at different universities saw their programmatic rubrics as adaptations of the VALUE rubric when they differed significantly, I noticed that some faculty used the word "rubric" to refer to any type of grading criteria. This appears to signal something about how faculty view and understand the rhetorical role of rubrics and their genre function within the classroom. As boss texts, drawing on rubrics adds a certain legitimacy to grading practice.

THE PROMISE OF CLASSROOM RUBRICS

Rubrics are a promise to teachers that grading can be quicker, more objective, and more focused (Wilson, 2006). Teachers can be "fair" if only they use a rubric. Under this objective epistemology, fairness is defined as a lack of bias and "ensured through reproducibility" (Lynne, 2004, p. 136). Brian Huot (2002) argued that equating reliability and replicability with fairness is "not only inaccurate," but also "dangerous" (p. 88). So, too, Inoue (2015) challenged this notion of fairness as a "White liberal value" that works to maintain racist practice (p. 56). However, this value of reproducibility is deeply embedded in the current system of higher education. The rubric also fits with promises made by neoliberal universities to students. As explained in Chapter 2, students are trained to make sure that their college experience offers them a good deal— one that is comparable to other universities and that will lead to a career—and promised that rubrics will keep their teachers objective and fair. Reproducibility might refer to scores on a rubric, but it also refers to the reproducibility of classroom experience. This need for objectivity and fairness has historically been tied to a system where students can demonstrate "proficiency" by testing out of a course or transferring one in from a different college (Behizadeh & Engelhard Jr., 2011). The course over here must be equivalent to the one over there, and rubrics, distributed *across* university contexts, work to meet this goal. The classroom rubric, particularly when based in a national or programmatic rubric, is meant to keep teachers consistent in their grading to ensure that all students have a similar classroom experience regardless of who their teacher is.

This attitude was reflected by multiple participants in my study. St. Rita's faculty member Patrice expressed that she is more consistent when using rubrics. She framed this consistency in terms of morality: "This forces me to be more honest." Kristen, too, uses rubrics because she values consistency in her grading. She sees rubrics as a means to help her discover her own expectations and be consistent with students. Shawna, a religious studies professor at Oak, said that she doesn't want to be "too subjective" in her grading, and the rubric helps her make sure she is "following the guidelines." Jeremy at St. Rita's tied this way of thinking to student expectations. He noted that students often complain about teacher subjectivity and that "providing a standard rubric across the curriculum was helping students see that there is a standard." Similarly, Wendy from Oak directly stated that rubrics are useful for justifying student grades. Across both institutions, faculty saw rubrics as performing this common function of making the inherently messy thing of grading student writing into a fair and consistent process.

The fact that grades need this sort of external justification speaks to their role in a system where teachers are viewed as subjects to be relegated rather than as expert readers of student texts. Going back to the beginnings of modern composition, early CCCCs workshops focused on methods to standardize grading, thus creating what Strickland (2011) called a "proper teaching subject" (p. 71). Strickland draws on a Foucaultian notion of the subject here as "someone who comes into being as a result of subjection" (p. 52). The writing teacher, for Strickland, is a position that requires systemic management and continued training in order to create "a better product" for student-consumers (p. 54). Rubric-use maintains this subject position and also asks that teachers self-regulate. As seen in the comments from my participants, instructors use rubrics to ensure *their own* consistency, to hold themselves accountable. In addition, the general education committee at St. Rita's is explicit about this use of both the rubrics and the outcomes they are creating. Dwayne told a story about a faculty member who would take off a point for every grammar error. Therefore, he values the language of the rubric, which directly states under the third level, sufficient: "the writer makes one or a few minor errors repeatedly." This language was specifically added to counter the practice of those like the faculty member in Dwayne's story.

The classroom rubric is also used as tool to get students to self-regulate, to be responsible for ensuring the consistency of their own educational process by adhering to the norms presented in the rubric. The classroom rubric is used as a tool to legitimize both qualities of student writing and the student themselves. Art History Professor Brad stated this best when he told me: "what we valorize in terms of writing habits and pedagogical habits in the classroom is embedded in the language of the rubric." Brad's English colleague Ronnie gives his students the assignment rubric during peer review and asks them to use it to evaluate their peer's work. "I want them to start thinking just a smidge like teachers themselves," he stated. Scientist Amelia, too, said that she expects students to use the rubric to write their assignment. Regardless of their discipline, Oak faculty saw the rubric as a way to get students thinking about the expectations of the assignment. Dwayne also embraced this self-regulatory function of the rubric but focuses more on the idea of behaviors and habits that could help the struggling students at St. Rita's. In my last interview with Dwayne before he left St. Rita's, he was working on building a rubric for his writing class that added a dimension that he hoped would convey the types of habits he wanted to instill in student learners. For this rubric dimension, he mentioned drawing not on the VALUE Written Communication rubric but on the VALUE rubrics for Lifelong Learning and Teamwork. However, unlike the Teamwork VALUE rubric that follows AAC&U asset-based approach by defining the lowest "benchmark" performance level in positive terms: "Completes all assigned task by deadline" (AAC&U, 2009a), Dwayne created the weakest row to communicate to students what not to do. In an interview, he shared part of this new rubric. In it, he titled the lowest performance level "absent or counterproductive" and used language such as "leaves the task incomplete, misses meetings, perhaps without notice, completes work late" to describe this level. He feels that these descriptions are necessary to communicate to the type of students at St. Rita's what it means to be "in the ballgame" of college. A similar issue of student behavior comes up at Oak but with less of a focus on preparedness. Ben, possibly drawing on Stephen North's (1984) famous writing center statement, has his students list not just qualities of good writing, but also "qualities of good writers." He then incorporates what they list into his classroom rubric.

While these discussions about writing process and college success are absolutely necessary to have with students, what is interesting is that these instructors find them also necessary to put on a rubric. The rubric, as a classroom genre, reifies and legitimizes these behaviors in a way a classroom discussion does not. Furthermore, rubrics shift the responsibility for regulation of these habits to the individual reading the text of the rubric. When this is the teacher grading the assignment, they must regulate their grading practice to be consistent with the rubric. Rather than start from the student text as a separate artifact, when guided by a rubric, the faculty member begins from a set of criteria, and this limits what they see in the student text itself. Rubrics are meant to "identify sameness, not surprises or difference" (Inoue, 2019, p. 71). Even if a rubric were to reward innovation as a dimension, an instructor would have to consider what levels of innovation looked like. Is the paper innovative or surprising enough for a "highly proficient" score or is it only "satisfactorily" innovative? Similarly, when students are asked to use a rubric to guide their writing, they are asked to read the assignment prompt through the lens of outcomes, and the rubric—as a genre—defines writing as steady progress toward the highest level of proficiency. Rather than accepting the assignment as an open invitation to writing or recognizing the degree to which failure is an important part of writing (Brooke & Carr, 2015), the student must become the writing subject who works to produce the writing the rubric calls for. They must *be* the writer whose behavior matches that of the rubric. Then, all traces of the ebbs and flows of the writing process are separated from the product of that work. Even if they become the writer invoked by the rubric, that writer is represented only by the final written product.

FACULTY DEFINE "RUBRICS"

While the rubric as a boss text asks teachers and students to take up generic subject positions in relation to the text, that does not necessarily imply uniformity in the genre. Devitt's (2004) views on genre fit well with institutional ethnography because they encourage researchers to study how individuals enact texts. While genres "exist institutionally and collectively," they "never operate independently of the actions of people" (Devitt, 2004, p. 49). Faculty use rubrics in great number, as the reference from FSSE above shows. So, too, they seem to agree on their function in the classroom—to guide both student work and teacher grading. However, without collecting these documents or discussing them with individual faculty members, it is difficult to define actual classroom practice. I found that faculty at Oak and St. Rita's sometimes used rubrics in the classroom in strikingly different ways, and those rubrics took vastly different forms. In particular, Kristen, the chair of the writing committee at Oak, had a very open perception of rubrics and how they could be designed and used in the classroom. Her "rubrics" are meant to share her expectations with students, but they are flexible and vary in both content and form depending on the course she is teaching and the assignment. In contrast, Patrice at St. Rita's felt a need to use the rubrics provided for her by her colleagues from English. She also saw rubrics as a means to give students a strict structure to follow in their essays—the five-paragraph form—and to dictate the content of those assignments. While I talked with others about their classroom rubric use, the contrast of these two participants in particular highlights how disparate classroom rubric use can be.

In one of my initial interviews with Kristen, she proclaimed her love of rubrics, followed by a list of all the different types of rubrics she could choose from:

> I love rubrics. And I have them in all kinds of forms. I have
> checklist rubrics. I have box rubrics. I have just general

question rubrics. I have narrative rubrics. For my senior seminar, I just use a narrative rubric where basically I'm sort of
explaining to students in a narrative how I approach grading
their papers.

As a follow up, Kristen sent me copies of her first-year writing "question
rubric" and her senior level "narrative rubric." Neither of these fit the definitions
of rubrics from O'Neill, Moore, and Huot's (2009) in that they do not have a
clear scale imbedded. The senior level evaluation criteria discussed grade levels
but did not organize them in any form of chart or table. Rather, it proceeded in
a fully narrative fashion:

> How I grade your final project: The first two questions I ask
> myself when I read your paper are: Is it based on primary
> sources? Does it have an argument? If the answer to the first
> question is no, if there are few or no citations of primary
> sources in your paper, the highest grade you can earn is a D. If
> your paper does not have an argument, the highest grade you
> can earn is a C.

Similarly, the "rubric" associated with her first-year writing assignment did
not have any kind of linear chart format. Rather, it divided a series of questions
into higher-order and lower-order concerns. For example:

> Higher-order questions: 3) Have you provided concrete exam-
> ples to support your points?

> Lower-order questions: 4) Have you followed the format for
> this assignment, as specified above?

The criteria then went on to explain that if the student can answer "yes" to all
the questions they will receive a "B." It also clarifies that the higher-order questions will be considered more heavily than the lower-order questions, though no
points are directly associated with either. While both artifacts mentioned performance, there is more discretion on the part of the instructor built into these
grading criteria than a typical rubric. There is an indication of what the teacher
should look for when grading and what the student should aspire to, but there
is no clear scale with performance levels.

In contrast, at St. Rita's, I collected grading criteria that was very focused
on specific points but did not have the dimensions we've come to associate with
the typical rubric. Here, the format of the five-paragraph essay is rewarded with
point values associated with each paragraph. This "rubric" was sent out by Dr.
Z to all the faculty in an attempt to get them to teach the five-paragraph essay

in their classrooms. It is titled "General Education Expository Essay Rubric" and begins with a paragraph stating the importance of all general education classes requiring the five-paragraph essay. The text states: "Here is a simplified rubric for grading an expository essay in any discipline." There is then a chart with the structure of the five-paragraph essay and a blank spot for point totals. And yet, this document does not specify levels of performance. Rather it tasks professors to set the point values based on their assignment (see Figure 6.1).

Although Patrice did not recall seeing this particular rubric (much to her chagrin), she is also very focused on points: "I give 15 points to responding to the assignment, 5 for structure, 3 for evidence." She also gives her government class an assignment sheet for a five-paragraph essay that dictates exactly what they should say in each paragraph, including the content. For example, the assignment states that the fifth paragraph is "where you restate your thesis statement (youth voter turnout matters) and repeat your three reasons why." Thinking about grading criteria without points is difficult for Patrice, and she struggles with the committee discussion of the VALUE rubric because of this. Dwayne, too, mentioned that when he attempted to bring a holistic rubric to St. Rita's faculty, many wondered, "What equals a B?" For many at St. Rita's, such as Patrice, rubrics are defined by having a very specific point-based form.

COMPETENCY	POINTS
Content (___ points) • Accurate, interesting, substantive ideas • Responds appropriately to assignment	
Thesis (___ points) • Clear and Focused/Asserts a Position	
Introduction (___ points) • Grabs Attention • Clearly States Thesis • Indicates how thesis will be supported	
Body Paragraphs (___ points) • States main idea in topic sentence that supports thesis • States specific, accurately-reported details that support topic sentence • Includes transition words that make logic of paragraph and essay clear, linking sentences within paragraph and paragraphs to one another.	
Conclusion (___ points) • Restates the thesis • Recaps the support for the thesis • Concludes with implications or look to future	
Sentence Grammar and Style (___ points) • Uses correct, appropriate grammar • Uses proper punctuation and spelling • Prose is concise and clear	
Total	

Note: *The weighting of different elements of the essay can vary from assignment to assignment but all elements of the essay should be assessed.*

Figure 6.1. WAC Rubric from St. Rita's.

Patrice's view of the purpose and form of a rubric is still very tied to a positivist testing mentality. Patrice is frustrated that her government students do poorly on the five-paragraph essay assignment when she "gives them what the answers are." In this case, Patrice is really testing students on their reading of an article not evaluating their writing ability. Rubrics, to her, function more as an answer key. In fact, she used this language again when telling me about helping a student on an essay about abortion. "I spend a whole hour and a half going over that article, and I go over the answers," Patrice lamented. This is perhaps why Patrice gets upset at the general education meeting when she thinks that introducing a new writing goal, and possibly a new writing rubric, will change what she is teaching. Several times in the meeting discussing general education goals for writing, Patrice complained, "That means I'm changing all my assignments!" Each time, the committee reminded her they were not discussing classroom level rubrics. "But if that's on the syllabus, if that's on, if that's the rubric I'm using to assess that assignment," Patrice continued to "no, no, no" responses from multiple committee members. Patrice's view of the rubric as answer key potentially impedes her ability to see them as anything other than a tool for the classroom.

Although both Kristen and Patrice valued the rubric for adding consistency to grading, this closer look at their criteria highlights the different views they hold on what a rubric looks like and how it functions. For Patrice, it is a very specific tool used to show students the answers and structures on which they will be graded. In contrast, Kristen sees the rubric as a diverse tool for evaluating student work, one that can take many different forms. Whether posed as a narrative description or a question, Kristen values these "rubrics" as a tool to communicate her expectations to students. Put in rhetorical genre theory terms, Kristen uses the same term—rubric— to refer to multiple types of assessment criteria because she views them all as responding to the same exigence and performing the same social action. That action is communicating to students about the grading process. Meanwhile, Patrice seems to draw on prior genre knowledge that comes from testing; just as essay writing replaced multiple-choice tests, rubrics have replaced answer keys.

With such disparate views on what even constitutes a rubric, it seems difficult to trace ruling relations. Identifying common word choices or common forms here is difficult. Yet, I would argue that simply the repeated use of the term "rubric" to describe this work signals something about how rubrics perform ruling relations in higher education. What is happening here seems similar to what I described in Chapter 4 where administrators drew on the ethos (and sometimes the funds) of the AAC&U to support their assessment efforts, even those that varied significantly from AAC&U best practice. So, too, faculty understand that rubrics carry a certain ethos on campus—among colleagues and among students. Whether or not their grading criteria fall neatly into the technical definition of a rubric, using the term carries with it a form of legitimacy. At the classroom level, rubrics legitimize teacher practice, just as they legitimize institutional practice at the national level.

WHERE FACULTY FIND RUBRICS

In order to see how ruling relations connect these disparate views on what a rubric is and what it should do, I turn to how faculty find example rubrics and learn about implementing them in the classroom. As reflected in the AAC&U's 2018 survey discussed in Chapter 5, administrators often pass down the VALUE rubrics as an example for faculty. However, it would be wrong to assume that faculty receiving these rubrics are a blank slate with no prior knowledge of rubrics. As with learning any genre or practice, a network of influences are at work here, including the influence of textbooks, training, and disciplinary colleagues. Sometimes faculty are aware of these influences; other times they are unsure where their practice comes from or how it evolved.

Several faculty members mentioned books that influenced their practice. At Oak, Kristen and Nina both use John Bean's (2011) well-known *Engaging Ideas*. Bean is a compositionist, and his book has been quite popular with faculty in different disciplines who teach writing. In chapter 14, Bean explained many different types of rubrics, and while most follow the standard grid form, he does include an example of a "gridless rubric." Unlike Kristen's rubrics, Bean's does still use points, but rather than using a scale of points, this example lists seven grading questions along with their point value (see Figure 6.2). Bean (2011) still called this a rubric but acknowledged that this form works well for teachers who find traditional rubrics "overly positivist and prescriptive" (p. 276). Nina, an environmental scientist, too, mentioned the book, although she couldn't remember what exactly she used from it. Unlike Kristen, Nina is not a fan of rubrics, which she associates with assigning numerical scores. "I read a paper, and I know this is an 83 or an 84," said Nina, "and when I've graded with rubrics before, I ultimately just end up making up numbers." However, Nina had saved an interesting document titled "Sample Rubric for Writing Program Assessment" that combined the "question rubric" format from Bean's book with the first goal of the Oak writing program (see Figure 6.3). Like with her reference to Bean's book, Nina was unsure where this document came from or how she used it. Returning to Dwayne's breadcrumb metaphor, we see that Kristen can clearly trace her path from Bean to classroom while Nina finds scattered crumbs, unsure how one thing leads to the next. Yet, we can see the connection to Bean by comparing this document to his example.

EXHIBIT 14.9

How I Assign Letter Grades

In grading "thesis papers" I ask myself the following set of questions:

1. Does the paper have a thesis?

2. Does the thesis address itself to an appropriate question or topic?

3. Is the paper free from long stretches of quotations and summaries that exist only for their own sakes and remain unanalyzed?

4. Can the writer produce complete sentences?

5. Is the paper free from basic grammatical errors?

   If the answer to any of these questions is "no," I give the paper some kind of C. If the answer to most of the questions is "no," its grade will be even lower.

   For papers which have emerged unscathed thus far, I add the following questions:

6. How thoughtful is the paper? Does it show real originality?

7. How adequate is the thesis? Does it respond to its question or topic in a full and interesting way? Does it have an appropriate degree of complexity?

8. How well organized is the paper? Does it stick to the point? Does every paragraph contain a clear topic sentence? If not, is another kind of organizing principle at work? Are the transitions well made? Does it have a real conclusion, not simply a stopping place?

9. Is the style efficient, not wordy or unclear?

10. Does the writing betray any special elegance?

11. Above all, can I hear a lively, intelligent, interesting human voice speaking to me (or to another audience, if that's what the writer intends) as I read the paper?

   Depending on my answers to such questions, I give the paper some kind of A or some kind of B [pp. 149–150].

Figure 6.2. Example from Bean's book (2011, p. 277). Reprinted with permission from Wiley.

1. Overall, has the author crafted and supported a cogent argument?

Excellent		Good		Satisfactory		Weak		Poor	
10	9	8	7	6	5	4	3	2	1

2. Has the author formulated a clear thesis?

Excellent		Good		Satisfactory		Weak		Poor	
10	9	8	7	6	5	4	3	2	1

3. Has the author used evidence appropriately?

Excellent		Good		Satisfactory		Weak		Poor	
10	9	8	7	6	5	4	3	2	1

4. Has the author organized his/her ideas effectively?

Excellent		Good		Satisfactory		Weak		Poor	
10	9	8	7	6	5	4	3	2	1

Figure 6.3: "Question rubric" from Oak.

Interestingly, the first draft of the writing program rubric at Oak that I collected from Ben also had a cover sheet that was formatted in this question and then scale format. While each performance descriptor was explained in detail on a separate page, this cover sheet represented a raters overall impression in each of the four assessment areas scored at Oak. Later drafts keep the cover sheet, but question-format is replaced by statements. For example, "How well does this paper demonstrate the student's ability to craft and support a cogent argument?" is replaced by "Based on this artifact, the student's ability to craft and support a cogent argument could best be characterized as:". In this case, the question-format was problematic because it would be impossible for the assessment committee to know how well one paper demonstrated a student's overall ability. Rather, the assessment at the programmatic level is entirely "based on this artifact," removed from the overall context of the classroom and the student.

Participants at Oak explained how rubrics are documents that frequently get passed around among faculty members. As such, they are documents that hold institutional power and influence practice. Using rubrics becomes tied to a discipline or a department. For example, Marisella noted that rubrics are a common disciplinary practice in the modern languages department. They are frequently used and shared by those who teach the same courses, although instructors often change them for their individual classrooms. Similarly, Amelia told me about a grid rubric that was developed and came through her chemistry department. Shirong in history also consulted rubrics from his department colleagues, although he had not yet ventured into creating his own. At Oak, it appears that the process of rubric-sharing is seen as a part of a collaborative, collegial driven practice, one that also values faculty autonomy in the classroom. Ronnie, the English department chair, appreciated the communal culture where people don't mind if you borrow their assignment or rubric.

In contrast, St. Rita's faculty expressed concern—and sometimes hope—that sharing rubrics was a way of dictating the pedagogical practice of others. Patrice felt like she must use the exact rubrics that are passed down to her by English faculty and this contributed to her resentment of English as a ruling faction as discussed in Chapter 5. Jeremy noted that he, too, had this misconception about what was required when he arrived at St. Rita's. He believed he had to use a rubric presented to him at his orientation. However, when he attempted to do so, he quickly discovered it wasn't "really an assignment level rubric." Thus, he opted for borrowing the basic format but adding specifics for his classroom, such as a row for "meeting the assignment." However, Jeremey didn't question that he should use *a rubric* to grade writing. Meanwhile, Heather had a different experience with orientation. When she began as adjunct faculty at St. Rita's, she noted that rubrics were provided at orientation but that she got the impression that "they never expected us to use them." However, as she grew into a full-time role and participated in the first-year writing portfolio review process, she changed her mind. She now feels that using the campus writing rubric in class is necessary so that students learn what is expected on the timed essay exam.

Whether the faculty at St. Rita's resent it or embrace it, there is a shared sense that rubrics are the way to evaluate classroom writing. That sense is reinforced through conversation and documents on campus. Even though Andrea, as co-chair of general education, strongly stated that she does not want to dictate classroom practice, the specifics of what she says reinforces the notion that rubrics should be used. She stated, "It is not for us to say what rubrics faculty use in their classroom for their assignments." Again, there is the desire to leave the specifics open to faculty, but there is an assumption that rubrics of some sort will be used. Emails, like the one Dr. Z sent with the general education expository essay rubric, have historically sent this message to faculty. Even though it was never an official practice, the top of that rubric states that "it is *necessary* [emphasis added] that all general education classes assign, assess, and submit to the general education committee one traditional five-paragraph expository essay." And although the document does not say the committee will look at it, it is clear that the attached rubric is meant for those instructors to use when grading the "necessary" essays. Although Dwayne feels that putting the VALUE rubrics in the university handbook had no real affect, the continued emphasis on rubrics at St. Rita's seems to teach faculty there that they have little choice but to adopt a rubric of some kind when assessing writing.

Whether rubrics are passed on as an act of collegial good-will or with the intent to dictate faculty practice, at both Oak and St. Rita's, faculty learn the use of rubrics from their colleagues. In addition, workshops about teaching served to reinforce rubric use. For Kristen, it is the VALUE workshops themselves that leave her thinking more about her own rubrics in the classroom. In particular, after scoring for "context and purpose" on the VALUE Written Communication rubric, Kristen realized that she needed to be clearer about what the context was and who the audience should be in her assignments. For others, local workshops significantly influenced their practice. Brad, who taught art history at Oak, solidified his writing pedagogy through attending writing across the curriculum (WAC) workshops. He noted that before these workshops, he did not use rubrics, but afterwards he began writing his own rubrics that were specific to his assignments. Even though there are few writing studies scholars on Oak's campus, several of these workshops brought in speakers from elsewhere, such as Carol Rutz, known for her WAC program at Carleton College. Rutz (2016), one of authors of the VALUE Written Communication rubric, is a big proponent of assessment as a means of faculty development in writing. Kristen followed this perspective and saw her test run of the rubrics with faculty in Summer 2017 and her full assessment process in Summer 2018 as a form of faculty development. She hoped to influence faculty practice through these assessment opportunities, while maintaining that the writing program rubric is meant for programmatic rather than classroom assessment. She is successful in this goal, as several faculty members who participated in these sessions commented that they would think more about audience and purpose in their own assignments after participating in the assessment process. Thus, rubrics used in an assessment workshop or programmatic setting influence the use of rubrics and/or the development of assignments in the classroom. These venues become a place where faculty not only work together to define programmatic goals, but they also learn skills and genres of assessment that they bring back to classroom practice.

Yet, St. Rita's is so small that this type of workshop never happens. I kept inquiring about attending a norming session for those who scored the first-year writing portfolios until I gradually realized that a session such as the one that I observed at Oak did not exist. Rather, only a few faculty members, the same ones who did it year after year, gathered and scored with little to no professional development piece to their assessment. Similarly, Dwayne and others talked about new faculty orientation, and I wondered if this was a place where professional development on rubrics might occur. Clearly the rubrics used across campus were presented to faculty there, but the message about the rubrics remained unclear as indicated in my interviews with Jeremey and Heather. Jeremy thought the rubrics presented at orientation were a mandate for classroom practice, while Heather got the impression that no one really cared about their use. Rather than a full professional development workshop on rubrics, they seem to be one very small piece shared with new faculty at a larger orientation. It is not only that faculty at St. Rita's often take a more confrontational stance with their colleagues than those at Oak, it is also that they do not have the same types of opportunities for collaboration and learning that happen at Oak. These institutional factors affect how the faculty learn about rubrics and how they view them as a part of both institutional and classroom practice.

THE INFLUENCE OF CLASSROOM PRACTICE ON PROGRAMMATIC RUBRICS

As we see rubrics shift from being classroom-based to programmatic, the rubric as a genre and its relationship to other texts also shifts. In the classroom, faculty seek to hold both themselves and their students accountable by creating a coherent genre set: the rubric reinforces the assignment prompt, and the two work in conjunction to define the student artifact. Because these genres are closely connected in the classroom, when faculty use a rubric for programmatic assessment, they often consider how it might affect not only their classroom rubrics but also their classroom assignments. Yet, at both Oak and St. Rita's those guiding larger committee meetings and assessment workshops encouraged faculty to set these thoughts about teaching aside. Individual classroom assignments are separated from the design of rubrics and outcomes. In the programmatic setting, it is the goals of the program, not the classroom, that are paramount; yet each faculty member participates on these committees as a representative of a particular field of study. They are asked to speak as a generic teacher within their department in order to make sure that the rubric is disciplinarily inclusive.

In their study of faculty disciplinarity and assessment, Christopher Thaiss and Terry Meyers Zawacki (2006) found that terms on a generic rubric often had different meanings and applications within different departments on campus. Similarly, Adler-Kassner and O'Neill (2010) noted that even terms as common as "grammar" are often used differently by different faculty members. Both of these sources warn against the assumption that common terminology equals consensus or even common understanding. "Common terminology that faculty use," Thaiss and Zawacki (2006) noted, "often hides basic differences in rhetoric, exigency, epistemology, style, form, and formatting" (p. 59). From the perspective of institutional ethnography, that is inherently the role of common terminology. LaFrance (2019) explained that "key terms operate discursively to create a sense of unity and shared practice" (p. 112). These terms are "never accidental" (LaFrance, 2019, p. 113). They are the building blocks of boss texts; they organize, guide, and regulate our work. Compositionists may worry that faculty in the disciplines fail to recognize this; that they will take these generic terms and ideas about writing to heart, leading to a lack of rhetorical awareness, poor assignment design, and generic rubrics applied uncritically to classroom writing. Yet, Broch Colombini and McBride (2012) felt that we do faculty a disservice by assuming that they lack the "facility to switch codes, adapt various rhetorical identities, [and] respond in appropriate ways to changing rhetorical constraints" (p. 194). Like our students, faculty possess a range of rhetorical awareness. Some clearly know how disciplinary difference affects their own understanding of the common terminology on the rubric, while others do subscribe to "universal," generic ideas about writing. Too, we should not assume that faculty who use common terminology do so uncritically or unaware of the political power of using that terminology to represent their work to external stakeholders.

In shifting to the epistemological stance of institutional ethnography, I became more interested in how faculty understandings of classroom practice interacted with their work building rubrics and outcomes at the committee level than with their definitions of terms. Campbell (2006) explained that institutional ethnographers use transcripts to ask questions about how an individual's work connects to other people as well as institutional processes. By examining how faculty negotiate their own work as classroom teachers in relationship with their work as committee members, we gain a fuller picture of how the work of assessment is coordinated on campuses. Faculty members at Oak and St. Rita's often use their experiences as classroom teachers strategically to guide the work of their committees in developing outcomes and rubrics, yet how they do so depends on how both individuals and institutions see that work aligning.

The institutional setting and the goals of Oak's writing committee versus St. Rita's general education committee made a significant difference in how their classroom experiences interacted with the work of building outcomes and rubrics. At Oak, the faculty were selected for the writing committee in order to represent their separate divisions or colleges. When I asked these faculty members if they would use the rubric created by the writing committee in their classes, they almost universally said they would not, particularly without significant revisions for their specific classroom context. Yet, these faculty viewed their classroom contexts as important to writing the rubric because they wanted the rubric to be able to assess artifacts from courses across the curriculum. Rather than change their classroom practice, these faculty presented their classrooms as test cases for whether or not the rubric was inclusive enough to capture pedagogical practice across campus. In contrast, at St. Rita's, the general education committee used the rubrics to create outcomes for general education. While they recognized that not every course would incorporate every outcome, they *did* have a goal to regulate classroom practice. They discussed how the next phase would be to "operationalize the outcomes." The committee discussed how these outcomes needed to be directly present in the core classes and how those classes needed to connect to one another to make up the overall general education curriculum. They, too, used current classroom practice as evidence of where the outcomes were already in operation, and thus clung to current practice rather than initiating change. In addition, since this school is so small, operationalizing outcomes means dictating practice in specific classes, and it was seen as the role of those classes to prepare students for an assessment process that ultimately has high stakes for the students. In this section, I examine the relationship between classroom practice and writing rubrics and outcomes on the committees I observed at these two different institutions.

OPERATIONALIZING OUTCOMES AT ST. RITA'S

At St. Rita's the general education committee was revising outcomes for their core curriculum based on the VALUE rubrics. While they did not see their reach going as far as to dictate what rubrics faculty used in the classroom, they did seek to build a curriculum in which the outcomes could be "operationalized." To do this, they envisioned a common assessment involving the same type of assignment repeated at multiple points in the core to see whether or not students improved. This scaffolded sequence depended on first-year writing courses at the entry level and a capstone theology course at the end of the core. As previously described, St. Rita's used what was referred to as a portfolio system, but their portfolio process fits with an outdated model of portfolio assessment as exit testing where students' portfolios are scored by a faculty member other than their instructor and that score determines whether or not the student passed the course (O'Neill, Moore, Huot, 2009). At St. Rita's, the work in these portfolios came from first-year courses and also from timed essay exams. One significant change that Dwayne and his colleagues made was to move the second first-year writing course to the sophomore year so that there was also a middle point for assessment of core goals. The process of assessing portfolios, or at least timed essays, then repeated at the capstone level, again as a high-stakes assessment where students passed based on scores assigned outside the classroom. The same rubric was used at these different points in the assessment process, but students had to score higher on the rubric to pass the junior level course than they did to pass the entry level course. The hope here was to have a through line of writing expectations in general education.

Because these assessments are high stakes for students, who must retake courses until they pass the portfolio process, instructors are particularly concerned with how their teaching prepares students for success as dictated by the rubric. Jeremy was the co-chair of the general education committee and a faculty member in English at the time I visited. He taught basic composition courses for students who are not prepared to begin in the regular composition sequence. He was concerned that these courses have traditionally taken an inordinate amount of time and that student skills don't improve quickly enough to help them pass other courses. Thus, when I spoke to him in 2016, he was piloting what he referred to as a "competency-based model" of the basic writing course. In this version, he worked with students to use grammar software (IXL) to drill grammar competencies at the student's own pace. Students in the class received a weekly progress report with a score showing how many exercises they had passed. While such a system may strike many as oppressive, for Jeremy, it is unethical to have students accruing debt by continually having to take and retake the first-year writing portfolio. So, too, is Jeremy aware that "traditional research has said that drilling grammar out of context doesn't work." However, he believes that his system is authentic because students must infer grammar rules from reading passages of writing. He also believes that by having students use this software in a classroom setting where he can answer questions as they work, he can get to the bottom of where students infer incorrect grammar rules. He can interrupt and correct their thinking, which the computer program can't "diagnose." This type of pedagogy fits the definition of eradicationist (Baker-Bell, 2020) or acculturationist pedagogy (Balester, 2012) where only White standard English is seen as acceptable, a point I will return to in Chapter 7. However, as long as the high-stakes portfolio process is in place and scored on a rubric with two out five sections focused on grammar and usage, Jeremy feels the pressure to get students to a point where they can pass this assessment. Thus, classroom practice is driven by assessment practice.

The general education committee used the VALUE rubrics to write general education outcomes. However, when it comes to written communication, they looked to their current portfolio rubric as well as the VALUE rubric. In doing so, they briefly considered whether both dimensions about sentence level concerns from their rubric should also become two separate general education objectives, a moment I discuss in Chapter 5 as well. They considered that the rubric might be more detailed than the general education goals need to be. To answer this question, they rely on current classroom practice to justify their decisions. Dwayne pointed out that the proposed objective about sentence variety, which corresponds to the "prose, style and syntax" part of the portfolio rubric, is more specific than general education objectives in other areas. He also wondered whether faculty themselves can "really name the sentence types." The ensuing conversation revealed how pervasive the assimilationist thinking and focus on grammar is across faculty members and courses at St. Rita's. Dwayne backed down when Thomas, a business professor, stressed the importance of these goals in his 300-level course (and does indeed name several sentence types). Dwayne's argument had been that sentence variety is a specific course goal, not an overall general education goal. Thomas, however, argued that he teaches sentence types and similar issues, like parallelism, in his 300-level business course, and that he hoped that students come to his class with some knowledge of this material already. He saw sentence variety as a general education outcome that is addressed in first-year writing and that his course will reinforce. Lucinda stated this directly, "if those objectives were introduced in [the FYC course], wouldn't it be great if they're reinforced in other general education courses? That would be where they would get to a level of mastery." The committee agreed with this sentiment and decided to keep sentence types as a part of the overall general education goals because they are *already* being taught in classrooms. Thus, the goals are written to fit current practice rather than to guide future classroom practice.

Assessment professionals often talk about "closing the loop" by using assessment data to improve classroom practice. What we see here is the circularity of that loop. Faculty justify their pedagogy because it prepares students for assessment while at the same time justifying assessment outcomes based on current pedagogy. When neither takes the lead, they feed off each other like the snake eating its tail. Pedagogical practice at St. Rita's fixates on grammar because it is necessary for the students to pass the high-stakes writing assessment scored on a rubric with multiple sentence-level dimensions. Yet, those categories remain because they fit with the current pedagogical practices in classrooms. Each one acts as a way to rule the other and keep it from changing.

OAK'S WRITING COMMITTEE & REPRESENTATION ACROSS THE CURRICULUM

At Oak, I was able to observe multiple meetings where the writing committee was discussing, revising, and testing their writing rubric. Since the writing committee was designed to include representation from each division on campus, members saw it as their role to speak for their discipline, including explaining how writing conventions in that discipline might vary. When I interviewed these committee members individually, they also talked about how their specific disciplinary approaches to teaching writing caused them to question the rubric. Faculty saw their role as making sure that the rubric and assessment process are inclusive of their discipline and classroom practice. This drive took precedence over changing classroom practice itself.

Arguing for rubric language that captures current practice is particularly prevalent in the discussion of the "research and sources" dimension, later changed to "evidence." The faculty at Oak are guided by an understanding that what qualifies as research varies by discipline. This is, I would argue, an assumption that guides faculty life on a broader scale. Not only does it apply to pedagogy, but it also guides discussion of faculty merit. For example, tenure and promotion committees draw on disciplinary experts to write letters on the merit of a candidate's scholarship because faculty recognize that what qualifies as good research is not always discernible to a disciplinary outsider. The faculty at Oak bring this assumption into their discussion of the rubric. In particular, they discussed whether the word research implies the use of external sources. The Oak writing program goals, not unlike writing curriculum elsewhere, specifies that students should "evaluate the credibility of potential research sources." However, Kristen does not believe this necessarily implies they are finding those sources on their own, but rather that they are evaluating sources provided within the classroom. Meanwhile, Amelia from chemistry is concerned about the lack of discussion of primary data in conjunction with sources. The overarching writing program goal specifies "synthesizing evidence," yet, the bullet point underneath this seems to define this as "integrat[ing] sources in rhetorically effective ways." For Amelia, chemistry papers must put data in the context of sources; integrating secondary research is not enough. Meanwhile, when the committee looked at a sample student artifact about a theater performance, they wondered what counts as research in this context as it seems the student bases their analysis solely on their observations as an audience member. "Does this meet the disciplinary standards for research?" they asked. Ultimately, the committee changed the dimension name, but the details here are also up for discussion. Shirong, a historian, is concerned that the weak performance descriptor under this dimension stated, "Students fail to accumulate a broad and reasonable spectrum of sources." He argued that while he sees the value of source variety, some assignments in history are about engaging deeply with only one or two sources.

Disciplinary difference also caused committee members to distrust moments of perceived consensus building. When Brad passionately launched into a story about how he limits his students from using direct quotation, and several faculty excitedly agreed, Kristen disrupted this moment with a simple statement: "See, this is the disciplinary thing." Quotes in history, she explained, are necessary and valued but only when dealing with primary source material. Even something seemingly neutral, like citation style, has disciplinary values attached to it. In a somewhat amusing committee moment, Brad expounded on the virtues of Chicago style and how it helps students synthesize their source material in sophisticated ways. The committee joked that the top level of the rubric should say "uses Chicago style."

These discussions highlight one of the main differences between the VALUE rubric and the modified version the Oak faculty create. Rather than attempt to specify all of these disciplinary conventions, the dimension for "sources and evidence" on the original VALUE Written Communication rubric simply states that sources and supporting ideas are "appropriate for the discipline and genre of the writing." Meanwhile, the faculty at Oak try to expound on this to define what that looks like while still being inclusive of all disciplinary possibilities. A key difference here is that original VALUE rubric was meant to be used with an assignment prompt. Thus, in the original VALUE model, the burden of describing disciplinary practice fell to each instructor as they composed their assignments. In the absence of this, it falls instead to representative committee members attempting to word the rubric to include the many possibilities of genre and disciplinary context. The committee members recognize, however, that no one person on the committee could reasonably know what the appropriate conventions are for every discipline and genre, not even those within the college or division they represent. Thus, the committee relies heavily on language, such as "consistency," to describe student work. If, they propose, the work is consistent in style, use of sources, and argument then the student must be aware of and following disciplinary standards, even when the specifics of those standards are unknown to the reader.

THE DEMOTION OF THE ASSIGNMENT PROMPT

Here we come to a bit of a catch-22 in the VALUE process: the assignment prompt. The AAC&U has walked a bit of a tightrope when it comes to assignment prompts and design. They have continually promoted that their rubrics can be used with authentic, classroom assignments, but they have also dabbled with common "signature assignments" and assignment design workshops to lead to more consistent artifacts. Common assignments lead to more reliability when using a generic rubric, but as we have seen in examples such as St. Rita's faculty member Patrice's use of the five-paragraph essay, they can resemble the testing the AAC&U seeks to move beyond. Yet, without a common assignment, artifacts sometimes don't fit the rubric at all.

This issue was on my radar from the start of my study when I heard stories from my own institution about raters trying to score dance performance videos with the Critical Thinking VALUE rubric. The VALUE rubrics were originally written to be used with the assignment prompt but collecting them has been both a logistical and philosophical challenge. The original VALUE Written Communication rubric (2009) is clear that the assignment prompt should be used for scoring: "Evaluators using the rubric must have information about the assignments or purposes for writing that guided the writer's work." Yet, that information is impractical to collect and does not always lend the clarity that assessors might wish for. In 2016, Kristen hoped to collect the assignment prompt, but by the actual assessment in 2018, she explained that scoring is meant to happen without it. Kristen encountered some of the logistical problems with the use of assignment prompts when she went through the AAC&U scoring process. In her experience with national scoring, she found that assignment prompts were inconsistently attached to artifacts. Also, when there was an assignment prompt, it was not always helpful. Kristen recalled: "Sometimes the assignment just was so general that it didn't speak to who the audience of a particular piece should be or what kinds of sources students should be using." When separated from the classroom context where the instructor often pairs an assignment prompt with classroom exercises, lectures, readings, and discussions; assignment prompts may not be helpful. Kristen also found that sometimes assignment prompts ended up incorrectly paired with artifacts. In talking with Terry Rhodes, then Executive Director of VALUE, Kristen got the sense that collecting assignment prompts and pairing them with artifacts was a "massive logistical challenge." Even on the smaller scale she encounters at

Oak, she worries about the logistics of collecting assignment prompts as well as the fact that all assignment prompts will not all include the same information, and thus will inconsistently affect the scoring process.

Philosophically, there is the need to distinguish large-scale, programmatic or university-wide assessments from classroom grading. Faculty raters need to shift their thinking away from grading, to take on a different role as a reader, and some argue that having an attached assignment sheet counters this goal. This is particularly true in the case of the VALUE rubric since it is meant to represent progress over a college degree rather than one course. If instructors know what course and what level of course the artifact stems from, that could very well skew how they read the artifact in relation to the rubric. Kristen comes to believe the assignment's connection with grading will hinder the assessment process. When the 2017 pilot assessment group wondered about the assignments and which courses artifacts came from, Kristen encouraged them to separate classroom grading and programmatic assessment:

> When we grade, the context usually for us is the specific assign-
> ment: how well did this student demonstrate the goals that I
> wanted them to demonstrate for this particular assignment.
> And then the other context when we are grading is the course:
> how well are they demonstrating the goals that I'm trying to
> teach them about writing and communication. So, of course,
> it's natural to think it's hard for me to react to this without the
> prompt. But with assessment, the context for us is the writing
> program. The context in which we're trying to evaluate stu-
> dents' writing is the goals of the writing program. So, it's not
> a, you know, so it doesn't matter if it's a first year or a senior.
> It doesn't matter if it's the beginning of the semester or later in
> the semester. In the context of assessment, none of that matters.

In the full 2018 assessment, Kristen continued to stress this point, remind-ing scorers: "It's not about the assignment, it's not about what was the student asked to do. It's about this rubric."

Yet,, it is difficult to score dimensions such as "context of and purpose for writing" or "genre and disciplinary conventions" without knowing the context of the writing or the discipline from which it hails. In the classroom, rubrics and assignment sheets are intertwined and meant to be genres that work together. When rubrics become disconnected from classroom practice, their relationship with the assignment becomes fraught. The boss-text rubric comes to "rule" over the assignment prompt. Even if it does not directly dictate classroom practice, it dictates how that practice is read and interpreted for stakeholders.

Rhetorical genre theory is helpful here in understanding the shift in the relationship of the genre of the rubric to the genre of the assignment sheet. In the classroom, the rubric, the assignment prompt, and the student artifact work together to dictate the terms of writing within that classroom, for both the student and the instructor. But in large-scale and programmatic assessment, the rubric and assignment prompt function as a part of a different system. The assignment prompt, student artifact, and rubric no longer work together or respond to one another. The student artifact—selected randomly, anonymized, and separated from the classroom—no longer belongs to that classroom or any particular student. Rather it is an exemplar text—a representation not of *a* student but of *the* student, a subject position within the institution of the university. The rubric, too, is not a specific teacher's expectations but fills in for all teacher expectations, for *programmatic* expectations, or even national expectations (agreed upon by *all* teachers, employers, and stakeholders).

Faculty raters are asked to take the position of representatives of faculty at large. They are chosen to represent the sciences or social sciences on the writing committee, to speak not for themselves as individuals but for the group. When they score, too, they are asked to represent the generic "faculty member" rather than draw on their own expertise. Classroom rubrics position faculty in readerly roles where the student work is read through the lens of the rubric, but the faculty member still has other texts to draw upon. Large-scale rubrics require the faculty to read the student text *only* in relation to the rubric. Gallagher (2012) argued that the process of norming "conditions what we are able (and unable) to see in the text" because it asks readers to start with the rubric as the primary text, not the student work (p. 46). Even those who take a more positive view on norming cannot deny that the rubric used for norming is the primary text under discussion. For example, Broch Colombini and McBride (2012) favored norming as means of community and consensus building, a process in which programmatic values and individual values are honored. So, too, Kristen is a generous workshop leader who facilitates this type of dialog about what the rubric means. How raters at Oak interpret the rubric is a matter of negotiation and discussion rather than top-down mandate, and yet, the reading still begins with and focuses on the rubric. The rubric is the dominant text, not student writing. The reader begins and ends with the rubric.

Assumptions about Assignments

Although large-scale assessment asks readers to sever the connection between the student artifact and the classroom assignment prompt, they have difficulty doing so. The assignment prompt acts a sort of phantom genre—faculty are aware of its existence but attempt to forget its role in relation to the student work in order to maintain a sense of objectivity when scoring. Assumptions about the assignment prompt or the course are seen as problematic—intrusive thoughts the neutral rater must put aside. Shawna, a faculty member in the pilot 2017 assessment at Oak, noted that this separation between the prompt and the artifact was particularly difficult when it came to scoring the "audience and community" dimension. Even though the dimension asked for her to assess how well the student "anticipates the audience needs," she tried not to imagine who that audience might be because she imagines that audience is something determined by the assignment prompt, not the student author. "I try not to imagine the assignment too much," she said, "or to imagine the community, who I think that community was."

Yet, even without the assignment prompt, faculty raters may be drawn to infer the assignment from seeing multiple artifacts from the same class. The smaller the institution and the sample size, the more likely this is to occur. Again, faculty often attempt to put this information aside, to forget what they have seen before and how it might connect to what they score next. Several participants mentioned how they had to purposefully try not to connect similar artifacts. When Ben participated in the 2018 Oak scoring session, he noted that it was difficult when he got two papers in row that seemed to respond to the same assignment prompt. He would have to purposefully make sure he wasn't confusing the two papers and misremembering which said what. Kristen encouraged raters to turn off the part of their brains that thinks about whether or not they have seen this assignment before. Ben suggested that re-norming in the middle of the assessment might be a good way to fight this bias. This overlap even occurs with the national VALUE scoring. Philip recalled scoring national artifacts using the Civic Engagement VALUE rubric, one for which the AAC&U collected far fewer artifacts than the more popular area of Written Communication. He noted that a number of the artifacts came from the same project, one in which students posted signs in parks, something that he did not consider fitting with the core of civic engagement.

In all these discussions, there is an underlying assumption that the assignment prompt specifies many decisions for the student writer, such as who the audience for the paper will be. This assumption does not account for student agency or teachers who deliberately incorporate a great deal of student choice into their assignments. Likely, the assumption that assignment prompts dictate student work comes from the way that faculty interact with assignments in their own classroom. After all, faculty take what they learn in assessment and apply it to their own assignments—like when Kristen adds the audience to her prompts after using the VALUE Written Communication rubric. There is also the assumption that the student work reflects the assignment prompt. Kristen, for example, tells the faculty raters: "That's something you can tell, whether or not the assignment specifies an audience. That's something you can actually assess in a given artifact." So, too, Nina from the writing committee thinks that "a well-written paper" will be one where you can understand the assignment from just reading the student text. Thus, the student artifact becomes the bridge between the absent assignment prompt and the rubric, a way to infer the context of the classroom. While specific inferences about the assignment prompt are not welcome, the process rests on an unstated assumption about the relationship of the assignment prompt and the student artifact.

Assumptions about Writers and Readers

In addition to not wanting the assignment prompt to influence scoring, so too, is knowledge of the student forbidden. While data on their class standing, race, gender, and other demographics may be collected and analyzed as a larger part of the assessment, it is not often provided to those reading and scoring the student work, a point I return to in Chapter 7. Faculty raters fill in this knowledge with assumptions, and even complete reconstructions of student identity in their minds, perhaps even more so than of the assignment prompt. Broad (2003) explained, "constructing writers is a widespread and perhaps inescapable feature of reading" (p. 83). The most glaring example of this from Oak was when Wendy, the coordinator of multilingual learning, shared detailed false memories of meeting one-on-one with the author of a sample paper, even though Kristen tells her multiple times that there is no way she did so. In addition, Wendy used this false memory in her scoring: "I scored this person fairly high on process and style because the person came to see me." She went as far as to say she remembered a young man coming in with the paper some time ago but can't remember who. Even after Kristen assured her that this is simply not possible, Wendy continued to explain her memory of talking to the student about the specific points made in the paper and about how it was organized. Kristen noted that she may have seen a paper on a similar topic, but that she has not seen this specific paper. That finally convinced Wendy that she should ignore the context that she believes she brings to scoring the paper. Kristen then told the committee that if they do happen to see a paper from their own class, they should ignore it and score a backup artifact. So, too, at St. Rita's, the faculty scoring the portfolios are different than the professor for those students. Knowledge of the student is seen as a hinderance to the scoring process.

Yet, assumptions about the student writer permeate the scoring process in less direct, but perhaps even more problematic ways when faculty assume a particular default identity for student writers. It's a small moment during the norming session that begins Oak's 2018 assessment, but one I keep returning to. Erin, a sociology professor, was discussing a sample paper and stops herself mid-sentence: "I thought he . . . I want to keep saying he, I don't know why." Erin then worked to use gender-neutral language in describing the student author, but this moment shows how these assumptions about the student author are impossible to completely remove from the scoring process. Davila (2012) outlined the way that language use in student papers led to assumptions on the part of faculty about the identity of the student. While her participants were able to identify specific features in the text that led them to draw conclusions about the socioeconomic status and race of the students, she found that when making assumptions about student gender faculty "relied on their intuition" (p. 192). Perhaps this is why Erin is unable to say why she used the pronoun "he" when referring to the student author.

So, too, the reader's identity is assumed to be a generalized White, academic reader whose is fluent in English. Although Shirong's background allows him to recognize errors in usage that come from translation from Chinese to English, there is no way for him to read for this if he begins with only the rubric in mind. His own experience with languages other than English is not relevant to the assessment process. Even the assumption that English is the dominant language of the artifacts can be challenged. Marisella teaches Spanish, including a Spanish course that carries the writing designation. Officially, this is a writing program course, but Marisella is not contacted to provide artifacts for the assessment. Marisella challenged the committee on this matter but was not taken seriously. Kristen expressed concern that it would be difficult to get a reader who was able to score those papers but who wasn't already the instructor for that course. Marisella maintained that there are plenty of qualified faculty to read a Spanish paper, but Kristen still worries that this would not be true for other modern language courses. So, too, this would violate the principle of not knowing what course the artifact comes from, as a Spanish artifact would be unlikely to come from a course outside of the modern language department. After a brief interchange between Marisella and Kristen, Ben interjected with the playful suggestion that the entire committee needed to go to France and ask French speakers to score artifacts. The committee engaged more with this joke than with Marisella's concern, imagining themselves on a tour of Europe, eating croissants and asking native speakers to score essays for them. This fantasy was evoked in fun, and yet, it devalues the linguistic expertise of Marisella and other faculty members on campus. English is the language of the writing program, it seems, and an assignment in another language is excluded. On the national level, even though the VALUE rubrics have been translated into multiple languages

(AAC&U, n.d., "Japanese"), at the time of this writing, the VALUE Institute does not offer scoring of any non-English language artifacts.

Relocating the Assignment Prompt Genre

Anson et al. (2012) discussed at length their concerns that assignment prompts that stem from generic rubrics lose important aspects of situated practice. "Such rubrics," they argued "can drive the creation of assignments and communication experiences from the 'outside in'" (para 38). The relationship between assignments and large-scale assessment at Oak and St. Rita's affected the classroom, but neither school took an entirely top-down approach. Kristen explained that there was no common assignment for writing courses at Oak, nor did she want to impose one. Even if it would make assessment easier, Oak faculty value autonomy in the classroom. While St. Rita's did want more common practice across courses in their general education curriculum, they saw this as a part of dictating common outcomes, not common assignments. The committee repeatedly assuaged Patrice's concerns that her specific assignments would need to change when the outcomes or the rubric changed. Rather, this would be up to her. However, that is not to say these processes had no effect on the classroom. For example, Kristen and others on her committee became more aware that they should talk to students about audience, genre, and disciplinary conventions, and that some of this information should be specified on their assignment prompts. However, the genre of the assignment prompt remained under the control of the instructor, a genre associated with the classroom rather than with large-scale assessment.

But the story doesn't end there. The assignment prompt is the next target of the AAC&U's VALUE initiative, which may also move this genre outside the control of the individual classroom teacher. Since I finished my data collection in 2018, the AAC&U has become increasing involved in assignment design. A 2020 initiative titled VALUE ADD is just getting underway and will require further study. ADD stands for Assignment Design and Diagnostic. Although the AAC&U no longer pairs assignment prompts with artifacts for scoring, through the VALUE Institute they have collected assignment prompts for analysis (Rhodes & McConnell, 2021). The AAC&U is working on a set of tools that faculty can use to determine how to better craft assignments to fit with the outcomes assessed by the VALUE rubrics. The term "diagnostic" is troubling here, as it implies that assignments that do not fit the rubrics are in some way deficient. At the time of this writing, only the critical thinking tool has been released for publication; yet the path toward assignment design tools has been a long time coming.

The AAC&U is not alone in their involvement with assignment design at a national scale. Lumina and The National Institute for Learning Outcomes Assessment (NIOLA) worked together in 2016-17 to create an assignment database. The goal of this database is to "strengthen assignment alignment to specific DQP proficiencies" by showcasing "high-quality, peer-reviewed assignments linked to DQP outcomes" (Beld & Kuh, 2014). Within this database, one can even search specifically for assignments that are tagged with a "VALUE rubric" descriptor. As discussed in Chapter 2, it is often advocacy-based philanthropists who fund such efforts. In addition to Lumina, the Gates Foundation has historically been involved in funding assignment design initiatives. They began a grant program called "Assignments Matter" in 2014 as a part of their funding of the National Writing Project. This program enlisted writing project sites to create a "Literacy Design Collaborative" of "juried" writing assignments that align with secondary educations Common Core Standards. Addison (2015) critiqued this program, noting that while Gates claimed to put teachers at the forefront, those teachers were obligated to use the rubric created for the Literacy Design Collaborative. So, too, the assignments included in this project are valued and judged based on their fit with Common Core Standard outcomes.

While it is unclear how the ADD will work or if it will lead to another database of exemplar writing assignments, these precedents are concerning. Addison (2015) worried that organizations such as the Gates Foundation "may quickly position themselves to rival long-standing professional organizations such as the National Council of Teachers of English." The VALUE Written Communication rubric (2009) was originally tied to NCTE's statements about best practices in assessment, which were directly referenced in the framing language. Yet, as shown in Chapter 4, that language is wont to disappear as the rubric moves from national use to local institutional use. Of the 16 adapted Written Communication rubrics I collected in my 2016, nine included a note crediting the AAC&U for the original rubric, but none referenced NCTE. The rubric itself loses its connection to the original rhetorical situation and becomes a genre separated from its exigence. As assessment practice then shifts to the national level, the student artifact represents not only a particular classroom but an entire university, and assignment prompts from that university become exemplars for college-level classroom assignments at large. The rubric is a thin thread connecting classroom to program to national assessment, one that carries with it many assumptions about actual pedagogical practice and actual teachers and students. These assumptions then impact individual universities and their local practice. Although Oak's rubric includes the goals of the writing program as a whole, and St. Rita's rubric comes with a page-long description of their local practice, the breadcrumbs that lead back to national disciplinary practice have scattered in the wind.

CHAPTER 7.

INDIVIDUALISM, RACISM, AND THE ECOLOGY OF THE WRITING RUBRIC

Individualism is a hallmark of American (specifically US) thinking, and it permeates our educational system. This notion of "liberty, individualism, and equal opportunity in choice" or "abstract liberalism" is at odds with the historic, lived realities of people of color in the United States (Martinez, 2020, p. 5). When we tie assessment, as we have historically done, to this story of individualism and equal opportunity, we also tie it to Whiteness. If minoritized students have equivalent skills as White students, assessed by the same standards or the same rubric, this is seen as equitable education. But this notion of equity relies on definitions of replicability and fairness that are "dangerous" (Huot, 2002, p. 88). Success that is based on "power and access to the dominant discourse" only reinforces oppression (Inoue, 2015, p. 226). The dominant discourse here refers to habits of Whiteness and White language. While I did not originally consider race as a factor in my study, it would be negligent to ignore the ways that race and racism intersected with faculty attitudes, rubric design, and institutional power at Oak and St. Rita's. So, too, it is important to view these stories as part of a larger narrative about education in America.

Over time, the discourse about race and writing assessment in the U.S. has shifted from exclusion to inclusion. Yet that inclusion—both historically and currently—still stresses *individual* paths to success rather than systemic change, as described in Chapter 2. The first president of the Educational Testing Services (ETS), Henry Chancey, positioned the work of testing as a part of a mission to "secure individual freedom through education" (Elliot, 2005, p. 122). At this time, Black men, particularly those who served in World War II, began to enter college in greater numbers under the G.I. Bill (Elliot, 2005). Chancey predicted that education would become increasingly tailored to the individual and that college admissions testing would play a key role in this process (Elliot, 2005). While ETS and entrance testing came under critique in the 1960s, this focus on the individual continues. Any assessment system based on common competencies reinforces the ideology of American individualism. Gallagher (2016) defined competency-based education as "a highly individualized approach" where students gain credentials (p. 22). In this model of education, "writing is understood as a discrete, commodified, vocational skill," a skill that individual teachers coach individual students to master (p. 22). While students might take different routes to achieve a certain outcome/ competency/proficiency, the promise of a common, universal outcome or skill remains. But despite the perceived universality of these outcomes, it is individuals who are responsible for achieving them. Whether it is traditional testing or rubric-based assessment, the focus is on individual achievement within systems of education rather than on the system's themselves.

The AAC&U aligns itself with this discourse when they argue that equity in higher education means that those with different backgrounds still finish college with the same skills and proficiency levels (Maki, 2015). They use the phrase "inclusive excellence" to means that education is inclusive when all students meet the same standards of excellence. Excellence itself, however, is a problematic term. It is often used in neoliberalism because "it *appears* so ideologically neutral" (Laubach Wright, 2017, p. 272). But such terminology is deeply linked to White ideologies. For Inoue (2015), evaluating writing on "so-called quality" maintains ruling relations. It is part of a larger assessment system that has historically manufactured what it means to be excellent (Elliot, 2005). Within this system standards are set and meeting those standards become synonymous with excellence (Yancey, 2005). As Inoue (2015) explained, these standards of excellence are grounded in White language supremacy and include linguistic markers that are often absent from the writing of non-White students. He has argued that labor is a more equitable measurement than excellence. Yet, the AAC&U believes it is "impossible to decouple quality from equity" (McConnell & Rhodes, 2017, p. 49). For the AAC&U, "inclusive excellence" is only achieved when each individual student completes the same "practical liberal education that prepares them for success" (AAC&U, 2015b, p. 7).

To identify inequities, the AAC&U calls for disaggregating student data. This data may indeed provide a clearer picture of inequity, but too often the solution is remediating the individual student rather than changing the criteria by which they are judged. In addition, individual faculty and administrators may be motivated by their own experiences and priorities, and the majority are White. Individual career moves can drive change just as much as consensus among experts (Trimbur, 1989). We see this particularly at St. Rita's. Here, students who fail the first-year writing portfolio must re-take the course. It is Dr. Gerald Z who controls the conversations about this assessment, using his own academic standing to do so. The role of individuals, like Dr. Z, who hold social, economic, and institutional power within their universities should not be overlooked in our discussion about how the work of assessment happens at specific universities. Therefore, placing these individuals within an ecology of assessment, the confluence of influences, allows us to name systems of power and identify White language ideologies at work.

This chapter directly addresses the way that faculty participants at St. Rita's and Oak operate within the racialized structures that rule U.S. higher education. While I did not ask questions specifically about race, I asked the majority of participants how they felt their institutional context and student population varied from other schools, and how that might affect writing instruction and assessment. In this chapter, I engage directly with how faculty talked about these student populations and institutional differences and how these views often assumed a White, prepared student as the default. So, too, my interviews touched on deeper racial and political tensions within the United States. The timing of my initial interviews and site visits was fortuitously placed within a week of President Trump's election in 2016. As seen in the sidewalk writings at Oak (pictured in my introduction), this tension was palpable at the time of my visits. In particular, my interview with Gerald Z at St. Rita's and my interview with Brad, the art history professor at Oak, struck me as representative of the larger tensions within the U.S. in Fall 2016. Both individuals acknowledged their power as White men: Gerald[7] was not shy about being "the big, bad, White guy," and Brad acknowledged his positionally as an "old fart of a White guy." Despite varying political views, both participants drew on an ideology of individualism that they saw as racially neutral. Gerald's belief in individualism and his bootstraps mentality caused him to believe that holding students to strict standards was in their best interest. Meanwhile, Brad's frustration with systems of power caused him to focus on changes in his own individual classroom rather than his institutional power. While sometimes challenging to engage with, both cases add much to our understanding of the way individuals interact with larger, systemic systems of race and power within higher education.

INSTITUTIONAL CONTEXT, STUDENT POPULATION, AND "PREPAREDNESS"

Local institutional context has played a significant role in this study and this book. I've addressed the ways that Oak benefits from funding sources and a

---

7   I refer to Gerald Z as Gerald in this chapter when I specifically draw from my interview with him. However, at other points I refer to him by the pseudonym Dr. Z because other colleagues often refer to him with the title Dr. and his surname initial. As other participants were commonly referred to by the first names in conversations with colleagues, I found this to be an interesting signal of the Dr. Z's status and power.

sense of faculty collaboration that is lacking at St. Rita's. These differences are significant, but in this section, I write more explicitly about the way that faculty at these institutions view their institutional context in terms of the student body. When we compare these institutions side-by-side using the national standard integrated post-secondary education data system (IPEDS), it is hard to argue that race or socioeconomic status is insignificant in the local experiences at these two institutions (see Table 7.3). The overall racial makeup of students varies significantly between the two schools, as does the admissions criteria. Oak's student body is 62 percent White with only a small number of Hispanic (8 percent) and Black students (6 percent). Meanwhile, St. Rita's undergraduate student population is more balanced among these three demographics at approximately 41 percent White, 27 percent Hispanic, and 29 percent Black. The population of Asian American students is small at both institutions: 4 percent at Oak and 1 percent at St. Rita's. Oak does attract a more international population with 14 percent of their students listed as non-resident aliens, while St. Rita's shows 0 percent in this category.

Table 7.3: IPEDS Data on Oak & St. Rita's

	Oak	St. Rita's
Student Population total	2,293	718
White students	62%	41%
Hispanic/Latino	8%	27%
Black students	6%	29%
Asian American students	4%	1%
Non-resident aliens	14%	0%
Acceptance Rate	29%	Open-access
Retention from first-second year	90%	47%
Graduation Rate (6-yr)	86%	24%
Graduation Rate (overall)	82%	44%
White students	83%	43%
Hispanic/Latino	84%	64%
Black	82%	14%
Instructional Staff		
Full-Time	252	21
Part-Time	26	66

Another key difference is admission qualifications. Oak is considered highly competitive with a 29 percent acceptance rate while St. Rita's is open-access. Although students take out loans at about equal rates, Oak is more than double the cost of St. Rita's. In addition, those who do take out loans for their education at Oak are much less likely to default on them, with only about two percent defaulting in comparison to 13 percent at St. Rita's. Finally, the graduation rate and how it varies by race is a significant factor distinguishing the two institutions. At Oak, minoritized students graduate at similar rates as White students. The overall graduate rate is 82 percent, and White, Black, and Hispanic populations rates are all within one percent of that average. Meanwhile, St. Rita's graduation rate is 44 percent overall but only 14 percent for Black students.

Although these numbers are striking, the way that institutional reporting structures influence them should be considered here. IPEDS is the standard for reporting such information, yet their overall graduate rates are based on full-time students, and nearly 40 percent of St. Rita's students are part-time. So, too, data is based on individual years, which can vary widely when the overall student population is as low as it is at St. Rita's. While it was my main informant at St. Rita's, Dwayne, who encouraged me to use the IPEDS statistics for comparison between institutions, he also collected his own data on these issues. He noted that other schools were unlikely to run this data "person by person" the way he does at St. Rita's; however, this is how he comes to a "real retention" number, one that is more around 25 percent than the 47 percent he acknowledges is reported through IPEDS. Thus, nationally reported numbers only tell part of the story about student population and the institutional context of these small schools. The data from my interviews adds a more dynamic view of institutional context but also shows how faculty ignore certain demographic realities, particularly race, in an attempt to present a neutral (and colorblind) representation of their institution.

The faculty at Oak almost unanimously answered my questions about their institutional context in terms of the academic prowess of their students. They mentioned that incoming students at Oak have "really polished skills," are "generally good students across the board," and have an "upward trajectory of preparation." Oak is traditionally a liberal arts school that sought to raise its profile in the 1980s when the president of the university stopped all residential fraternities. Ben, the former writing committee chair and dean of first-year students, noted that this was a turning point where Oak was able to recruit students who were "more seriously academically." He also explained that through a series of endowments in the past ten years, the university has been able to incorporate more diversity in its student population, particularly when it comes to socio-economic diversity.

When it comes to writing, the faculty at Oak viewed it as valued across the curriculum in that students are both asked to write in a lot of different classes and value that preparation. These comments reinforce a generalized idea of the default Oak student—well prepared, high-performing, engaged. So engaged that Ronnie, English department chair, said with a chuckle: "they take some keeping up with." No one says that they are also White—race does not readily enter these descriptions. Only Shirong and Wendy, both of whom work with and value international students, commented that some students come from different cultural and linguistic backgrounds and "didn't start at the same starting point as other students." Shirong explained that the challenges these students experience with writing are not about mechanics as much as they are about culture, and that language-learning is inherently tied to culture. Wendy, too, noted that the students she has worked with from China come with very different expectations of what a classroom environment is like. She explained that those students have often only written small papers of less than 250 words that were graded with very limited expectations, likely for grammar.

While the racial makeup of the student population at St. Rita's is entirely different than that of Oak, faculty members also frame their student body in terms of preparation and ability rather than race. Socio-economic status does enter the conversation more explicitly here, but it is the rare exception that race is directly mentioned. Students at St. Rita's are continually framed in opposition to the traditional college student. "Our freshman are different here," said composition-teacher Heather: "their perception of college is sort of like it's a continuation of high school." Heather, along with others, stressed that these students are also first-generation college students. Dwayne noted that since St. Rita's is open-access with rolling admissions, many of their students don't consider college until the last minute: "We've got kids that decided they were going to go to college the day before college." Gerald lamented that the students "don't have a culture of education at home." Lucinda also explained the impact of the non-residential nature of St. Rita's: their students are local and come from families that do not have a tradition of going away for college. So, too, many faculty stressed that their students come from "awful," "underperforming" high schools, and the teachers at those high schools "don't know writing well enough." In contrast to Oak, St. Rita's faculty see their students as "really disengaged" and "reluctant to ask for help."

Those at Oak refrain from discussing the finances of their students in general, only noting exceptions—those funded by specific outreach efforts to broaden the student population. However, the low socio-economic status of the students at St. Rita's is something many faculty members are actively aware of. In terms of local context, there is an understanding that St. Rita's exists within a depressed region of the country. Lucinda explained that it was the first school in the region to offer a four-year degree, and the school purposefully sought to provide such a degree to those working in the steel industry that surrounds the college. The building for the school was donated by British Petroleum (BP), and the order of Catholicism that established St. Rita's seeks to bring education (among other services) to economically deprived regions. Gerald explained that the students are poor and that they often work 30–40 hours a week to support their families. While he doesn't think that is feasible to pair full-time work with a full-time college education, he acknowledged that the state limits financial aid so that it is difficult to pursue college part-time and still receive financial assistance.[8] Jeremy, too, recognized the financial limitations of his students and how this interacts with financial aid and state funding. He believes that remedial courses are necessary but recognizes the financial burden they place on students. If they don't meet certain scores on placement exams, Jeremey explained, "the state is loath to fund them," and that aid may or may not be reinstated when those scores are achieved. He noted that the state does this because they see it as "paying twice" for what should be achieved in high school. Dwayne went further with this point, noting that the placement system is managed by admissions and that he finds higher performing students are sometimes placed in lower-level classes for no discernible reason. He is also the only one to directly link this inequity to race as well as socio-economic status: "It does seem like race and class could have played a role," he lamented.

As seen in other research, faculty define students, particularly Black students, in terms of deficit (Davila, 2017). This holds true of Latinx and Hispanic students as well. We repeatedly see the population of students at St. Rita's defined in opposition to the "normal," "prepared" college student. Meanwhile, the Oak faculty rarely mention the race or economic class of their students, noting only that they are high achieving and prepared. When faculty at both institutions talk about student population, they talk about preparedness and merit rather than their race or language backgrounds. They explicitly link good writing with preparedness and coming from good (aka wealthy) high schools. Bethany Davila (2012) noted that in her study this type of talk "ultimately functioned to create a stereotype of privileged White students who have had better educations and are therefore better writers" (p. 191). Davila's later (2017) study found that there were two main ways that "White talk" manifested in her interviews with faculty: avoiding the subject of race or asserting that it is not relevant to the subject at hand. While my participants did not directly argue that race is irrelevant to

---

8   Although he characterizes the students as full-time, as many as 40% of undergraduates at St. Rita's are actually part-time.

rubric-making, they did not discuss it as a factor either. This ideology of neutrality "may eclipse local meaning making" (Davila, 2017, p. 158). Thus, looking at how faculty talk about their local settings, including what they do *not* talk about, helps build a better picture of how power functions in those institutions.

ACCULTURATIONIST RUBRICS & ADAPTATION

These assumptions about neutrality and language play out in the text of the rubrics themselves. Although the AAC&U intends for their rubrics to represent an assets-based model, this is difficult to maintain at St. Rita's when the lowest benchmark category does not match with the texts that students there routinely produce. One way the AAC&U addresses this issue is to have a "zero" performance level that doesn't necessarily indicate poor performance, but rather indicates that a dimension of the rubric was not present in that artifact. The zero can mean that the student artifact is below the benchmark level, but it can also simply mean that dimension of the rubric was not present in that artifact. When used at the programmatic level, the zero can provide valuable information about what was collected, and theoretically, what is taught. For example, national scoring using the Written Communication rubric has a disproportionately high number (15 percent) of zero scores for "research and sources" (Rhodes & McConnell, 2021). This potentially shows us that faculty are not assigning writing that asks for research rather than that students are not succeeding in using sources. Thus, the "zero" does not assign blame for not fitting the rubric but leads to an open question of why the artifacts gathered do not show evidence of source use.

Although the national data from the VALUE Institute has shown that students at all levels of higher education can consistently reach the top performance levels on the rubric (Rhodes & McConnell, 2021), the notion of deficit, lower ability and/or unpreparedness is often translated to the rubrics when they are modified. As I described in Chapter 5, one of the most common changes to the VALUE rubric is to make the lowest performance level negative. This shift not only moves away from the asset-based model, but also shifts the responsibility for a low score from an unknown entity to the student author. At Oak, the lowest level is labeled "weak," while at St. Rita's, it is called "insufficient."

At Oak, raters long for the assignment sheets, often attempting to infer whether they should bump up the student score to account for something not being a factor of the assignment. For example, 2017 faculty-rater Eshaal said she tried to be "more lenient" because she didn't know what the assignment prompt was asking for. While she was encouraged not to do this, I would argue that the definition of the artifact as "weak" rather than simply a non-represented "zero" score encourages this kind of emotional investment on the part of the rater, who does not want the student labeled as "weak" when the assignment is to blame. Meanwhile, at St. Rita's, the rubric is used to actually determine whether or not students pass certain general education courses, and so "insufficient" is exactly what it says—that student will be held back from progressing to the next level of their degree if their writing falls within this portion of the rubric. The AAC&U does define the "benchmark" level as the skills often found in beginning level college students, but they are also clear that they do not intend the rubrics to represent "college readiness standards" (Rhodes, 2010, p. 3). Nevertheless, when applied in an environment where students are viewed primarily in terms of preparation, the benchmark becomes just that—a sign of who is prepared and who is "weak" or "insufficient."

In addition, both the original rubric and the ones used at Oak and St. Rita's reinforce the view that "SEAE is widely accessible and not affiliated with any one group of people" (Davila, 2012, p, 196). The original VALUE rubric for Written Communication (2009) uses terminology in the "Control of Syntax and Mechanics" section that is coded for Whiteness. The capstone dimension reads:

> Uses graceful language that skillfully communicates meaning
> to readers with clarity and fluency and is virtually error free.

Clarity, in particular, has been noted as a stand-in for Standardized Edited American English (SEAE), which is depicted as "neutral, clear, widely accessible" (Davila, 2017, p. 168). So, too, Davila (2017) argued that using the generic term *language* on outcomes and rubrics "leaves SEAE unnamed and contributes to its position as neutral" (p. 168). The notion of a text being "error-free" fits with Valerie Balester's (2012) definition of the "acculturationist rubric," which assumes errors are easily quantified. Such rubrics convey the message that SEAE is "stable and easily identifiable" to both writers and readers (p. 66).

While the rubric at Oak changed over the course of my study, the language under the dimension titled "process and style" maintained a similar acculturationist stance. Oak's rubric defined the "process and style" dimension in terms of a "polished state." This state included the "refinement of ideas" as well as style but linked the two together under an assumption that well-developed ideas are to be presented using SEAE. The 2016 version of the rubric equated maturity with White language practice and assumed that it is a mere matter of "attention to clarity and concision" that allows students to reach the performance category of "mature." Although the 2018 revised rubric clearly labels the use of SEAE as "adherence to convention," rather than as morally or developmentally superior, it still sees clarity and conciseness as a matter of "sustained attention" and a feature of "engaging prose." By linking process and style, there is the assumption that all writers have equal access to SEAE conventions if only they take the time to edit.

The rubric at St. Rita's has two dimensions for sentence level error: 1) prose style and syntax; 2) spelling, word-choice, grammar, and punctuation. As discussed in both Chapter 5 and 6, the faculty at St. Rita's do not agree that there is the need for two separate dimensions, particularly on a rubric with only five total dimensions. Yet, Gerald Z's insistence that these elements are key to good writing prevails. The language of this rubric appears to recognize that students at St. Rita's come from different language backgrounds, yet it clearly labels those forms of English as inappropriate for writing in an academic setting. The rubric associates written prose with SEAE and contrasts that with speaking, calling for "standard written English rather than spoken English." Furthermore, the "prose and syntax" dimension clearly and deliberately shows a progression from "insufficient" and "distorted" English to "slang or dialects of English" to "standard written English," which is "sufficient."

These statements fit with Balester's (2012) description of acculturationist rubrics in that it calls for SEAE to be "the sole language variety to be used in schools" (p. 66). However, I would argue that this rubric takes a more outwardly eradicationist view of language. As defined by April Baker-Bell (2020), eradicationist language pedagogy is when:

> Black Language is not acknowledged as a language and gets treated as linguistic, morally, and intellectually inferior. The goal of this approach is to eradicate Black Language from students' linguistic repertoire and replace it with White Mainstream English. (p. 28)

The rubric at St. Rita's recognizes variety but does not recognize that multiple Englishes can be written or that they are not simply "slang." Rather, it outright calls for the elimination of non-White, non-standard English. This eradicationist stance has real-world consequences for the students at St. Rita's. Dwayne studied the correlation between the two sentence-level dimensions of the rubric and found that while there was a high variance among the other areas, students consistently received the same score on these two dimensions. Furthermore, he explained that if students had two scores of "insufficient" on the rubric, they would need to retake the first-year writing course, even if they had high scores on other areas of the rubric. Although the university decided not to charge the students for the course the second time, it added to their load and kept them in school longer or discouraged them from continuing at all.

Regardless of the AAC&U's call for inclusive excellence in relation to the VALUE rubrics, current writing scales continue to exclude language variety. The acculturationist, even eradicationist, wording of these rubrics signals a need to erase the individual identity of the student and depict the performance of students, faculty, and entire universities in a "neutral" way that itself "actively creates continued White dominance" (Davila, 2012, p. 184). It is impossible to fully embrace the asset-based approach advocated for by the AAC&U or acknowledge the needs of local student populations while maintaining this focus on standardized, White English within the dimensions of the rubric.

WHITE MEN TALKING: THE INFLUENCE OF INDIVIDUAL FACULTY MEMBERS

As demonstrated throughout this book, faculty play a significant role in designing local assessment practice, even when using national documents for guidance. Therefore, any discussion of individual demographics and power is incomplete without a look at faculty. When we talk about diversity, we often talk about student population. IPEDs provides statistics on the racial makeup of student bodies by individual institution and year. They disaggregate graduation statistics by race and can thus identify inequities such as the much lower graduation rate for Black students at St. Rita's. So, too, the AAC&U advocates for disaggregating data based on race, socioeconomic status, and other demographic factors. They see disaggregation of student data as key to working against a deficit model of higher education and working toward inclusive excellence (McConnell & Rhodes, 2017, p. 49). But who is in charge of looking at this data, using it, and working toward more equitable practices within higher education? The answer is: still primarily White faculty members and administrators.

While IPEDS does not provide the racial data on faculty members per institution, the National Center for Education Statistics does give demographic data for faculty across institutions (IES, n.d.). As of 2018, they found that 40 percent of full-time faculty were White males, and 35 percent were White females. Twelve percent were Asian/Pacific Islander. Only *three* percent of full-time faculty were Black or Hispanic with those statistics combined. Like IPEDS data, the focus is on full-time faculty, and again, this ignores a significant portion of St. Rita's population. While Oak has only 21 part-time faculty to 252 full-time, at St. Rita's, the majority are part-time. They have only 26 full-time faculty members and 66 part-time (IPEDS, n.d.). However, as reflected in my interview with Heather at St. Rita's, full-time faculty still make the decisions. When I asked Heather if she was involved in the initial creation of the rubric used there, she said, "I wasn't full-time when we started this, so they wouldn't have asked me." So, too, the general education committee wanted to have clear outcomes because they recognized that their reliance on adjunct labor means that outcomes are not consistently met. At best, the general education outcomes can be seen as a means to guide adjuncts; at worst, they also control and discipline them. Meanwhile, Gerald Z is full-time and tenured, and Dwayne feels that he can do nothing to get him to align his courses with what he knows to be good composition pedagogy. It is clear that certain individuals have far more power within this system than others.

I did not ask my participants to identify their race or ethnicity. However, the demographics within my study appeared to fit with the overall makeup of faculty within academia. The majority of my participants were White with a few exceptions, most notably international faculty members. My one Black female participant was present for the assessment at Oak but did not consent to an interview. Although institutional ethnography attempts to avoid falling into the trap of presenting only the standpoint of the ruling (Rankin, 2017b), the truth of my study is that White voices dominated the discourse. This section shows how two particular White male faculty members talk about their own relationship to race, power, and the institution. I present these two White male points of view not to valorize them but as examples of how racial and individual power interacts with institutional power to influence writing assessment at these particular institutions. These individuals hold institutional power, and because they do, their acts are ultimately the acts of the institution.

GERALD'S STORY OF HIMSELF: SON OF A COP SAVES WORKING CLASS KIDS FROM THE DANGERS OF RHETORIC

As we have seen at St. Rita's, competency-based education and the desire for all students to achieve certain levels of "success" dominates the thinking. Jeremy drills grammar but justifies his basic writing course through the notion that students proceed at their own individual pace until they have reached the necessary competency to complete the regular first-year writing course. This mindset was pervasive at St. Rita's. However, there was one individual there who was particularly influential in determining assessment practice at St. Rita's, not because he directed the writing program, chaired the general education committee, or had particular relevant expertise, but because he asserted his individual control. Gerald, or Dr. Z as his colleagues refer to him, frequently asserted himself as a privileged member of society, in his own words: the "big, bad White guy." One might assume, then, that Gerald closely identifies with the institutional structures of the academy, but in many ways, he does not.

When analyzing my interview transcripts as a whole, I rarely used my code for external or personal influences, yet it appeared frequently in my interview with Gerald. I wondered, at first, how relevant these moments were to a book about rubrics and writing assessment. Campbell (2006) warned against institutional ethnographers' tendency to get too caught up in the competing stories of participants. Yet, Gerald's own view of his relationship to systems of powers is complex. So, too, I believe his point of view—while potentially traumatizing to those who have been subjected to bullying, racism, sexism, and other oppression within the academia—helps us "expose" how individual lives "come under the influence of specific ruling practice" (Campbell, 2006, p. 95). Gerald's point of view on grammar and rubrics remains unchallenged at St. Rita's. If Gerald rules St. Rita's, who or what rules Gerald? And how do we ultimately disrupt those systems of power and their influence on both those who are harmed by them and those who cause harm because of them? Knowing how Gerald views himself within this system may offer us some answers to these questions.

This section's subheading might be one version of how Gerald frames his own story at St. Rita's. In this story, Gerald, of course, is the hero. Through both long tangents and short interjections during our interview, I learned a great deal about Gerald's background and life experiences. Not once, but *four* times in the interview, Gerald identified as the son of a cop. He uses this identity to tie himself to the working class and to set himself up in opposition to academia. "I don't think I'm smart," he said, "I'm just a cop's kid." But he's not any cop's kid, either. He's "a cop's son who ended up getting his Ph.D. in English" from a prestigious university. He sees himself, then, as the embodiment of the American bootstraps narrative. He grew up "working class"[9] but succeeded, and he did so by learning basic competencies. In fact, he may have had to subvert his own language background to do so—although he doesn't mention this outright, when he gets angry/passionate, a bit of dialect seems to creep into his speech.

In addition to being a son, Gerald is a father, which also came up several times in the interview. In particular, Gerald told me about his regrets in not bringing his son up Catholic. While seemingly out of the blue, this story connects with Gerald's own feelings about working at a Catholic institution. He values the "mission oriented" nature of St. Rita's and thinks it is good for the students. He noted that parents sometimes send their students to St. Rita's in hopes that their children will receive traditional Catholic discipline. He seems to see it as his place, then, to subject students to this discipline. For example, he makes students revise their first paper as many times as it takes to get an A. More than any other participant, Gerald talked about specific students, those who succeeded and thanked him for this discipline. "I'm still Facebook friends with some of them," Gerald told me, "And they say, well, this guy taught me

---

9   This is Gerald's definition. I recognized that police officer is not seen as a universally "working class" profession.

how to write. For the first time, somebody forced me." This discipline, this *forced* writing, is not only what he thinks students need, but also what he thinks they value. He even goes as far as to say that a student who was a Marine particularly liked this approach because those in the military "like abuse."

Whether or not it is this discipline that Gerald seeks for his own son, Gerald sees his role as a teacher as similar to his role as a parent. Not only does he mention how his parenting relates to his teaching, but he also consistently infantilizes his students. He believes strongly that questioning conventions is not meant for his students/children. "If you think it is," he said in a chilling, but telling statement: "You don't know what it means to bring up children. You don't know what it means to educate young people." This connection is solidified with the story he tells me about how he regrets not raising his son Catholic. Gerald was raised Catholic but later came to question and leave his faith. He said: "It's a lot different growing up with a God and then deconstructing your Gods later." By not bringing his own son up Catholic, he feels that his son has had to deal with philosophical questions at a younger age and that this has made things more difficult than they were for Gerald who only came to question religion as an adult. So, too, he believes in teaching writing as teaching traditional structures first and questioning them later. "It's okay to deconstruct [conventions] after you've learned them," is an idea he repeats throughout the interview.

Although Gerald's words are particularly infantilizing, I should note that referring to students as "kids" is the norm at St. Rita's. Also worthy of note is that Gerald does not always seem to associate this status with youth but rather with being at the beginning stages of learning a subject. He frequently compares teaching writing to his own experience learning art, which he has been studying for the past five years. He explained that the artist can't draw a portrait until they know basic structures, like a nose. For Gerald, SEAE grammar is to composition what anatomy is to art. He knows that the way he treats students is seen as demeaning. In fact, he complains that most educators these days are too focused on empowering students. For Gerald, there is nothing demeaning about being seen as a beginner, and to imply so is in itself demeaning. "I go to art class in the city with men who are a lot more practiced, professional artists than I am," he said, "and there's no demeaning me when they treat me as a beginner." He even went as far as to imply that it is dangerous not to do so, also comparing writing to hunting. He indicated that students must write for an "artificial situation" first just as a hunter must practice on a target.

Gerald is keenly aware that his pedagogical approach does not fit with advances in composition theory and pedagogy. Rather, he actively and aggressively resists those pedagogies by asserting his version of moral rightness. When I asked Gerald one of my standard questions, "How do you define good writing?" he began by placing his answer in opposition to the answer he likely believed I wanted:

> I know it's very fashionable to answer that good writing, it does its thing. It does what it's supposed to do. It meets its audience and has its effect on the audience it's supposed to, which is a very rhetorical understanding of writing.

Gerald knows which practices are disciplinary consensus, but he goes on to outright reject them, even demean them. He described the progression of composition as a field as a grab for disciplinary power, as creating a field "out of thin air." He went as far to accuse writing instructors of "laziness," noting that they are driven by a "careerism" rather than concern for students, and thus they won't take the time to "actually correct" student writing.

His critique is not only of composition, but also of academia as whole, thus fitting into the wider conservative attack on intellectualism and expertise. He believes that academic prose is "the worst prose in America right now." And despite receiving a Ph.D. from an elite institution, he complained that most universities follow the "Harvard model" where academics, thinking they are better than everyone else, seek only self-replication, favoring students who go to graduate school and perpetuate their discipline. This is a ridiculous approach for St. Rita's, he argued, where he has never had an English major continue to graduate school. This concern of overly focusing on the academy is not lost on Dwayne and Heather. Yet, they approach it entirely differently. In keeping with composition pedagogy, they design assignments that have students writing for community and public audiences rather than academic ones whereas Gerald believes that he is doing his students a favor by having them write five-paragraph essays in an artificial setting.

I argued in Chapter 2 that a "great books" philosophy of liberal education has morphed into a "great skills" approach. This shift is clearly shown in Gerald's exercise of power at St. Rita's. Gerald sees his mission as providing foundational competencies to underprepared, first-generation students. He holds similar views as those proponents of the "great books approach," who tied the success of a democracy to the development of a cultured individual (Russell, 2002, p. 170). In this view, only White, Western views are considered cultured, a view Gerald perpetuates when he describes his students' upbringing as "culturally thin." This approach is also tied to his own identity as a professor. While he says he loves teaching at St. Rita's, he noted that at "a normal institution" he would be teaching far more Shakespeare, and that he would have to teach at least four of his plays to "be considered a serious professor." Most keenly, we saw this view enacted in his outburst in the general education meeting. When discussing the reading outcomes in the general education committee, Dwayne noted that Gerald clearly wanted all general education classes to read three books, and he defined those books as "a title across the spine, and was on paper, and was, you know, a dead White male." Gerald can't enact the great books approach by requiring his colleagues in the sciences to teach books, so he calls them names and storms off the committee. After that incident, he is no longer a member of the committee, nor is he allowed to continue as department chair. Gerald's individual power, his ability to successfully bully his colleagues, is thus not unlimited. His colleagues recognize that the "great books" approach to general education is no longer acceptable.

But the great skills approach to writing—specifically the skill of SEAE grammar—is one where he is allowed to assert his influence. Even though he was absent from the general education committee meeting on writing that I attended, his will was palpable. When the limitations of the current writing "portfolio" model comes up in the general education meeting, Dwayne hesitated saying: "I agree, but he, he, he was playing nice with that assessment." No one needs to ask who "he" is. Dwayne's tentativeness here as well as the uncomfortable laughter that follows show the power that Gerald holds over others at his institution. Because competency-based education is viewed as being colorblind and is seen as current best practice, Gerald is able to push toward his own views in this arena. Those views, we could argue, take competency-based learning to an extreme, but they do not fall completely outside the bounds of current thinking the way the "great books" approach does.

Gerald's power is both individual and institutional. He is forceful about his own views, and his verbal abuse causes his colleagues to fall in line even when they disagree with him. But no matter how much he sees those views as connected to his own identity—that of a son, a father, an artist—they are historically rooted in institutional systems of power and White supremacy. As seen in Chapter 2, writing scales were originally created by eugenicists and have historically excluded students of color and those from language backgrounds other than SEAE. Gerald noted the racial diversity at St. Rita's as something he values, and yet, he does not consider how that diversity might impact his practice. Race is simply erased from his thinking about language and pedagogy. Gerald sees White Mainstream English as the "target," the basic competency to reach. He sees his students, perhaps beginning academic writers, as merely children; thus, eradicating their own language expertise, agency, and maturity. His anti-academic, anti-intellectual stance allows him to discredit practices within composition that value language diversity and take a rhetorical approach to language. Yet, he is willing to use that institutional power to reinforce his own ideology. He's not naive to the role that rubrics play in this, hence his email to all faculty with the rubric for grading five-paragraph essays. Rubrics, he stated, "institutionalize writing pedagogy." Thus, he fights his fight for two sections of sentence-level errors on the St. Rita's rubric, purposefully institutionalizing his view that students are not ready to progress without mastering these great skills.

BRAD'S SELF NARRATIVE: FRONT-LINE WRITING PEDAGOGUE BLOWS UP THE SYLLABUS

The relationship between individualism and institutional power at Oak manifests differently than it does at St. Rita's, and yet it is no less White. According to Kenneth Jones and Tema Okun (2001), fear of conflict and individualism are both elements of White supremacy culture. These two elements of Whiteness limit how progressive the writing committee at Oak is able to be despite good intentions. Faculty members at Oak seek professional standards and "best" practices[10] from a variety of sources, including the VALUE rubrics as well as workshops by specialists in the field of composition. They seek consensus. And yet, they are limited in their influence over actual classroom practice. Philip, the associate provost, noted that there is "a great deal of sovereignty given faculty in their own courses." The word sovereignty here clearly links faculty practice with ruling relations: it is clear that *individual* faculty rule individual classrooms.

Kristen and the writing committee value this individual sovereignty over collective action. As seen in Chapter 6, when developing the rubric, they attempt to account for as many different pedagogical practices as possible rather than use the power of the rubric to change those practices. They do not want to impose any common assignments in writing classes but rather want an open-ended rubric that accounts for individualism in classroom practice. Barbara, the writing center director, feels that this valuing of classroom sovereignty limits the ability of the writing committee to make positive change on campus. She expressed disappointment that the writing committee hadn't been able to do more to assess writing instructors and move toward better practices in the classroom. When I asked her what limited the power of the writing committee, she replied: "good feelings." On a small campus, she explained, you have to pick your battles, and "there's always a price."

This tension between individual classroom sovereignty and institutional power plays out in the story of Brad, an art historian who was on the 2016 Oak writing committee that was revising the rubric. Brad desperately wants to upend a system of White language supremacy and revolutionize education.

---

10 Wilson (2006) challenged the notion of "best" practice, noting that it assumes a fixed set of practices and closes off options (p. xxii). As shown throughout this book, the notion that particular practices are best across contexts is one I also wish to challenge.

He is another White male with tenure, and he recognizes his own privilege. At first, I saw him as a direct contrast to Gerald, as they seem to represent two sides of a political spectrum. While Gerald insists on the importance of "conventions," when I talked to Brad in November 2016, he was ready to "blow up" everything from the syllabus to capitalism. Yet, as I delved further into their interviews, I found multiple similarities. Like Gerald, Brad volunteered a great deal of personal opinions and experiences, although his commentary was often more abstract. Both have a complex relationship with power based, in part, on individual experiences. Both see themselves in opposition to institutional power structures. However, both also operate within a White ideology that values individualism and self-reliance. Thus, I offer their stories not in opposition, but in concert, to show how White individualism ultimately impedes systemic, institutional change.

A sesquipedalian, Brad's interview was filled with complex, philosophical statements about critical pedagogy, language and politics. I prodded him to tell more of his personal backstory as well. How had this "classic old White guy" come to the place where he recognized his own power and privilege and wanted to "blow up" the system? Brad explained that his resistance to systems of power originated early in his life. Although he grew up in a White middle-class suburb, he noted that as a Southerner, he was aware of racial tension from an early age. In particular, he played football with "Black kids from the other side of town." During the same formative years, he watched on TV as the Vietnam War and race riots happened. He watched "Black people getting shot up" and became "intensively aware of cultural difference." Then, in the late 1970s, Brad had the opportunity to do graduate study abroad, an experience he returned to multiple times throughout his interview. During his study in Romania, he needed to do academic work in another language, as a language learner. For Brad, writing a graduate-level academic paper in Romanian was one of the hardest things he's ever had to do, but it led him to think about how language, culture, and writing interact. In light of the political environment surrounding Trump's election in November 2016, Brad expressed a desire to renew his commitment to issues of language diversity and pedagogy. "Language matters in every realm of social engagement," Brad said, "if we didn't know it before, after last Wednesday [the day of Trump's election], we know it now." Brad criticized what he called the "ultimate entitlement" in North America: "I speak English, everybody else needs to." He expressed frustration that the "dialect of English constructed through the 19th and 20th centuries driven by White Anglo capitalist economic interests" is the default language of academia.

Brad was the only one of my participants to directly invoke "critical pedagogy," and he talked at length about what this means for the writing classroom.

For Brad, critical writing pedagogy needs to not only look different in practice but also come from "a vastly different cultural and political position" on the "part of the pedagogue." A critical writing pedagogue, he articulated, "approaches ASE from an L2 plus point of view." He questioned whether anyone with a mono-lingual background can really engage with the important issues of language and writing. Rather, he wondered if the person teaching writing shouldn't be "this wonderful person from Singapore who speaks both at home . . . and here on campus, three or four different languages." Although he focuses on international students as English language learners, Brad also recognized that this diversity is not uniquely foreign: "We live in a multi-glossal North American culture." Thus, he argued that pedagogical practice needs to be reexamined with a multi-lingual and multi-glossal lens.

Brad recognized that this reexamination is not an easy task: he is bound within an academic system—ruled by boss texts—that is difficult and slow to change. At times, Brad sees this challenge as overwhelming. At multiple points in our interview, he expressed frustration with the ability to work within the system to create change:

> Normativity in the classroom is really something that needs
> to be not simply problematized but fucking blown up and
> recreated. Sorry. There it is. Just blow it up. You know, but
> how do you do that? When I need to write up the syllabus for
> next semester. . . .

His own role as an agent of change within this system is something that Brad struggles with and raises questions that get to the heart of this book, questions I will return to in the conclusion. What can Brad do within this system when assessment keeps accreditors happy and his paycheck coming in? Some ques-tions, like whether or not a college degree is worth the money, he designates as over his pay grade.

In this interview, Brad and I shared the frustration that while admitting that academic language is steeped in Whiteness is a step, it isn't enough. Yet, Brad also believes that an individual instructor can make a difference:

> If we're going to do anything different, it starts with one
> professor, one class, throwing out the syllabus and rewriting it
> in a different way. And frankly, that may simply happen next
> semester in every fucking course I run, and I don't really know
> how to do this.

Brad's vision of throwing out the syllabus might be appealing to some readers, as it initially was to me. And yet, Brad is a long-time, tenured faculty member.

Meanwhile, the proportion of minoritized faculty in adjunct or contract faculty roles is higher than those in tenure-line positions (IES, n.d.). These faculty may be given a particular syllabus to teach or at the very least be regularly renewed based on how well they follow a "master" syllabus designed by others. Tenure-line faculty are shielded from, but also not immune to, the way external power structures dictate these classroom texts. Associate Provost at Oak, Philip was concerned that the next stage for accreditors will be "saying every syllabus has to have certain things on it," something that he worries will cause a lot of push back from Oak faculty, most of whom are full-time, tenure-line faculty members. Yet, at other institutions, non-tenure line faculty syllabi are already routinely examined for such adherence to institutional norms.

As a tenured faculty member at an institution like Oak, Brad has a lot of power within this system to change his own classroom practice. While he maintains a profound skepticism of the institution as a whole, he is profoundly optimistic about his own ability to separate his classroom from such structures. When I asked him about the VALUE Written Communication rubric, he strongly expressed that he did not care at all about "assessment with a capital A." Rather, he said: "I'm interested in teaching in my classroom. That's what I care about." I asked if that made it difficult for him to be on the writing committee, to which he responded that he recognized the need for it because of the accreditation. While he says he'd be completely fine with Oak giving up their accreditation, he recognized that assessment is something the institution does to maintain its standing with accreditation agencies, and "that's what keeps the doors open."

Thus, Brad separates himself from the systems that allow him to continue his work, to keep the university running. Rather than seeing himself as a part of—as complicit with those systems—he sees himself as a "front-line writing pedagogue." He has taught writing courses at Oak since the 1990s. During that time, he has participated in many writing workshops and revised his own pedagogy extensively. Brad clarified that he is at least somewhat interested in the collaboration with other members of the writing committee in writing the rubric, and yet he frames this interest in terms of how it will help him better evaluate and give feedback in writing in his own classroom. He is very willing to change his own pedagogy to reflect what he learns about writing, but he is unwilling to use his position to ask others to do so as well. Rather than see the writing committee as a place where he can use his influence to change writing pedagogy across the program, Brad falls back on the *individual* control he has over his own classroom. Even as a senior faculty member, he does not embrace the power he holds within the university as a whole.

Perhaps it is his feeling that assessment is a means for accreditation rather than for improving pedagogy that holds Brad back from being as vocal about linguistic justice in the committee as he is in his interview. He does offer suggestions for the writing rubric, but none of them meet the goal he expressed to me of revisiting the rubric from a "poly-glossal, culturally diverse, and global perspective." He does challenge the notion of "correctness" but remains in the realm of convention: "I don't care about correctness; I care about if you're writing in the formal register of academic English." In fact, he reinforced the idea that "process and style" includes grammar because correct grammar is merely a product of careful revision. He agreed that a "developing" paper is one that lacks "clarity and precisions at the sentence level . . . that results from revision." So, too, he reinforced the idea that the way to evaluate style is whether or not it is understood by the audience, noting that if he has to "work at understanding," he will assess a paper lower.

As discussed here and in Chapter 5, this notion of a text being understandable to a generalized audience is problematic and relies on the default assumption of a White, native-English speaking audience. It is committee-member Shirong who questions this in his interview with me when he discusses the way that he can understand the argument made by a Chinese-speaking author when his White American colleagues miss it due to translation errors. Yet, this point never comes up in the writing committee meetings. Ironically, Brad's hypothetical multi-linguistic person from Singapore who he believes should be teaching writing is there in the flesh on the writing committee at Oak. In fact, Shirong joined the writing committee for this very purpose, hoping he could "talk to people about ways to help especially international students to grow into better writers." And yet, Shirong spoke only three times in a one-hour meeting I recorded, while Brad spoke 33 times (not including small expressions such as agreement with others). Brad learns a lot from the meetings about disciplinary diversity and how other fields handle evidence, quotation, or other writing variations, but he does not ultimately learn what he needs to know to blow up either the system, the syllabus, or the writing program rubric.

HYPER-INDIVIDUALISM, WHITE RACIAL HABITUS & RUBRICS

It's easy to read the stories of Gerald and Brad and see one as the villain and one as the hero. But doing so only reinforces a view of Gerald as an *individual* racist and Brad as not racist, when both operate within systems of White supremacy. White supremacy is not individual racist acts or ideas, but rather institutional. It exists in the habits of language and grading that perpetuate our schools *as institutions*. One such habit of Whiteness is hyper-individualism, which puts the rights of the individual above all else, focusing on self-determination and self-reliance

(Inoue, 2019). This habit is present throughout the data presented in this chapter. Hyper-individualism is clearly reflected in Gerald's self-narrative. He rose from a "working class" background as the "son of a cop" to be a professor, and he believes that learning standard White language is the means for others to gain similar social mobility. Although Brad calls for a "poly-glossal" perspective, in practice, he too defaults to hyper-individualism when he expresses a belief that he can *individually* rise above the constraints of the system. Brad focuses on the teacher's individual power to change their syllabus, while not recognizing the collective power of groups such as the writing committee. This ultimately prevents him from enacting the change he seeks or making this change possible for other faculty members who may not share his individual status in the classroom.

Aja Martinez (2020) asked us to consider how we might focus on changing the institution rather than the individual classroom. For her, the former is a precursor to the latter. Similarly, Inoue (2015) reminded us that the consequences of our assessment practice do not occur because of "individual actions by students or a teacher or a rubric alone" (p. 120). It is true that Gerald has more power than many in dictating that the rubric at St. Rita's stresses grammar and mechanics, and that this power has direct consequences for the students who fail the portfolio assessment. But Gerald is granted that power because of his own status as a full-time tenured faculty member who is also White and male. For example, even though Gerald's female colleague Lucinda now occupies a higher status than him in the academic hierarchy, she backs off from challenging Gerald's view in the general education committee. Exercising one's individual prowess, then, is only possible because of where one ranks in the collective.

Similarly, the larger institution of higher education views individual students in terms of their status within a collective, as either prepared or unprepared. Outcomes and rubrics work to define a "benchmark" for preparedness, one that often draws on habits of White language. Faculty who comment on the preparedness of students do not openly consider race but assume a White default. So, too, they assume White writers and White readers when they design their rubrics. BIPOC students are the *exception* to the White norm. Of course, all students (and humans) should be valued for their individual backgrounds and perspectives, but the perspective we see here is that race comes in only as a factor that affects *individuals*. The individual is defined by their diverse characteristics while the collective is assumed to be White, prepared with the socio-economic status necessary to afford higher education. It is then up to those individuals to make up for what is perceived to be a deficit—to take remedial courses at their own expense to "catch up" to the level of other students. These students exist within a White, colonial narrative of progress that states that if non-White individuals only achieve the same outcomes as White individuals, they can overcome the systemic obstacles in their way and forward the progress of the nation as a whole.

Within this system, students only have the power to meet outcomes, while faculty and administrators have the power to change the outcomes. Although, the AAC&U (2020) has argued that their methods "empower the liberal learner" to take the LEAP outcomes and "make them his or her own" (p. 15), this rarely happens in actual practice. Rather the rubrics were designed for scoring artifacts at a programmatic or university level where students are often unaware their work is even being read. To the extent that this work does impact actual practice at colleges and universities, that practice is not something the student has access to or can "make their own." To their credit, the AAC&U does recognize this oversite and hopes to include student voices in future revisions of the VALUE rubrics (personal communication, K. McConnell, October 25, 2021). However, even if student involvement in rubric development does occur, it occurs within a larger ecology of assessment that involves "a confluence of many structures in language, school, and society" that students, teachers, and assessors "have little control over" (Inoue, 2015, p. 19).

The rubric is a tool created within a larger system of historic racism within universities. As a genre, the rubric presupposes a linear progression of learning that ends in the same place for all learners, not a diversity of outcomes to be achieved. That end place is a matter of quality, of excellence, that is often synonymous with habits of White languaging. Though McConnell and Rhodes (2017) hoped that the VALUE rubric approach to assessment would "raise up, not wash out, the inherent diversity found on campuses" (p. 32), traditional rubrics are not well-positioned for this goal. Furthermore, the process of rubric development and adaptation is centered around reaching consensus rather than highlighting diversity. As I've shown throughout this study, rubrics rely on consensus on key outcomes and terminology. In order to make any rubric work in actual practice, the language of the rubric becomes generalized, and with it comes generalized rather than diverse assumptions about writers and readers. Faculty who adapt the rubrics may be diverse, but as a part of the process, they are valued for their role in consensus-building, for their ability to be *representative* of all faculty, not for their individual diversity. Similarly, even if diverse students are engaged in the process of rubric adaptation, they, too, will be representatives of the student population at large. Finally, without systemic change to our institutions, those individuals with more power—whether that power is due to race, gender, or institutional status—will have the most say in determining our actual assessment practices.

CHAPTER 8.

THE INDIVIDUAL, THE INSTITUTION, AND THE ADMINISTRATOR'S DILEMMA

> "Power was not the province of those who made choices. Power was the ability to set the context in which those choices were made."
>
> -Baru Cormorant, *The Monster Baru Cormorant* (2018) by Seth Dickinson

Narrative—particularly western narratives—often end in a heroic outcome for the narrator. Often the story of assessment ends with the heroic writing administrator who resists standardization and develops local, meaningful writing assessments (Kelly-Riley, 2012, p. 34). This book is not that kind of story. You will find no heroes in this conclusion. Dr. Z does not get his comeuppance as one of my peer reviewers hoped; no writing specialist saves the students who fail the portfolio at St. Rita's; nor does Brad suddenly involve Shirong in radicalizing the writing program at Oak. Rather, by telling multiple stories from different institutional standpoints, institutional ethnography resists a heroic narrative. There are no heroes in the story of writing assessment, only complex individuals carrying out the everyday work of writing assessment within complex systems of institutional power.

So, too, does IE resist final conclusions. Upon the completion of an institutional ethnography, the problematic is explored, but the researcher resists arriving at the *answer* to a question—doing so implies a positivist stance that such an answer can be defined rather than the post-positive approach taken by IE (Smith, 2005). As defined in Chapter 3, the problematic that grounded this study was non-writing specialists adapting national writing rubrics, specifically the AAC&U's Written Communication VALUE rubric. Nearly every part of the problematic invites further questions, from who is a writing specialist to what "adapting" actually means. However, one solid conclusion is that rubrics, whether national or local, are boss texts that are inextricable from systems of power. Even if we feel rubrics do not reflect our values as a discipline (Broad, 2003), the values they do import affect the work of writing assessment and instruction across higher education.

Using IE to study the adaptation of national writing rubrics brought forth many additional questions regarding how power manifests at institutions of higher education—from how mega philanthropists fund educational initiatives to how individual bullies enact White racial privilege within their personal interactions. Adding genre theory to institutional ethnography helps us place rubrics within these systems of power. Rubrics are neither agents themselves, nor are they neutral tools. Rather rubrics are designed—and activated—by individuals and organizations with particular political purposes in mind. As a genre, rubrics exist at the "nexus between an individual's action and a socially defined context" (Devitt, 2004, p. 31). Individuals at the AAC&U may write and assess the VALUE rubrics but are constrained by larger systems of power, including philanthropy in higher education as well as national policy. Individuals on the writing committee at Oak and the general education committee at St. Rita's adapt the rubric but are constrained by the funding they receive from grants and the need for accreditation. Individual teachers, such as Jeremy who teaches basic writing at St. Rita's, then teach in ways that students need to "pass" the rubric, balancing pedagogical needs and the very real financial needs of students who may not be able to pay the tuition to retake the course. Studying rubrics as a genre that is activated by individuals invites us to connect individual actions to larger institutional contexts. Whether viewed from the perspective of national organizations, local universities, or even the classroom, rubrics are formed at this nexus of individual and institutional power.

For LaFrance (2019), "one of the most powerful imaginative moves of IE is its insistence that we are the institution" (p. 133). The concluding question then becomes: what power do individuals have within the broader institution of higher education? How do administrators and instructors exist at the nexus of the individual and the institution, and how to they channel this power to make institutional change? Inoue (2015) noted that "consequences . . . occur because of the ecology or complex system, not because of individual actions by students or a teacher or a rubric alone" (p. 120). Yet, the data from this institutional ethnography shows the "undeniable influence of local conditions to reshape the pedagogies championed by national standards and statements" (LaFrance, 2019, p. 130). While consequences never occur in a vacuum and individual power is inherently tied to institutional systems, it is still valuable to recognize local conditions. The catch-22 is this: How do we shape our institutions for more ethical practice while also existing within the power structure? I dub this the administrator's dilemma.

Here I invoke the epigraph to this chapter, which comes from the fantasy series *The Masquerade* by Seth Dickenson. Dickenson's series engages with philosophical questions about the role of education as a means of colonization, and his main character Baru Cormorant finds herself at this intersection of power, both a part of the institution and working against it. Baru learns that real power is not in making choices but in setting the *context* that allows for and constrains choices. This theme permeates my study. As seen at both Oak and St. Rita's, the faculty make choices about what to include in their outcomes and their rubrics, but they do not challenge the very notion that outcomes and rubrics should guide their practice. To do so is to challenge the dominant institutional logic currently ruling education. But if we are, in fact, the institution, then we can also use our individual power to shape the institution—if we can only step back, "look up" as LaFrance calls for, and see how we enact ruling relations in our own everyday practice. This step back is nearly impossible to do when we limit ourselves to only one institutional context, which is why a key practice in IE is studying multiple institutions outside the home context of the researcher. Yet, such research can be used to shape our interactions with and within institutions: "Our research doesn't just describe social realities, it creates them" (LaFrance, 2019, p. 132). In this conclusion, then, I offer a combination of stories from this study and thoughts about how national, local/programmatic, and classroom settings work together to create the institution. I hope to spark ideas and discussion about how we then intervene in and shape power through our national institutions, our local institutions, and our classrooms.

SHAPING THE INSTITUTION NATIONALLY

The literature in writing assessment asks us to "rethink rubrics" (Wilson, 2006), to "reframe writing assessment" (Alder-Kassner & O'Neill, 2010), and even to "reclaim accountability" (Sharer et al., 2016). Sometimes that call has been connected to issues of equity and race in college classrooms (Balester, 2012). But new rubrics and new terminology have not solved our administrator's dilemma—we are each constrained by our position within the power structure. It is easy to critique national practice and then move on to how we can and should influence local practice—to say that we should just change, adapt, or ignore national rubrics in our local programs or classrooms. Yet, such arguments fall into the same trap that Brad (the art history professor at Oak) defaulted to, thinking that his classroom *could* be a space separate from assessment with a capital A, that his role as pedagogue could be pure in a way that academia as a whole could not. The narratives of local practice in this book show no fewer flaws than national practice. They are no less acts of institutional power than those we see at the national level. So, too, national efforts are no less acts of individual agents— real people with their own everyday work lives and institutional constraints. I thus challenge the oft-heard wisdom of our field that local assessment inherently equals good assessment, that it is somehow not subject to the same pitfalls we see at the national level. Rather, I ask how we can shape assessment at all levels of the institution in ways that best serve us and our students.

Since the emergence of writing assessment as its own field in the 1990s, the field has sought to balance critique of traditional assessment practice with collaboration between composition and educational measurement (Behizadeh & Engelhard Jr., 2011, p. 204). Those who focus on collaboration stress the need to bring our expertise to national efforts and to build alliances with national assessment professionals. Wendy Sharer et al. (2016) argued that those involved in administering writing programs need to "be involved in defining the terms and setting the parameters of large-scale writing assessment" (p. 3). Adler-Kassner and O'Neill (2010) provided extensive advice on how to move beyond our traditional role as academics and engage in community, organizing with those in more public sectors of education. When those in composition operate at this national level—whether it is on a faculty team constructing the VALUE rubric for Written Communication or creating the CWPA Outcomes Statement—they seek to make the values of our field transparent to a wider circle. But not all writing scholars agree that collaboration is a useful strategy. Patricia Lynne (2004) argued that "large-scale assessment is conflicted at the level of theory," and that writing professionals operate under a different paradigm that is irreconcilable with that of assessment professionals (p. 167).

Whether we call for opposing or working with national assessment professionals, the literature within writing assessment tends to separate an "us" (composition scholars) from "them" (educational measurement/assessment professionals), despite our mutual everyday involvement with the work of writing assessment. There are two ways of looking at the history of writing assessment. One is to define a historical "lack of alignment between writing theories and the practice of writing assessment in the United States" (Behizadeh & Engelhard Jr., 2011, pp. 205–206). The other is to note that "our" work has *always* been intertwined with "their" work. This second view is hard. It means owning the historical failures in assessment and the history of White supremacist ideology from which they sprung. Elliot (2005) does not shy away from either the historical connection with eugenicists that created early writing assessment nor the real impact writing assessment has had on students over time, such as the role literacy testing has played in limiting immigration or determining which individuals are placed on the front lines in war-time. Yet, the effects of these practices are not only historical; they are also current.

White writing program administrators are likely to say they work toward anti-racist practices, but teachers and administrators of color challenge that these efforts go deeper than surface level. Carmen Kynard (2021) stated, "I have never worked in a writing program where Whiteness was not the fait accompli of its structure and yet . . . the folk at the helm would tell you they are striving toward and have achieved justice" (p. 187). Similarly, when Genevieve García de Müeller and Iris Ruiz (2017) conducted a survey about race and racism in writing programs they found that there was a "perception gap" between White survey participants and participants of color on whether or not diversity efforts in writing programs are successful (p. 36). Tyler Branson and James Chase Sanchez (2021) noted that the strategies presented by participants in this survey for combating racism "happened more or less at the *individual level*" (p. 72). As shown throughout my study, the individual is always intertwined with the institution. Thus, change must go beyond the individual to the institutional, even the national level. On this front, the most promising development is the creation of the *Institute of Race, Rhetoric, and Literacy* in 2021 to make race a central issue in national writing studies organizations. Addressing the systemic harm done by writing assessment and writing professionals must be a national effort.

BEYOND THE TERMS OF ASSESSMENT

Writing scholars have long concerned ourselves with influencing *terms* of assessment—the words we use and put in outcomes and on rubrics. Anderson et al. (2013) noted the similarities between the VALUE Written Communication rubric and the CWPA Outcomes Statement, saying that they are "almost indistinguishable" from one another (p. 95). This connection is not surprising considering that the faculty team creating the VALUE Written Communication rubric began with existing practice in the field and referenced such norms in the preface to the rubric itself. Some might say that this similarity is a positive attribute of the VALUE rubric. Yet, genre matters. The original CWPA Outcomes were meant to provide *guidance* for curriculum, they were not meant to "require agreement on the best way to achieve those outcomes" (White, 2005). Is the similarity between the VALUE Written Communication rubric and the CWPA Outcomes then a cause for concern as it seems to corrupt this original intent?

We must go beyond terms to examine the *circulation* and use of these national texts. In 2010, Adler-Kassner and O'Neill lauded the AAC&U for their LEAP initiative and its initial focus on educators shaping and adapting a set of open-ended outcomes. In both this book and elsewhere, I have expressed concern that the use of the rubrics is diverging from this initial purpose and moving toward certifying mastery (Grouling, 2017). We see this happening when administrators and faculty change the language of the dimensions to deficit-based language, establishing a category that reifies students as "insufficient," "unsatisfactory," or otherwise lacking. Too, we often find slippage between using the data from rubric-based assessment as "discovering and improving what students are doing" to a "demonstration of achievement" (Adler-Kassner & O'Neill, 2010, p. 86). As I describe in Chapter 7, observing that a large number of zero scores were issued in the area of "Evidence and Sources" can give us a clue that something further should be investigated in that area. However, it does *not* tell us that students are unable to use evidence and sources. This point is one I have not only written about here but have stressed in presentations I have done at the state level through our LEAP organization.

The key becomes not the original words used on the rubrics but how the rubrics are used in everyday assessment practice. Lynne (2004) worried that by using psychometric terminology, we are subject to a "ventriloquist's trick" where educational measurement theorists have put words in the mouths of compositionists (p. 16). Her metaphor also works in the opposite direction. Over time, our words become used in ways that are unfamiliar to us. Gallagher (2012) described an event at which he interacted with accreditors who seemed to be using our theories about writing portfolios only to find that it was "a Trojan horse" (p. 23). The accreditors used writing studies terms but twisted them to their own agendas. Is this not what we have seen happen with the VALUE Written Communication rubric? The rubric, created by a team of writing professionals, using our disciplinary terms, was meant to be used with portfolios, with assignment prompts, with student reflections that established the context for writing that writing specialists so highly value. We did our part. We worked together. But we do not ultimately define the context in which our work is used without further action.

To continue the metaphor, to enact change we must not fixate on the ventriloquial figure but to the ventriloquists themselves. When we look at the philanthropic forces behind higher ed, we often see only a large number of impenetrable institutions. It is true that "these movements are larger, more powerful, and better funded than any writing teachers, or even any group of writing teachers, will ever be" (Alder-Kassner, 2012, p. 136). But it is also true that individuals working with institutions have agency. For example, Terry Rhodes, the first Executive Director of VALUE and Vice President of AAC&U's Office of Quality, Curriculum, and Assessment, often expressed an interest in e-portfolios, and I suspect that his connection to Kathleen Blake Yancey—composition e-portfolio specialist and a member of the VALUE Advisory Board—has been influential to his thinking. Similarly, the former Director of LEAP, Susan Albertine taught composition at multiple colleges and universities, no doubt rubbing elbows with multiple compositionists and WPAs. In a talk titled "Writing for Lives Our Students Will Live" in 2016, Albertine drew heavily on her own background as a composition teacher. She argued for "boundary pushing writing assignments" and told of a project where a woman literally wrote on her own body to make an argument about body positivity. She also advocated for Black English being as valid as SEAE. When Adler-Kassner (2017) talks about the EIC, it is easy to see a number of powerful entities working for their own interests in higher education, but it is important to remember that all institutions are made up of actual individuals, and they, too, are agents behind movements such as the VALUE initiative.

That relationship is also not one way—these individuals also interact with and influence our discipline. A 2021 book on outcomes edited by Kelly-Riley and Elliot concluded with a chapter on accreditation and the VALUE multi-state collaborative by Terry Rhodes. Meanwhile, on April 1, 2021, the Association for Writing Across the Curriculum held a virtual event for members that engaged with issues of equity and assessment. On the program was current Executive Director of VALUE, Kate McConnell with a presentation about equity and the VALUE rubrics (Johnson, 2021). Those who directly impact national practice through the VALUE rubrics are participating in our disciplinary venues and doing the work of writing assessment. By interacting meaningfully with these individuals on a professional level—whether they are temporary teachers at our institutions or presenters at our conferences—we influence the forward direction of higher education as a larger, national institution.

Yet, they too are individuals with limited means to act within these power structures. In a personal conversation I had with McConnell, she also expressed frustration with ways the VALUE rubrics had been used outside of their intended purpose, sometimes without the knowledge of the organization itself (personal communication, October 25, 2021). In a follow-up email, McConnell told me that she often sees people cite this misuse to make the argument that the rubrics are not helpful tools. For her and the AAC&U, partnering with those using the rubrics and creating resources with and for them is key to "making sure these pieces are working in concert" (personal communication, February 17, 2022). McConnell is conscious of the way the VALUE rubrics exist within their own system, one that she hopes to intentionally support: "While we can't, of course, control how rubrics get used 'out there,' we do nonetheless feel responsible to ensure that 'bad' or unintended uses are not resulting from a lack of support or guidance from the initiative itself" (personal communication, February 17, 2022). The frustration and concern about how boss texts circulate within power structures, then, is also something that impacts the work of the "bosses" themselves. The AAC&U takes their call as stewards seriously, but part of having a freely available and widely used resource means it will be implemented outside of the overall framework. In fact, it may be that those that most lack support, such as the faculty at St. Rita's, are the most likely to find and implement an approach they do not have the resources to fully use. To distribute the rubrics only to those who undergo training in how to use them, like Kristen and others at Oak did, would mean the resources are less widely distributed.

What I have often characterized in this book at a means of exerting control or power is not done with malintent but rather from a desire for what McConnell refers to as "implementation fidelity," an issue she sees not only with the VALUE rubrics but with any assessment tool. The administrator's dilemma at this national level is how to make sure that the tools provided are adaptable while still ensuring that they are used the way they were designed. In my study, we see how difficult that balance can be when faculty from all disciplines, backgrounds, and opinions on assessment are involved in the process. So, too, the AAC&U relies on a variety of entities with their own agendas for funding and support themselves. Currently, the AAC&U is committed to revising the rubrics and are in the process of seeking funding to do so. If funding is secured, then another group of stakeholders and their views will need to be considered as a part of the process. McConnell is passionate about the revisions going forward, with or without funding. She sees the need to think about equity and involve both students and faculty in the process. Like local leaders, it is important for key officials at national organizations to think deeply about their own role in higher education and the power embedded within those roles, and McConnell is interested in such conversations.

It is not only interaction with the members of national organizations that matters, but also who these individuals are and what backgrounds they bring to their work that matters. Inoue (2021b) reminded us that the authors of the CWPA outcomes statement "are White academics, most of whom do not specialize in racial theories." So, too, are the faculty teams writing the VALUE rubrics. When authorship of these boss texts is granted only to the organization, it obscures both the expertise of these authors and their Whiteness. I call on organizations, such as the AAC&U, to make the individual names behind these documents visible: to list the faculty teams as authors on the rubrics themselves so that all can have a better understanding of what backgrounds—both helpful and harmful—they may have brought to their writing. Such transparency can also help us identify what expertise is missing from the conversation, whether that is the lived experiences of scholars of color, of contract faculty members, or of international English speakers. Organizational authorship implies consensus. Yet, consensus is itself a grand narrative, one steeped in White assumptions (Martinez, 2020). The assumption that a boss text represents consensus shuts down critique of systems, and the inability to contact individual authors curbs future discussion.

Cutting Our Strings

In addition to recognizing that those who speak for and through national organizations, such as the AAC&U, are also individuals, we must recognize that the national organizations within our own discipline are not homogenous. When we rally behind the values of composition, we assume and promote a consensus that is unlikely at best and dangerous at worse. While there are threshold concepts that connect us as a discipline, we are a diverse set of individuals with our own standpoints in relation to higher education and the field itself. We have often failed to recognize and honor these differences, and thus it comes as a shock to some—a disruption—when someone challenges our assumed consensus. Rather, such challenges should be an integral part of our regular practices.

For example, for years there has been an assumption that the CWPA outcomes are common wisdom in the field and are what first-year composition students should be striving for. Much like the LEAP outcomes and VALUE rubrics, the CWPA Outcomes Statement began as a way to resist movement toward standards in higher education (Ericsson, 2005). Yet, they circulate in similar ways as other boss texts. As Gallagher (2012) maintained: "Outcome statements take on an aura of finality, of achieved and unimpeachable institutional authority" (p. 45). Perhaps this is why when the CWPA created a task force co-chaired by Asao Inoue and Beth Brunk-Chaves to apply anti-racism to the outcomes, the result was not what the board seemed to expect. That is, the recommendations of the task force did more than reword the outcomes; the task force challenged the very notion of outcomes to begin with. They attempted to change the very context of the choices presented to WPAs by their national organization, and they encountered enough resistance to this change that they ultimately split off from the CWPA and formed their own national organization, the *Institute of Race, Rhetoric, and Literacy.*

In June 2021, this group released their statement on first-year writing goals, clearly stating: "Each goal is structured after the previous CWPA outcomes, but they are not outcomes. They do not identity preconceived ideas about what students will produce in a writing course" (Beavers, et al., 2021). Interestingly, like the original LEAP outcomes, these "goals" are vague areas rather than statements that lead with "students will" and begin with verbs. Such work can begin to change the context of our choices. Yet, it is still too early to know how this work will grow, shift, and be applied by WPAs. Although I personally hope to apply this new work to the curriculum in my home writing program, I am skeptical that any new syllabus that breaks from "students will" plus Bloom's taxonomy verb format will be approved through official channels and curriculum committees at my university. This genre is too entrenched in academia. Are we willing to go as far as to *not* have our first-year writing courses approved as a part of a core curriculum? This is a potential real consequence and one that we should examine carefully.

Or do we propose one set of "outcomes" for the official documents of the university, knowing the audience is committee members and accreditors, and another set of "goals" for students? If so, does this do anything to actually change the context of writing across the university? Does it create any kind of real, sustainable change within the practice of teaching writing beyond our own classrooms? I agree with Inoue (2021a) that: "Doing antiracist and anti-White supremacist work in an organization is about *dismantling the structures and policies that those in the org have heard dearly*, such as the Outcomes Statement." But I am curious how, and if, this work can ultimately shift the actual practice of everyday administrators as well. Will we soon see these new antiracist goals turned into outcome statements turned into rubrics, or can we cut the strings binding us once and for all? If we were to bring these goals to the revision of the VALUE rubrics, for instance, could that produce meaningful change, or would it only twist the good work of our newest professional organization in unintended directions?

Perhaps more importantly, how will this work reach those who do the work of writing assessment but who do not circulate in writing studies arenas. It is important to remember that at both Oak and St. Rita's administrators went looking for national practice in writing assessment for a reason. They did not necessarily seek out best or most current practice but sought *national* practices that would bring them the social capital their schools needed. In this age of austerity, philanthropists provide funding that these schools may not otherwise have to gain recognition, meet accreditors standards, and stay in business. In the case of the AAC&U VALUE rubrics, funding and assessment work is linked to the collection of student artifacts and their assessment with rubrics. While some faculty may have no idea where the rubrics they use stem from, in this study we have also seen faculty invoke these systems of power strategically for their own ends. Dwayne purposefully and strategically puts St. Rita's on the radar of the AAC&U. He writes a piece about St. Rita's for them to publish, and even though it ends up being more aspirational than he hoped, it helps his own tenure case. Even surly Gerald notes that what Dwayne is doing with the VALUE rubrics is important for the recognition of a school like theirs. And when the VALUE rubrics are not implemented, they are "re-discovered" by the next St. Rita's administrator, also wanting to link to national norms.

Meanwhile at Oak, Associate Provost Philip takes advantage of the funding provided by the AAC&U grant to give the writing program support to build their own rubric—one that ultimately bears very little resemblance to the VALUE rubric. While Brad scoffs at assessment on the national level, even he admits that it keeps the doors open and his paycheck coming in. It allows him to do the work he values as an individual teacher, not through providing rubrics for his own classroom but by placing the burden of assessment on other shoulders. Because the university performs well for accreditors, he can do what he wants in his classroom—throw out the syllabus, bring in translingual pedagogy: take risks. Meanwhile, Jeremy at St. Rita's is tied to a competency-based model of basic writing in part because St. Rita's has not solidified their status in the way that Oak has. Closure was, and remains, a very real threat at St. Rita's. That anxiety manifested multiple times in the interviews I conducted.

The ones setting the context for these practices that compositionists may find problematic are those who fund and cut funding to higher education in the first place. Nicholas Behm and Keith Miller (2012) called for "the rebuke of public policy makers and accrediting agencies who attempt to prescribe Standard English—the language of Whiteness—as the ultimate template and touchstone for evaluating all student writing" (p. 137). Being able to take up this call means better understanding systems of power. It means understanding both social and *financial* power structures. It also means being aware of national sources of data that carry institutional weight. For example, I have frequently used the National Census on Writing to gather data that may be persuasive to administrators. Yet, my own WPA training did not include learning about where to get such data or how to use it. It was only in talking to Dwayne during this research project that I learned about the Integrated Postsecondary Education Data System (IPEDS) and the wealth of data that is collected nationally on institutions there. Such knowledge has allowed me to counter dubious claims made by administrators about how our institution compares to other institutions. As WPAs, faculty, and administrators, we need training on these national data sources—what the boss texts are and who the bosses are—and how to use them strategically. And then we must use them to talk back to systems of power and to fight misinterpretation and misuse of boss texts like the VALUE rubrics. So, too, we must become voices within organizations like the AAC&U, publishing work in the *Chronicle of Higher Education* and well-read publications and forwarding what we know to the wide-spread audiences engaged in writing assessment decision making. Even so, for any one individual, it may not be enough to change the context, not without our national organizations also changing theirs, listening to diverse voices, and advocating for national policy changes in higher education.

SHAPING LOCAL INSTITUTIONS

At times, institutional power may appear unidirectional—money flows from philanthropists to intermediaries to local institutions. Local institutions, such as Oak and St. Rita's, rely on national organizations, such as the AAC&U, to fund assessment initiatives, and these organizations rely on philanthropists, such as Gates and Lumina for their financial capital. However, social capital or "reputation, status, stature, or prestige" operates differently. In her definition of social capital, Seawright (2017) drew on Bourdieu, who used the example of a father figure as someone with social capital—someone who is authorized to speak on behalf of the family as a whole (p. xxiv). So, too, are national organizations, whether it is the AAC&U or the CWPA, authorized to speak for all WPAs, teachers, and administrators through their common outcomes and rubrics. To extend the father metaphor, though, there are different approaches to this role.

The AAC&U has historically taken the position of stewards of higher education rather than technocrats. The primary difference in this approach is that steward's emphasis on nurturing individual choice rather than dictating practice from above (Adler-Kassner, 2008). Therefore, the AAC&U's social capital—their reputation as stewards—relies on local institutions and individuals using and adapting the VALUE rubrics for their own assessment practices. Just as administrators at Oak and St. Rita's draw upon the AAC&U to gain social capital for their institutions, the AAC&U solidifies their social capital through the position that their rubrics are adaptable. The fact that local assessment experts are sharing the rubric at their institutions is seen by the AAC&U as evidence of their validity. There is, then, a certain social power granted to local institutions and the groups that conduct assessment at them.

Local committees do have an impact on local practice. For example, the writing committee at Oak and the general education committee at St. Rita's decide on writing and assessment practice for their institutions. At Oak, the committee approves which courses count as writing designated; at St. Rita's, the committee determines which courses are a part of the core curriculum. These decisions have real institutional power. At St. Rita's, for example, there is concern that certain courses—even certain disciplines—will not survive if they are not required classes. Thus, the way that St. Rita's uses the VALUE rubrics to determine the outcomes of the core curriculum has real effects on the working lives of faculty. Oak's committee may have a less immediate effect since they only determine whether the course counts for the writing credit; however, to the extent that faculty follow approved syllabi, they determine what counts as enough writing to qualify. Furthermore, they specify pedagogical practices, such as peer review, as key to writing pedagogy and look for reference to these in course proposals.

Ultimately, these groups determine how they will use the VALUE rubrics. Devitt (2004) explained that with any genre, groups accept or reject variations. This may become more difficult as specific genres become more entrenched in institutions, but the groups do have power over genre variation. We see this power used at Oak when Associate Provost Philip provided the AAC&U funding to the writing program to create a rubric, but the writing committee created one that is vastly different from the VALUE Written Communication rubric. We see it used at St. Rita's when the general education committee rejects the suggestion to make the writing outcomes more like the VALUE rubric but instead sticks to the outcome about sentence variety to reflect actual practice and appease Dr. Z. These committees may not challenge the idea of outcomes or rubrics, but they set the context for those outcomes and rubrics to be applied in core courses and writing designated courses.

Participation and interaction with these committees is often seen as tedious by faculty. Dr. Z states that he does committee work "under duress," and Brad says he only cares about his own classroom. Both see this type of work as extra and annoying rather than as a key part of their own institutional role. Yet, these committees are key to connecting national institutional practice to local institutional power. For example, as WPA at an institution with upper-level writing designated courses but no WAC program, I have long hoped for a way to impact those courses. I offered workshops through our office of Strategic Learning and have presented about writing assessment at our local university assessment forums. Using data from the National Census on Writing and documents produced by the CCCCs and NCTE, I wrote a document specifying what counts nationally as a writing course for my department chair. Yet, I found my participation on the university core curriculum committee to be the best way to subtly influence these courses. Here I drew on boss texts, such as the form for core approval, and modified them to clearly state that writing courses needed to involve a process of feedback and revision. Whether or not this impacts actual classroom practice is another matter, but this change will impact how the committee evaluates and approves courses as writing designated.

Local Institutional Standpoints

Just as individual faculty members occupy a particular standpoint in relation to the power of their institutions, so do local institutions occupy a particular standpoint within the institution of higher education. It is a myth that national practice—whether the VALUE rubrics or CWPA outcomes—can be applied evenly or will be seen the same across these local institutional standpoints. As seen throughout this study, Oak and St. Rita's occupy significantly different standpoints. As an open-access school in a depressed region of the country, St. Rita's serves an economically and racially diverse student population, many of whom would be denied access at other institutions. Yet, rather than recognize this as one particular standpoint within the institution of higher education, St. Rita's draws on national practice to compare itself with institutions that occupy different standpoints. In so doing, the faculty view their students as "underprepared" or "insufficient" rather than seeing the value added by their particular student population. Thus, their strategy is to try and be more like a "normal" college. Gerald mentioned that St. Rita's is acquiring land for a dorm and build-ing an athletic center in an attempt to be more of a traditional college. St. Rita's attempts to enact the institution of higher education through these practices as well as through attempting to get their students up to the standards they per-ceive as the norm across higher education.

While we should hold those at St. Rita's accountable for their practice, we should also remember that they lack many of the privileges enjoyed by faculty members at Oak. At Oak, facilitators are regularly brought in to run work-shops on writing pedagogy and assessment, faculty are funded for participating in assessment initiatives, and the majority are protected by tenure. No mat-ter how involved writing and assessment professionals are at the national level, when local institutions don't have funding to send faculty to conferences or to bring workshop leaders to campus, then we rely on local professionals to inter-pret and apply documents, such as the VALUE rubrics, when they find them freely available online.[11] So, too, national organizations such as the CWPA have offered evaluator services that, while valuable, are out of reach financially for the typical writing program. When we look at somewhere like St. Rita's that has only a handful of English faculty operating within a humanities department without a program or program director, we must acknowledge that they simply do not have the access to resources larger departments and programs benefit from. Thus, our own financial and social structures privilege the education of some students over others.

Elizabeth Kleinfeld (2020) called for a recalibration of expectations within writing programs to be in line with both material and emotional resources. Such a recalibration is necessary, but it also begs the question of how our national organizations get resources to those who might most benefit from them. Could, perhaps, evaluator services be tied to accreditation efforts, or provide a sliding scale of services at different price points? While I do not begrudge any speakers or workshop facilitators for being paid by their labor, like systems of publication, this can curtail the distribution of ideas. Furthermore, as seen in Chapter 7, White faculty still dominate our local institutions and are more likely to be pro-tected by tenure and to make their voices heard. In reality, it is these individuals (often White and male) who benefit from academic freedom, which they in turn may use to maintain outmoded, racist pedagogies (Branson & Sanchez, 2021). We must work to diversify our faculty lines and to fight against the labor ineq-uities that allow some individuals to hide behind academic freedom and tenure while keeping teaching faculty from enacting anti-racist pedagogies.

---

11   As the pandemic has moved us into more virtual spaces, we can hope that these workshop and conference opportunities may become more accessible and more affordable for those at institutions such as St. Rita's.

COMPOSITIONISTS ON CAMPUS

Part of the impetus for this study was to see how national rubrics created by specialists in writing were applied and adapted by non-writing specialists. There has historically been a narrative that the compositionist on campus must get involved in writing assessment and guide local application, and that when they do, all is well. But aside from the writing center director at Oak who was not involved with the writing committee or curriculum, there were no faculty who were affiliated with the discipline of rhetoric and composition at the two institutions I studied. It would be simple to say that writing at both St. Rita's and Oak is operating outside of our discipline. In many ways, this does seem to be true. Kristen is a history professor. Her predecessor, Ben, is a computer science professor. At St. Rita's, Dr. Z actively separates himself from the field of composition and seems to run off compositionists: Jessica worked as a compositionist at St. Rita's but left after a few years when she could not make the change she wanted. Dwayne took up the charge of composition, but he is a creative writer by training. These factors made the two schools ideal for my desire to study institutions where non-disciplinary experts implemented the VALUE rubrics for writing assessment. Yet, who is "in" our discipline and who is "out" is more complex. As seen throughout this study, what is on paper is not always representative of actual practice. A degree in rhetoric and composition may not mean any expertise in assessment, while those from other degrees may come to acquire both training and experience in writing pedagogy and evaluation.

At Oak, several of the faculty members who I interviewed talked about their experience with writing and assessment as graduate students. In each case, I recognized the program and/or the director as someone well-known in our field. Shawna, a professor of religious studies, participated in the first assessment of writing at Oak in Summer 2018. As a graduate assistant in her Ph.D. program, she taught writing, and she now teaches an upper-level writing intensive course on race and religion. In this class, she has implemented a portfolio, a practice she took from her graduate training. She was curious to participate in the writing assessment at Oak because she found it fascinating when she attended a campus-wide forum on writing conducted by Linda Adler-Kassner during her graduate studies. This was her first experience in seeing how writing conventions varied significantly across the disciplines, and she brings this understanding to her work as a rater in the assessment at Oak. Similarly, Wendy, the coordinator of multilingual learning at Oak, drew on her experience in graduate school when she participated in the 2018 assessment. Although her focus as a scholar is on German linguistics, Wendy has a graduate certificate in teaching ESL and has taught composition courses at multiple institutions. When I interviewed her, she was teaching a first-year writing section at Oak that focused on bilingualism. Before coming to Oak, Wendy worked in a prestigious writing center where she applied her knowledge of language acquisition to writing. She brings this background into her teaching at Oak and works to make her classroom a place that "builds bridges between the international community and the domestic community." Finally, at St. Rita's, Dwayne continued to draw on his training as a graduate student in a composition program run by Andrea Lunsford. His view of error was influenced by this background, and while he is unable to fully resist Dr. Z's focus on error, he does at least change practice at St. Rita's so that faculty do not repeatedly count the same "error" against students.

These faculty members had training in writing instruction and assessment beyond what was offered at their current institution. Those of us who work as WPAs in first-year writing or WAC programs should consider, then, how our institutional role is often influential beyond our local institutional context. If practicum courses and TA training only focuses on the immediate need to train TAs in our programs, if we only focus on teaching writing at research institutions, then we neglect the chance to influence practice more broadly. Handing a TA a syllabus to teach or a rubric to assess writing may solve the immediate need for an instructor, but it does not prepare that instructor to think in new educational settings. So, too, must writing across the curriculum efforts focus on training graduate students as well as faculty. These opportunities as graduate students may be the only direct interaction future faculty have with writing pedagogy and assessment, and it is highly influential to their future practice.

The training we provide in WAC workshops and TA practicums can also help these future faculty think about the institution of higher education itself. If we see the goal of these opportunities as actually changing the institution, then we must teach the ability to read and resist institutional power. As Seawright (2017) stated: "Teaching our students to read institutions empowers them to decide what role they will play in supporting or deconstructing those institutions" (p. 101). While her book discussed the implications for professional writing pedagogy, such instruction is paramount for graduate studies. This questioning of institutional power and our place within it is also inherently tied to race relations in the United States. Inoue (2021b) perfectly posed the question: "Good assessment is local assessment, but what happens when we cannot count on our local teachers to be trained in race theories?" Local assessment stories, such as the ones I've shared in this book, show that we cannot expect this training, and worse, some local teachers may actively promote White supremacist ideology. Gerald Z directly called the students at St. Rita's background, "culturally thin," but he was not alone in promoting White ideology, stressing White languaging or even making racialized assumptions about students' preparation and backgrounds. When faculty and administrators have the tools they need to examine assessment from the lens of race, then they can make important adaptations to national texts. For example, one respondent to my 2016 survey about the Written Communication rubric, noted that they planned to modify the "Control of Syntax and Mechanics" dimension of the VALUE rubric because it maintained "the White privilege of standard English speakers."

Yet, this knowledge—of writing, of assessment, of race theory—is often the responsibility of the individual rather than the institution. Martinez (2020) pointed out that minoritized perspectives are often found in elective course offerings rather than core classes. The same is often true within graduate programs. Adding these perspectives and introducing critical race theories in all graduate training, particularly TA training, is key to providing the foundation that future faculty need to interact with and question the authority of boss texts. This training is often not a part of practicum courses, or when it is, it is addressed in problematic ways (de Müeller & Ruiz, 2017). Addressing racial injustice is the work of every discipline, but compositionists are particularly well-suited because of our involvement in TA training and WAC efforts on campuses. We may not be present at every institution, but as seen with many faculty members interviewed for this study, those who hear our words and attend our trainings often take that with them to their own careers.

Here we also need to take individual responsibility for what was institutionally lacking in our own educational histories. Although Black feminists have always made pro-Black work central to their careers (Jones et al. 2021), compositionists as a whole have not been trained in race or assessment. To make this change, then, we must ourselves seek out the perspectives our own education has lacked. As Natasha Jones, Laura Gonzales, and Angela Haas (2021) recently reminded us, we must ask, "What expertise do we need in order to address anti-Blackness that has been present in our program or organization from the start?" (p. 31). Too often we assume that if we teach and work from our own values that we will not be contributing to the ecology of assessment that is steeped in Whiteness. But as Patti Poblete (2021) noted in her own response to the 2021 CWPA outcomes debate: we should not be surprised when "we get called out for saying things that reflect White supremacy. **Because we do.** It's what we're trained to do. It's what we've been doing. It's the air we breathe and the water we wade through" (p. 182–183). We, too, have been trained in systems of White supremacist language ideology and until we re-train ourselves by listening to diverse voices in our field, reading critical race theory, and interrogating our own institutional power, the real work cannot begin. The responsibility for this work lies with both us as individuals and with the institution at large. Politically, it may seem more acceptable to fund training in assessment than training in critical race theory. But we must make the argument that to ethically do assessment—if that is even a possibility—we must be trained to look at race and its interaction with our systems of assessment and power.

SHAPING THE INSTITUTION IN THE CLASSROOM

Even though groups such as core curriculum and writing committees are involved in deciding how the VALUE rubrics are used on their campuses, there is no guarantee this affects individual classroom practice. As with all boss texts, "Individuals must *actively* take up the discourses a text presents" (LaFrance, 2019, p. 44). Those in writing program administration sometimes talk about curriculum or assessment in programmatic terms without acknowledging individual, lived, material realities. Institutional ethnography helps us see the ways that pedagogy is "a highly individualized and material process" (LaFrance, 2019, p. 49). Even Gerald acknowledged, "Curriculum isn't on a piece of paper. It's in the classroom where people are acting it out and doing it." Within assessment, we often note a tension between what we call the institution—the external forces and administrators who require accountability, assessment, reporting—and the individual—the lone pedagogue at work in their classroom. But it is together that they make up the institution. Thus, we must take institutional critique to "the actualities of an individual's everyday work" (LaFrance, 2019, p. 15).

Chapter 7 focused on this connection with the individual by telling the stories of Gerald Z at St. Rita's and Brad at Oak. While Gerald and Brad are not meant to represent all White male professors, or even particular archetypes, the overlap we see in their stories is that they operate from a viewpoint in which the classroom instructor is at odds with institutional structures. Gerald rails against disciplinary norms in composition as well as norms in academia as a whole. Although Brad's definition of the problems with academia are opposite of Gerald's, he too finds fault with academia as a system. It's not that these challenges are unwarranted—they often are—it's that both Gerald and Brad see themselves as *external* to the institutional power of higher education while occupying a standpoint of ruling within that institution. For better or worse, they do not recognize their own institutional power. Even though Gerald exerts his influence frequently, the extent to which he recognizes his own bullying behavior is unclear. He knows he's "an opinionated guy," but Dwayne commented that "Dr. Z has no idea how much he has interfered" with the assessment procedures at St. Rita's. Similarly, Brad expresses a deep commitment to critical pedagogy and linguistic justice in his classroom while enacting the role of White male professor on the writing committee, unaware of the valuable perspective on writing that his colleague from Singapore brings to the table. By separating the role of the instructor from the power of the institution, we deny the way that individual and idiosyncratic preferences become institutionalized, particularly when those individuals have status within the institution due to position and racial privilege.

For students, who usually do not see the inner workings of the institution of higher education, who may never know that their writing is taken from the classroom and passed to national assessors in order to hold the university accountable for their learning, the instructor is the face of the institution. Often administrators dictate policies that go on syllabi, but students may not be aware of what material their instructors create and what is handed down to them. When they see a strict attendance policy or cell phone policy, they see an individual teacher enacting the role of cop in the classroom. As Gannon (2020) reminded us, when we tell students to trust us but then state in bold in the syllabus that they must provide documentation for every absence, we reinforce that the institution of education is about legalese not trust. Whether guided by common administrative language or not, when instructors act as police in the classroom—attendance police, cell phone police, or grammar police—they reinforce that policing is an everyday practice within the university.

So, too, when students are given rubrics—perhaps ones made by writing committees, perhaps by individual teachers—that include a dimension labeled "unacceptable" and then produce work that the teacher marks in that area of the rubric, no amount of teacher feedback or revision opportunities can entirely counter the power of that language. Rubrics, by their very structure, imply that students should reach a particular end point that is not of their own determining. We can remove the letters A, B, C, D from a rubric and replace them with 4, 3, 2, and 1, but these changes make little difference in communicating to students that they should be progressing linearly through their studies. The form of the rubric indicates that students should aim for the top dimension of the rubric, even if it asks them to enact an identity that is counter to their own. In much the same way as our policy may communicate a lack of trust in students, so, too, an instructor can ask students to set their own goals for writing and can tell them they do not need to change everything to please the teacher, but it is difficult for the genre of the rubric to convey that same message. Rubrics place student work, and students themselves, in categories, in boxes, and thus constrain them to a particular role within the system of their education.

Creating rubrics with students is a solution for some. A limitation of my particular study is the lack of data from students adapting a rubric. However, if the same trends exist that we've seen here with faculty adapting a rubric, then this solution is suspect. When faculty adapt rubrics as a committee, they bring their own biases to this process. Their social dynamics and privileges inherently interact with these adaptations. So, too, would it be difficult to remove the racial, gender, and class dynamics from the classroom setting itself when creating or adapting a rubric with students. Students, too, have ideas of how writing should be evaluated that come from years in our educational system. In addition, creating a rubric collaboratively with students continues to reinforce the value of consensus, that we all need to agree on common outcomes and standards for our writing. Inoue (2015) challenged us to think about how students might understand the evaluation of their own texts "as more than an individual's failure to meet expectations or goals, but also as a confluence of many other structures in language, school, and society" (p. 19). For students to understand this requires an understanding of institutions and institutional racism that must be explicitly taught. It requires far more than a class period of collaborative rubric-making, and it is a big ask for teachers who may not be well versed in these issues themselves.

INDIVIDUAL STANDPOINTS & LABOR

The individual position of any given instructor and how they interact with local and national boss texts is paramount to understanding how institutional power functions (LaFrance, 2019). Individual standpoint affects the choices available to individual pedagogues. Instructors themselves do not set the context in which they make their choices, and our valorization of the individual professor masks this fact. As Martinez (2020) reminded us, the idea that an individual can choose happiness—or success—for themselves ignores the historical realities of oppression. This statement is true whether we are talking about upper mobility within society, student successes within educational systems, or instructors so-called "academic freedom."

In a technical sense, standpoint refers to the particular role that an individual occupies within a system. Institutional ethnographers thus pay attention to references to position titles as signals of how institutions function (Rankin, 2017b). It is telling in this study that neither Kristen nor Dwayne have the titles that are common to writing program administrators. Both Kristen and former writing committee chair Ben refer to their role as "director," but Barbara, who occupies the position of a writing center *director*, clearly calls Kristen "chair" of the writing committee. While this missing title doesn't affect her day-to-day work, Kristen expressed concern that it signals a lack of long-term institutional support for writing. However, faculty often defer and refer to her as the person responsible for writing pedagogy and assessment on campus. Although Dwayne later became department chair, at the time I visited St. Rita's he had been trying to promote the VALUE rubrics for years only as a member of the general education committee. He tried to advocate for the WPA Outcomes, and what he believed to be best practice in writing pedagogy without any official role related to writing on campus. Perhaps it is not surprising, then, that his own individual success is limited. He lamented that even after everything he did with the VALUE rubrics, a new dean found the AAC&U and LEAP movement independently and presented it like something new on campus. So, too, the newest co-chairs of the general education are repeating work that Dwayne attempted years before. This leaves Dwayne with a sense that the institution does not follow through on its promises and leads to frustration that his efforts go unnoticed. This frustration is magnified when faculty with even less institutional power attempt to make change. Dwayne and Kristen are both White, tenured faculty members.

To resist the frame of the institution takes its toll. Dwayne is exhausted and burnt out after years of challenging the system and his colleagues. His experiences fit with what Kate Navickas (2020) recognized as identity-based emotional labor, which occurs when "previous values and narratives com[e] into conflict with new institutional context, narratives, and roles" (p. 57). Dwayne struggles with attempting to balance what he believes the institution wants with what he believes will benefit students. He struggles with his role on the general education committee, and later as department chair, in conjunction with his role as someone who has a background in rhetorical pedagogy. In the beginning, he hopes for outcomes that match assessment, but by 2018, he admits that using rubrics to create those outcomes might not have been best. What Dwayne really wants is to talk about content of courses, but he rarely attempts that conversation because he does not see it fitting the institutional frame. The discussion of general education at St. Rita's fixates on what Dwayne calls "developmental order." As I outlined in Chapter 2, this conversation is a part of the "great skills" approach to liberal education now dominant in higher education and reinforced by rubrics and skill-based outcomes. No one wants to talk about content at the general education committee meetings because it doesn't fit with this frame.

So, too, are faculty, in Dwayne's words "not wanting to step on each other's toes in terms of academic freedom." Content is the purview of the individual pedagogue, and thus, a more rhetorical first-year writing pedagogy is seen as something for Dwayne to do in his *own* classroom and not something to be changed at the institutional level. Dr. Z, Jeremy, and others across the curriculum at St. Rita's continue their focus on development and skills, viewing sentence-level error as something that must be corrected before focusing on rhetoric. While Dwayne ascribes these views to the individuals at his institution, they too exist within a larger institutional frame. For example, we see this view that error correction must precede rhetoric reflected in VALUE Written Communication rubric. The "Control of Syntax and Mechanics" performance descriptors progress from a benchmark level where language might impede meaning to a capstone level where such language is "graceful." Rhetorical acumen is viewed as an accomplishment that comes from conquering error rather than something can co-exist with error. The rubric alongside other boss texts sets that developmental frame for discussion, and thus Dwayne's colleagues cannot see how he can teach rhetoric when the students "can't even write a sentence." It is only by working within this developmental frame that Dwayne is able to change the curriculum: he is able to move one first-year writing course to the second year. This move is, he stated, "an example of getting my way and still not being happy about it." It is not enough for Dwayne when he continues to see how many students, particularly students of color, don't make it past the first-year course. The vast amounts of labor that Dwayne puts into this change is not ultimately satisfying emotionally because Dwayne's administrator identity is still in conflict with his values as a pedagogue.

It is also important to recognize that while any individual *can* act counter to a group they are in, there are consequences for some more than for others. For example, Dr. Z's outburst at the general education committee results in a decrease in his own labor and responsibilities. He is no longer on the committee and is removed from his role as department head. Since my interview with him was before this incident, I did not get a sense how this affected him emotionally, but we should note that his actual labor load certainly decreased. The ability to resist the institution, and the consequences to doing so are linked heavily with institutional standpoint and privilege.

In contrast, even when the content of a particular class is seen as an issue of academic freedom, the means of assessment are often not. Instructors in first-year classes may be asked to adopt a common rubric, or their own students work may be assessed through an external portfolio completely outside the purview of that classroom or instructor. Even when classroom grading is left to the individual teacher, they may face institutional challenges to implementing alternative assessment. For example, if we look at a classroom practice of using contract grading over rubrics, we run into multiple institutional issues from explaining the practice to our students to defending our grades to administrators. These are not reasons to abandon alternative forms of assessment, but we should realize that they come with a labor cost that some cannot as readily pay as others.

If we stay with using rubrics, then local creation or adaptation is a key practice. Still, adapting or creating a rubric takes a great deal of labor. As Anderson et al. (2013) said about adapting the WPA Outcomes to WAC: "Nothing about adapting outcomes to local contexts is easy; no statement should promise anything but the rewards of that labor-intensive adaptation" (p. 102). Broch Colombi and McBride (2012) described an intense process of team development where faculty take multiple days to disagree about writing assessment before even beginning to move toward a collaborative assessment process. At

Oak, time and resources were dedicated to this process and the faculty had energy to invest on the writing committee, particularly Kristen. Over the course of three years of checking in with Kristen and visiting Oak, I saw her move the committee through multiple rubric drafts, to a summer "test run," to another revision, and then to a first roll-out of the rubric and assessment process. Every faculty member I interviewed at Oak was also on the tenure track. Kristen had a course release. And the summer assessors were compensated with a stipend for their labor. The sheer amount of labor involved in creating local assessment processes is daunting. It's no wonder, then, that so many faculty at St. Rita's, and elsewhere, are tepid in the face of these discussions.

What are the rewards for this labor-intensive process? For Broch Colombi and McBride (2012) it is an assessment that both meets the needs of faculty across the disciplines and the needs of higher administrators. For others, the benefit lies in faculty development. Zawacki et al. (2009) believe that faculty gain the most from collaborating on rubric creation. So, too, Kristen values the role that rubric development can play in faculty development, although Barbara laments the lack of the kind of full-scale faculty development she had at a former institution where she worked in a WAC program. In this study, I did see some positive effects of the rubric-adaptation process on faculty's own pedagogy. For example, Kristen herself began thinking about the context of her assignments, and about how to present students with a "purpose and audience" for their writing. Anson et al. (2012) also believed that better assessment processes would lead to better assignments, and the AAC&U, too, is exploring the relationship between assignment prompts and assessment. This potential benefit of collaborative rubric making or adaptation should not be dismissed. And yet, such benefits should also not be assumed. In my pilot study at my own institution, where the adapted VALUE rubric included "context and purpose" but eliminated "genre and disciplinary conventions," faculty I interviewed expressed a newfound need to have students make their writing readable by all audiences rather than help them learn disciplinary-specific conventions. Nor is this study free from examples where a quick dabbling with assessment led to its misapplication in the classroom. Jeremy at St. Rita's sees the grammar categories on the rubric and then primarily focuses on this area in his instruction. And even though Kristen is clear that the rubric created by the writing committee is not for direct classroom use, the feedback she received from the summer assessment process included comments from faculty members who wanted to take it directly to their classrooms. When collaborative rubric-development and assessment workshops are paired with other professional development, they can be a powerful means of connecting classroom practice to assessment across the institution. However, they should not stand alone or in place of other faculty development. So, too, if the only outcome of assessment practices is faculty development, then participants and writing administrators may find that it is better to focus that time and labor elsewhere.

A part of the administrator's dilemma is how to value assessment labor knowing full well that the systems of accountability often mean that the intellectual contributions of a local assessment team may remain unrecognized by the institution as a whole. For Jacob Babb and Courtney Adams Wooten (2017), a part of recognizing contingent faculty members' contributions to a program is to include them in rubric development and assessment. Yet, even for tenure-line faculty, such labor is not often rewarded in the promotion or annual review process. When faculty participate in such efforts but never see meaningful results or feedback come from them, this can add to their feelings of isolation and frustration. In her dissertation on writing center assessment reports, Kelsie Walker (2018) found that the primary impact of the reports was financial. Institutions used the reports to verify the success of writing centers and renew their funding. The same may be true for writing programs. In Kristen's case, she received financial support for her assessment, but she lacked meaningful dialog with higher administrators about the process. After three years of perfecting her assessment process, she submitted her first report to the university assessment coordinator and the associate provost.[12] I asked her what the response had been to the report, and she replied with a bit of disappointment in her voice: "They both just email responded and told me they got it and appreciated it because we're coming up on accreditation." Dwayne does not get even that. He mentioned a university senate meeting where he wasn't even asked for his report. "It just doesn't make a difference what I say," he told me; "So, I'm just not even saying anything." Here we see the impact on real individuals from the way boss texts operate to uphold institutional power rather than to make meaningful change or even lead to meaningful dialog. To name this frustration is to be able to act upon it, whether that action means pushing for more meaningful responses between levels of the institution or deciding to re-focus our labor on areas we find more productive in the long-term.

SETTING THE CONTEXT: FINDING VALUES

Many in composition have questioned the primacy of the rubric (e.g., Anson et al., 2012; Broad, 2003; Wilson, 2006). This debate is important, but to fully question the power of the rubric, we must locate it within the larger ecology of assessment and uncover the hold it has on systems of higher education. Doing

---

12   By this time, Philip was no longer in the Associate Provost role.

so does not so much question whether or not rubrics *should* be used, but rather asks: who determines whether or not rubrics are used? How do rubrics, as a genre, perpetuate ways of thinking and conventions that fall in line with dominant power systems? The work of this book has been descriptive: to show how these power systems interact within the actual assessment processes at two different institutions. In so doing, I have made suggestions about how power and boss texts may operate at large, but the results here are not meant to be fully generalizable.

I have explored the notion of the rubric as a boss text that interacts with other genres within a larger ecology. Such ecological work is not new but is often discussed in theoretical terms. For example, Inoue (2015) reminded us that each text involved in assessment can only be understood in meaningful ways when seen as a part of the larger assessment ecology. For example, "a rubric, some feedback, a paper, inter-is with the other ecological elements" (p. 126). Genre theory helps us see how the texts within this assessment ecology interact. Devitt (2004) explained that "each genre encourages some actions and not others" (p. 77). By selecting the genre of the rubric for assessment, a committee thus limits themselves to certain actions while encouraging others.

Institutional ethnography adds qualitative research to our theories of genre to show how these limitations play out in actual assessment processes. Within literature that critiques the VALUE movement, there is a concern that the initiative may "be used to justify the continuation of ineffective practices" (Eubanks, 2018, p. 30). The qualitative data added through institutional ethnography can elucidate how and why this happens. Specifically, this study has shown how rubrics have become a stand in for teacher judgement across classroom and university contexts. And following that, student texts—while "authentically" produced within the classroom context—are removed from that context for the purposes of assessment. Assignment prompts are removed from assessment processes as is other contextual information about student writing. Rubrics are no longer genres that work in conjunction with classroom genres, like the assignment prompt or teacher feedback, but are rather stand-ins for all student work in all classrooms across institutional context. This awareness of how genres operate within systems is something we often don't always consider in large-scale or national assessment efforts. So, too, we must include racial privilege as one of the many forces influencing these systems of power. My study has added to what Behm and Miller (2012) called a fourth wave in writing assessment, one that elucidates "the intersection of race and writing assessment" (p. 136). Qualitative studies that explore the impact of assessment practice on the everyday lives of students and faculty working in variety of institutional contexts add to this important discussion of labor and equity in relationship to assessment.

Higher education has historically put too much hope in the genre of the rubric. We have been sold on the idea that it will save us time while still being a meaningful part of an assessment loop meant to improve curriculum and instruction. While a rubric-based assessment can be a piece of this puzzle, we must recognize that the data we gather from large-scale rubric use is extremely limited. Without returning to the context of writing, without returning to what teachers are assigning and what is happening when students write those papers, we know very little about why we are getting the results we see. We need to adjust our own expectations for what we can learn through large-scale, rubric-based assessment, what decisions we can and should make based on it, and how it might lead to follow up research. Over the years I interviewed her, Kristen began to realize the extreme limits of her assessment process. She began in 2016 by stressing that the rubric needed to reflect the writing program outcomes. But in 2018, she realized "it's not actually an assessment of the writing program, it's not an assessment of the writing courses at Oak . . . it is just a place to start." Kristen completes the assessment, turns in her report, and thus satisfies the requirements of the institution. It does not answer the questions she began with about how the outcomes of the program are being taught or learned. While the continued use of this particular assessment at Oak is beyond the scope of this one three-year study, we know how this story often plays out. The assessment is conducted again next year. The director changes. Some tweaks are made to the rubric. And we do it all again. The assessment loop doesn't close, we just become swept up in it, running on hamster wheel, gathering artifacts, scoring with rubrics, writing reports, unable to escape the assessment cycle that has embedded itself in the logic of the neoliberal university.

Returning to the epigraph of this chapter: how do we break free of that cycle and change the context of our choices about assessment? Bob Broad's (2003) method of dynamic criteria mapping (DCM) is appealing for its attempt to disrupt the assessment cycle and focus on the values brought to the assessment over the qualities of student texts. Broad encourages writing programs to host "articulation" sessions over norming sessions. Such sessions are designed to uncover faculty values and provoke discussion rather than to make sure that all faculty align in their scoring practice. Yet, as demonstrated here, we should not assume that local practice is equitable practice. The product of these articulation sessions is still often a rubric or rubric-like scoring criteria that fails to challenge the thinking behind rubrics. A more thorough analysis of such texts is warranted, but a short look at the contributions in Broad et al.'s (2009) edited collection on DCM in practice illustrates this point. In this book, Barry Alford (2009) admitted that the faculty who participated in DCM at his institution wanted a rubric. So, Mid Michigan Community College created one, and with phrasing such as "cannot grasp the key ideas," it maintains deficit-based language (p. 47). Susanmarie Harrington and Scott Weeden (2009) created what they dub an "unrubric." They even ask themselves: "Is the UnRubric a rubric?" (p. 96). They argue it is not because it is meant to be framework for the program, not dictate grading practice. Yet, it looks very much like a holistic rubric, and it appears to dictate a particular relationship between the student author and the faculty reader with language such as this description of a "below passing" final product: "A reader may come away from the essay thinking, 'I expected more'" (p. 117). Thus, they seem to assume that there is nothing problematic about valuing the reader's expectations in the assessment process. But that reader may be Brad or it may be Dr. Z, and their expectations vary drastically.

At one point, I too, helped create what I insisted were "assessment guidelines" and not a rubric for my local writing program. I made the same argument that Harrington and Weeden (2009) do: such a document would give faculty guidance but was not meant to be used directly in the classroom. Yet, year after year I see it linked on syllabi and assignment sheets as the only criteria on which students are graded. Using DCM may shift the context in which the assessment is conducted, but faculty and administrators often still apply the logic of rubrics to the resulting assessment documents. This logic suggests a hierarchy of written products that can be separated from the social conditions of their writing, products that can be read objectively by a reader, whose expectations are also assumed to operate outside this conglomeration of social, political, and racial biases. Our local values are no less suspect than the values of our culture at large. To change the context of our assessment means questioning the values under which higher education operates.

Contract grading has, perhaps, had more success in breaking the frame of assessment. In particular, Inoue's (2019) version of labor-based contract grading operates from the notion that setting a single standard for student writing perpetuates White supremacy. Rather than grading writing on a scale that meets a (often White) reader's expectations, we should grade on labor. This idea resists the very frame of our current assessment ecology. Yet, we still need more studies of how faculty at different institutions use these contracts. Shane Wood (2020) explained that if commenting practices do not change along with the implementation of labor-based contract grading teachers may still perpetuate the larger assessment ecology based on a White habitus. Sherri Craig (2021) argued that contract grading only does more injustice as it "attempts to convince them [Black students and faculty] that the university cares" while in reality, "we cannot correct the violence and the potential for violence in our universities" (p. 146). Further, Ellen Carillo (2021) reminded us that labor as a standard of measurement is not neutral, particularly when we approach it from the angle of disability studies. In my own experience, I have seen new instructors attempt a contract-based system without fully adopting a different ideology than the one they have previously held. We are again stuck in the administrator's dilemma, making changes that ultimately do not change the violence done in our society and thus in our institutions.

When we think of rubrics as a rhetorical genre, we must ask what is the situation to which they respond? As covered in Chapter 2, early writing scales were designed as a labor-saving aid. It takes far less labor to use an already existing rubric for university-wide, programmatic, or even classroom assessment than to make a new one. At my university, the VALUE Written Communication rubric was adapted and implemented in just two brief meetings. Kristen and the writing committee took two-years or more on the process. And yet, they still saw rubrics as less labor-intensive than portfolios. I asked multiple faculty at Oak about a portfolio-based assessment, but I repeatedly was told that such a system would require too much labor, an argument I have encountered on my own campus as well. The portfolio-grading at St. Rita's is labor-intensive, as instructors score all first-year writing portfolios in a day-long marathon. Perhaps this is why the timed essays remain the central focus of the portfolio there, and why the portfolios are scored on a rubric. To offer meaningful feedback to each student would be an impossible task, even at an institution with fewer than 1,000 students. Moreover, the logic of outcomes focuses on the end point of an education, not on the experiences along the way or the embodied labor of learning (Brannon, 2016). These practices exist within a neoliberal capitalist system that values saving labor rather than rewarding it. This mindset is too often a part of WPA work, which has historically been about seeking administrative solutions that "involved shaping the behavior of teachers rather than in any sort of systemic change" (Strickland, 2011, p. 68). Arguments against rubrics must go beyond creating un-rubrics or using contract grading. We must resist the very logic that makes rubrics attractive: the logic of efficiency and accountability, the logic of neoliberalism and austerity, the logic of Whiteness.

Perhaps to hope that we can resist the logic of this system is naive or unrealistic. But at the very least, every time someone proposes a labor-saving measure, I ask: "What if we valued that labor instead?" Too often I hear that teachers should cut down their time responding to student work or that if they take too long grading it is their own fault. The problem of the labor needed for meaningful practice is not only found in education. For example, in a time of high need our university counseling center used a rubric to assess which students received immediate one-on-one services and which could be funneled into group counseling sessions. We've seen the way that the COVID-19 pandemic has stretched our labor thin and has led to difficult decisions. In a time of crisis, relying on time-saving measures can be key. I won't argue that we aren't currently experiencing a crisis in higher education. However, we must also recognize that neoliberalism relies on a rhetoric of crisis to justify austere measures (Scott & Welch, 2016).

Institutional ethnography allows us a means to tie institutional critique to everyday labor practices. LaFrance (2019) noted that our critiques rarely examine "the actualities of an individual's everyday work" (p. 15). Even when they do, the actualities that are written about are the actualities of those who already have position and privilege in the field. The pages of our journals are filled with stories of WPAs and WAC directors who successfully implement new assessment measures in their programs or their classrooms. They are often disciplinary experts with tenure and research releases, not the Kristens and Dwaynes of the WPA world. To fully describe actual assessment practices, our research must go beyond our own experiences and theories to qualitative research at multiple and varied institutions. Whether intended or not, this distancing from the lived experiences of students and faculty—operating in very different local, embodied contexts—works to solidify the place of rubrics within ruling relations. Institutional ethnography asks how these boss texts are put into practice and interpreted by individuals. This institutional perspective can inform our perspective on other genres as well. LaFrance (2019) noted that annual reviews tied to writing center director's official job descriptions can "erase, minimize, and diminish work" (p. 83). Much of our frustration with such processes comes from the lack of meaningful response, but this expectation may be a misconstruction of the role of the boss text, which functions generically to maintain systems not to change them. Whether it is a rubric or another boss text, we must always ask where texts come from and how their context in larger ecologies affects their meaning.

Brad called rubrics a "pastiche." They are always a patchwork of local and institutional power, a combination of compromises, and thus they are never neutral tools. Rather, like Seawright's (2017) example of the police report genre, the genre of the rubric creates cultural capital, capital that benefits both individuals and institutions. To understand that power—and perhaps resist it—we must return to the "text-reader conversations" to see how real material conditions activate these power relations (Smith, 2005, p. 184). When I have critiqued the AAC&U or my participants in this book, it is to invite us all to consider how we all exist and act within systems of power that permeate our work and our everyday interactions. We must continue to interrogate those systems and our role within them.

REFERENCES

Adelman, C., Ewell, P., Gaston, P. & Schneider, C. G. (2014). *The Degree Qualifications Profile*. Lumina Foundation.

Addison, J. (2015). Shifting the locus of control: Why the Common Core State Standards and emerging standardized tests may reshape college writing classrooms. *Journal of Writing Assessment, 8*(1). https://escholarship.org/uc/item/2w69x0w5.

Adler-Kassner, L. (2008). *The activist WPA: Changing stories about writing and writers*. Utah State University Press.

Adler-Kassner, L. (2012). The companies we keep or the companies we would like to try to keep: Strategies and tactics in challenging times. *WPA: Writing Program Administration, 36*(1), 119–140.

Adler-Kassner, L. (2017). 2017 *CCCCs* Chair's Address: Because writing is never just writing. *College Composition and Communication, 69*(2), 317–340. https://www.jstor.org/stable/44783617.

Adler-Kassner, L. & O'Neill, P. (2010). *Reframing writing assessment to improve teaching and learning*. Utah State University Press.

Adler-Kassner, L., Rutz, C. & Harrington, S. (2010). A guide for how faculty can get started using the VALUE rubrics. In T. L. Rhodes. (Ed.), *Assessing outcomes and improving achievement: Tips and tools for using rubrics* (p. 19). American Association of Colleges and Universities.

Adsit, J. & Doe, S. (2020). Educating the faculty writer to "Dance with Resistance": Rethinking faculty development as institutional transformation. In L. Micciche, C. Wooten, J. Babb, K. Costello & K. Navickas (Eds.), *The things we carry: Strategies for recognizing and negotiating emotional labor in writing program administration* (pp. 75–95). Utah State University Press.

Albertine, S. (2016, Sept. 16). Writing for the lives our students will live. [Conference presentation]. Writing Pathways to Disciplinary Learning Conference. Indianapolis, IN, United States.

Alford, B. (2009). DCM as the assessment program: Mid Michigan Community College. In B. Broad, L. Adler-Kassner, B. Alford, J. Detweiler, H. Estrem, S. Harrington, M. McBride, E Stalions & S. Weeden (Eds.), *Organic writing assessment: Dynamic criteria mapping in action* (pp. 37–50). Utah State University Press.

American Association of Colleges and Universities. (n.d.). *Parts of a VALUE rubric*. Association of American Colleges & Universities: A voice and a force for liberal education.

American Association of Colleges and Universities. (n.d.). *Japanese translation of the VALUE rubrics*. Association of American Colleges & Universities: A voice and a force for liberal education. Retrieved March 10, 2022, from https://secure.aacu.org/iMIS/ItemDetail?iProductCode=E-VRALLJAP&Category=RUBRICS.

American Association of Colleges and Universities. (2009a). *Teamwork VALUE rubric*. https://www.aacu.org/value/rubrics/teamwork.

American Association of Colleges and Universities. (2009b). *Written communication VALUE rubric.* https://www.aacu.org/value/rubrics/written-communication.

American Association of Colleges and Universities. (2022) *About AAC&U.* https://www.aacu.org/about.

Anderson, P., Anson, C. M., Townsend, M. & Yancey, K. B. (2013). Beyond composition: Developing a national outcomes statement for writing across the curriculum. In N. N. Behm, G. R. Glau, D. H. Holdstein, D. Roen & E. M. White (Eds.), *The WPA outcomes statement: A decade later.* Parlor Press.

Anson, C. M., Dannels, D. P., Flash, P. & Housley Gaffney, A. L. (2012). Big rubrics and weird genres: The futility of using generic assessment tools across diverse instructional contexts. *The Journal of Writing Assessment, 5*(1). https://escholarship.org/us/item/93b9g3t6.

Association of American Colleges and Universities. (2006). *Communicating commitment to liberal education: A self-study guide for institutions.* Association of American Colleges & Universities.

Association of American Colleges and Universities. (2007). *College learning and the new global century: Executive summary with findings from employer survey.* Association of American Colleges & Universities.

Association of American Colleges and Universities. (2015a, March 21). Integrating signature assignments into the curriculum and inspiring design. *Tool Kit Resources.* Association of American Colleges & Universities. https://web.archive.org/web/20150321221536/http://aacu.org/sites/default/files/Signature-Assignment-Tool.pdf.

Association of American Colleges and Universities. (2015b). *The LEAP challenge: Education for a world of unscripted problems.* Association of American Colleges & Universities.

Association of American Colleges and Universities. (2017). *The VALUE Institute: Learning outcomes assessment at its best.* Association of American Colleges & Universities. https://www.aacu.org/VALUEInstitute.

Association of American Colleges and Universities. (2020). What liberal education looks like: What it is, who it's for & where it happens. American Association of Colleges and Universities.

Babb, J.; & Wooten, C.A. (2017). Traveling on the assessment loop: The role of contingent labor in curriculum development. In S. Kahn, W. B. Lalicker & A. Lynch-Biniek (Eds.), *Contingency, exploitation, and solidarity: Labor and action in English composition.* The WAC Clearinghouse; University Press of Colorado. https://doi.org/10.37514/PER-B.2017.0858

Baker-Bell, A. (2020). *Linguistic justice: Black language, literacy, identity, and pedagogy.* National Council of Teachers of English.

Balester, V. (2012). How writing rubrics fail: Toward a multicultural model. In M. Poe & A. Inoue (Eds.), *Race and writing assessment* (pp. 63–77). Peter Lang.

Bawarshi, A. (2000). The genre function. *College English, 62*(3), 335–360. https://doi.org/10.2307/378935.

Bazerman, C. (2004). Speech acts, genres, and activity systems: How texts organize activity and people. In C. Bazerman & P. Prior (Eds.), *What writing does and how it does it: An introduction to analyzing texts and textual practices* (pp. 309-356). Lawrence Erlbaum Associates.

Bean, J. (2011). *Engaging ideas: The professor's guide to integrating writing, critical thinking, and active learning in the classroom* (2nd ed.). Jossey-Bass.

Beavers, M., Brunk-Chaves, B.L., Green, N., Inoue, A.B., Ruiz, I., Saenkhum, T. & Young, V.A. (2021, June 11). Abbreviated statement toward first-year composition goals. *Institute of Race, Rhetoric, and Literacy.* https://tinyurl.com/IRRL-FYCGoals.

Behizadeh, N. & Engelhard, Jr., G. (2011). Historical view of the influences of measurement and writing theories on the practice of writing assessment in the United States. *Assessing Writing, 16,* 189–211. https://doi.org/10.1016/j.asw.2011 .03.001.

Behm, N. & Miller, K.D. (2012). Challenging the frameworks of color-blind racism: Why we need a fourth wave of writing assessment scholarship. In M. Poe & A. Inoue (Eds.), *Race and writing assessment* (pp. 127–138). Peter Lang.

Beld, J.M. & Kuh, G.D. (2014, October 20). *Making assessment matter: How not to let your data die on the vine.* [Conference presentation]. Assessment Institute, Indianapolis, IN, United States.

Bennett, M. & Brady, J. (2014). A radical critique of the learning outcomes assessment movement. *Radical Teacher: A Socialist, Feminist, and Anti-Racist Journal on the Theory and Practice of Learning, 100,* 146–153. https://doi.org/10.5195/rt.2014.171.

Brannon, L. (2016). Afterward: Hacking the body politic. In N. Welch & Scott, Tony (Eds.), *Composition in the age of austerity* (pp. 220–229). Utah State University Press.

Branson, T.S. & Sanchez, J.C. (2021). Programmatic approaches to antiracist writing program policy. *WPA: Writing Program Administration 44* (3), 71–76. https:// wpacouncil.org/aws/CWPA/asset_manager/get_file/604393?ver=1.

Broad, B. (2003). *What we really value: Beyond rubrics in teaching and assessing writing.* Utah State University Press.

Broad, B.; Adler-Kassner, L.; Alford, B.; Detweiler, J.; Estrem, H.; Harrington, S.; McBride, M.; Stalions, E.; & Weeden, S. (Eds.), (2009). *Organic writing assessment: Dynamic criteria mapping in action.* Utah State University Press.

Broch Colombini, C. & McBride, M. (2012). "Storming and norming": Exploring the value of group development models in addressing conflict in communal writing assessment. *Assessing Writing, 17,* 191–207. https://doi.org/10.1016/j.asw.2012 .05.002.

Brooke, C. & Carr, A. (2015). Failure can be an important part of writing development. In L. Adler-Kassner & E. Wardle (Eds.), *Naming what we know: Threshold concepts of writing studies.* Utah State University Press.

Campbell, M. L. (2006). Institutional ethnography and experience as data. In D. E. Smith (Ed.)., *Institutional ethnography as practice* (pp. 91–108). Rowman & Littlefield.

Campbell, M.L. & Gregor, F. (2004). *Mapping social relations: A primer in doing institutional ethnography*. AltaMira Press.

Carillo, E.C. (2021). *The hidden inequities in labor-based contract grading*. Utah State University Press.

Craig, S. (2021). Your contract grading ain't it. *WPA: Writing Program Administration 44* (3), 145–146. https://wpacouncil.org/aws/CWPA/asset_manager/get_file /604397?ver=1.

Crowley, S. (1998). *Composition in the university: Historical and polemical essays*. University of Pittsburgh Press.

Crusan, D. J. (2015). Dance, ten; looks, three: Why rubrics matter. *Assessing Writing, 26*, 1–4. https://doi.org/10.1016/j.asw.2015.08.002

Davila, B. (2012). Indexicality and "Standard" Edited American English: Examining the link between conceptions of standardness and perceived authorial identity. *Written Communication, 29*(2), 180–207. https://doi.org/10.1177/0741088312438691.

Davila, B. (2017). Standard English and colorblindness in composition studies: Rhetorical constructions of racial and linguistic neutrality. *WPA: Writing Program Administration, 40*(2), 154–173. http://associationdatabase.co/archives/40n2 /40n2davila.pdf

Davila, B. & Elder, C. (2019). "Shocked by Incivility": A survey of bullying in the WPA workplace. In C. Elder & B. Davila (Eds.), *Defining, locating, and addressing bullying in the WPA workplace* (pp. 18–33). Utah State University Press.

de Müller, G. G. & Ruiz, I. (2017). Race, silence, and writing program administration: A qualitative study of US college writing programs. *WPA: Writing Program Administration 40* (2), 19–39. http://associationdatabase.co/archives/40n2/40n2 mueller_ruiz.pdf.

DeVault, M. L. & McCoy, L. (2006). Institutional ethnography: Using interviews to investigate ruling relations. In D.E. Smith (Ed.). *Institutional ethnography as practice* (pp. 15–44). Rowman & Littlefield.

Devitt, A. J. (2004). *Writing genres*. Southern Illinois University Press.

Dickenson, S. (2018). *The Monster Baru Cormorant (The Masquerade Book 2)*. Tor Books.

Dryer, D. (2013). Scaling writing ability: A corpus-driven inquiry. *Written Communication, 30*(1), 3–35. https://doi.org/10.1177/0741088312466992.

East, M. & Cushing, S. (2016). Editorial: Innovation in rubric use: Exploring different dimensions. *Assessing Writing, 30*, 1–2. https://doi.org/10.1016/j.asw.2016.09.001.

Elliot, N. (2005). *On a scale: A social history of writing assessments in America*. Peter Lang.

Ericsson, P. F. (2005). Celebrating through interrogation: Considering the outcomes statement through theoretical lenses. In S. Harrington, K. Rhodes, R. O. Fischer & R. Malenczyk (Eds.), *The outcomes book: Debate and consensus after the WPA outcomes statement*. Utah State University Press.

Eubanks, D. (2018). Addressing the assessment paradox. *Peer Review, 20* (4), 30–31. https://d38xzozy36dxrv.cloudfront.net/qa/content/magazines/PR_FA18_ Vol20No4.pdf.

Gannon, K. M. (2020). *Radical hope: A teaching manifesto.* West Virginia University.

Gallagher, C. W. (2012). The trouble with outcomes: Pragmatic inquiry and educational aims. *College English, 75*(1), 42–60. https://www.jstor.org/stable /24238306.

Gallagher, C. W. (2016). Our Trojan horse: Outcomes assessment and the resurrection of competency-based education. In N. Welch & T. Scott (Eds.), *Composition in the age of austerity* (pp. 21–34). Utah State University Press.

Grace, L., Zurawski, C. & Sinding, C. (2014). A workshop dialogue: Institutional circuits and the front-line work of self-governance. In A. Griffith & D. Smith (Eds.), *Under new public management: Institutional ethnography of changing front-line work.* University of Toronto Press.

Griffin, M. (2010). What is a rubric? In T. L. Rhodes (Ed.). *Assessing outcomes and improving achievement: Tips and tools for using rubrics* (pp. 9–10). Association of American Colleges and Universities.

Griffith, A. (2006). Constructing single parent families for schooling: Discovering an institutional discourse. In D. E. Smith (Ed.). *Institutional ethnography as practice* (pp. 127–138). Rowman & Littlefield.

Griffith, A. & Smith, D. (Eds.). (2014). *Under new public management: Institutional ethnographies of changing front-line work.* University of Toronto Press.

Grouling, J. (2017). The path to competency-based certification: A look at the LEAP Challenge and the VALUE rubric for written communication. *Journal of Writing Assessment, 10*(1). https://escholarship.org/uc/item/5575w31k.

Hall, C. & Thomas, S. (2012). *"Advocacy philanthropy" and the public policy agenda: The role of modern foundations in American higher education.* American Educational Research Association.

Harrington, S., Rhodes, K., Fischer, R. & Malenczyk, R. (Eds.). (2005). *Outcomes book: Debate and consensus after the WPA outcomes statement.* Utah State University Press.

Harrington, S. & Weeden, S. (2009). Assessment changes for the long haul: Dynamic criteria mapping at Indiana University Purdue University Indianapolis. In B. Broad, L. Adler-Kassner, B. Alford, J. Detweiler, H. Estrem, S. Harrington, M. McBride, E. Stalions & S. Weeden (Eds.), *Organic writing assessment: Dynamic criteria mapping in action* (pp. 75–118). Utah State University Press.

Haswell, R. H. (2014). Paul B. Diederich? Which Paul B. Diederich? *Journal of Writing Assessment, 7*(1). http://www.journalofwritingassessment.org/article.php?article=58.

Hawthorne, J. (2008). Accountability & comparability: What's wrong with the VSA approach. *Liberal Education. 94*(2).

Hudelson, E. (1923). The development and comparative values of composition studies. *The English Journal, 12*(3), 163–168.

Huot, B. (2002). (Re)articulating writing assessment for teaching and learning. Utah State University Press.

Inoue, A. B. (2015). *Antiracist writing assessment ecologies: Teaching and assessing writing for a socially just future.* The WAC Clearinghouse; Parlor Press. https://doi.org/10 .37514/PER-B.2015.0698.

Inoue, A. B. (2019). *Labor-Based Grading Contracts: Building Equity and Inclusion in the Compassionate Writing Classroom*. The WAC Clearinghouse; University Press of Colorado. https://doi.org/10.37514/PER-B.2019.0216.0.

Inoue, A.B. (2021a, April 24). Update—CWPA response to my call for a boycott. *Asao B. Inoue's Infrequent Words*. [Blog post] https://asaobinoue.blogspot.com/2021/04/update-cwpa-response-to-my-call-for.html.

Inoue, A.B. (2021b, Oct. 1). *How writing teachers dismantle White language supremacy* [Conference Presentation]. 2021 Conference for Antiracist Teaching, Language, and Assessment. Virtual.

Institute of Education Sciences (IES). (n.d.). Fast facts: Race/ethnicity of college faculty. National Center for Educational Statistics. Retrieved April 19, 2021 from https://nces.ed.gov/fastfacts/display.asp?id=61#

Integrated Postsecondary Education Data System (IPEDS). (n.d.). National Center for Education Statistics. Retrieved April 19, 2021, from https://nces.ed.gov/ipeds/.

Johnson, F. W. (1913). The Hillegas-Thorndike scale for measurement of quality in English composition by young people. *The School Review*, *21*(1), 39–49.

Johnson, J. (2021, March 20). *Event: AWAC Workshop: WAC pedagogy, equity, and anti-racism*. [Electronic mailing list message] WPA-Announcements.

Jones, K. & Okun, T. (2001). The characteristics of White supremacy culture. In *Dismantling racism: A workbook for social change*. https://surj.org/resources/white-supremacy-culture-characteristics/.

Jones, N. N., Gonzales, L. & Hass, A.M. (2021). "So you think you're ready to build new social justice initiatives?" Intentional and coalitional pro-Black programmatic and organizational leadership in writing studies. *WPA: Writing Program Administration 44* (3), 29–35. https://wpacouncil.org/aws/CWPA/asset_manager/get_file/604407?ver=1.

Kelly-Riley, D. (2012). Getting off the boat and onto the bank: Exploring the validity of shared evaluation methods for students of color in college writing assessment. In A. B. Inoue & M. Poe (Eds.), *Race and Writing Assessment* (pp. 29–43). Peter Lang.

Kelly-Riley, D. & Elliot, N. (Eds.). (2021). *Improving outcomes: Disciplinary writing, local assessment, and the aim of fairness*. The Modern Language Association of America.

Killen, R. (2016, March 2). William Spady: A paradigm pioneer. [Fact sheet]. Department for Education South Australia. https://www.education.sa.gov.au/doc/william-spady-paradigm-pioneer.

Kleinfeld, E. (2020). From great to good enough: Recalibrating expectations as WPA. In L. Micciche, C. Wooten, J. Babb, K. Costello & K. Navickas (Eds.), *The things we carry: Strategies for recognizing and negotiating emotional labor in writing program administration* (pp. 237–250). Utah State University Press.

Kynard, C. (2021). Afterword: "Troubling the boundaries" of Anti-racism: The clarity of Black radical visions and racial erasure. *WPA: Writing Program Administration 44* (3), 185–192. https://wpacouncil.org/aws/CWPA/asset_manager/get_file/604410?ver=1.

LaFrance, M. (2019). *Institutional ethnography: A theory of practice for Writing Studies researchers*. Utah State University Press.

LaFrance, M. & Nicolas, M. (2012). Institutional ethnography as materialist framework for writing program research and the faculty-staff work standpoints project. *College Composition and Communication, 64*(1), 130–150. https://www.jstor.org/stable/23264923.

Laubach Wright, A. (2017). The rhetoric of excellence and the erasure of graduate labor. In S. Kahn, W. Lalicker & A. Lynch-Biniek (Eds.), *Contingency, exploitation, and solidarity: Labor and action in English composition* (pp. 271–278). The WAC Clearinghouse; University Press of Colorado. https://doi.org/10.37514/PER-B.2017.0858.2.17.

Levi, A.J. & Stevens, D. D. (2010). Assessment of the academy, for the academy, by the academy. In T. L. Rhodes, T. L. (Ed.). (2010). *Assessing outcomes and improving achievement: Tips and tools for using rubrics.* Association of American Colleges and Universities.

Lynne, P. (2004). *Coming to terms: A theory of writing assessment.* Utah State University Press.

MacNealy, M. S. (1998). *Strategies for empirical research in writing.* Pearson.

Maki, P. (2015) Assessment that works: A national call, a twenty-first-century response. Association of American Colleges and Universities.

Martinez, A. Y. (2020). *Counterstory: The rhetoric and writing of critical race theory.* National Council of Teachers of English.

McClellan, E. (2016). What a long, strange trip it's been: Three decades of outcomes assessment in higher education. *PS: Political Science & Politics, 49*(1), 88–92. https://doi.org/10.1017/S1049096515001298.

McConnell, K.D., Horan, E.M., Zimmerman, B. & Rhodes, T.L. (2019). We have a rubric for that: The VALUE approach to assessment. Association of American Colleges and Universities.

McConnell, K. D. & Rhodes, T. L. (2017). *On solid ground: VALUE report 2017.* Association of American Colleges and Universities. https://www.aacu.org/research/on-solid-ground.

McCoy, L. (2014). Producing "What the Deans Know": Cost accounting and restructuring of post-secondary education. In D. E. Smith & S. M. Tuner (Eds.), *Incorporating texts into institutional ethnographies* (pp. 93–119). University of Toronto Press.

Merisotis, J.P. (2014). Foreword: It's time to define quality—for student's sake. In C. Adelman, P. Ewell, P. Gaston & C. G. Schneider. *The Degree Qualifications Profile.* Lumina Foundation. https://www.learningoutcomesassessment.org/dqp/.

Mette Morcke, A., Dornan, T. & Eika, B. (2013). Outcome (competency) based education: An exploration of its origins, theoretical basis, and empirical evidence. *Advances in Health Science Education, 18*, 851–863. https://doi.org/10.1007/s10459-012-9405-9.

Miller, C. (2017). Where do genres come from? In C. Miller & A. R. Kelly (Eds.), *Emerging Genres in New Media Environments.* https://doi.org/10.1007/978-3-319-40295-6_1.

Mutnick, D. (2016). Confessions of an assessment fellow. In N. Welch & T. Scott (Eds.), *Composition in the age of austerity.* Utah State University Press.

Navickas, K. (2020). The emotional labor of becoming: Lessons from the exiting writing center director. In L. Micciche, C. Wooten, J. Babb, K. Costello & K. Navickas (Eds.), *The things we carry: Strategies for recognizing and negotiating emotional labor in writing program administration* (pp. 56–74). Utah State University Press.

Newkirk, T. (1992). Narrative roots of case study. In G. Kirsch & Sullivan (Eds.), *Methods and methodology: Issues in composition research* (pp. 139–152). Southern Illinois University Press.

Nichols, N., Griffith, A. & McLarnon, M. (2017). Community-based and participatory approaches in institutional ethnography. In J. Reid & L. Russell (Eds.), *Perspectives on and from institutional ethnography* (Vol. 15, pp. 107–123). Bingley: Emerald.

North, S. M. (1984). The idea of a writing center. *College English, 46*(5), 433–446. https://doi.org/10.2307/377047.

O'Neill, P., Moore, C. & Huot, B. (2009). *A guide to college writing assessment.* Utah State University Press.

Peacock, D. (2017). Institutional ethnography, critical discourse analysis and the discursive coordination of organizational activity. In J. Reid & L. Russell (Eds.), *Perspectives on and from institutional ethnography* (Vol. 15, pp. 91–106). Emerald.

Poblete, P. (2021, April 21). How to respond when you're BIPOC and your organization is called out for racism. *WPA: Writing Program Administration 44* (3), 181–184. https://wpacouncil.org/aws/CWPA/asset_manager/get_file/604418?ver=1.

Rankin, J. (December 2017a). Conducting analysis in institutional ethnography: Analytical work prior to commencing data collection. *The International Journal of Qualitative Methods, 16*(1). https://doi.org/10.1177/1609406917734484.

Rankin, J. (October 2017b). Conducting analysis in institutional ethnography: Guidance and cautions. *International Journal of Qualitative Methods, 16*(1), 1–11. https://doi.org/10.1177/1609406917734472.

Reid, J. (2017). Relfexivity and praxis: The redress of "I" poems in revealing standpoint. In L. Russell & J. Reid (Eds.), *Perspectives on and from institutional ethnography* (pp. 29–48). Emerald.

Rhodes, K., Peckman, I., Bergmann, L. & Condon, W. (2005). The outcomes project: The insiders' history. In S. Harrington, K. Rhodes, R. O. Fischer & R. Malenczyk (Eds.), *Outcomes book: Debate and consensus after the WPA outcomes statement* (pp. 8–17). Utah State University Press.

Rhodes, T. L. (Ed.). (2010). *Assessing outcomes and improving achievement: Tips and tools for using rubrics.* Association of American Colleges and Universities.

Rhodes, T.L. (2012). Show me the learning: Value, accreditation, and the quality of the degree. *Planning for Higher Education, 40,* 36-42.

Rhodes, T. L. & Finley, A. (2013). *Using the VALUE rubrics for improvement of learning and authentic assessment.* Association of American Colleges and Universities.

Rhodes, T.L. & McConnell, K.D. (2021, February 12). *The landscape of learning: Findings from 5 years of AAC&U's Nationwide VALUE assessment initiative* [Conference presentation]. 2021 Conference on General Education, Pedagogy, and Assessment: Embracing the Best Practices for Quality and Equity. Virtual.

Rhodes, T.L., Watson, C.E., Hathcoat, J.D., Orcutt, B. & Stout, S. (2019, October 30). *The emerging landscape of learning: A review of five years of AAC&U's VALUE Initiative.* [Webinar]. Show me the learning: Value, accreditation, and the quality of the degree.

Rice, J. M. (1914). *Scientific management in education.* Hinds, Noble & Eldredge.

Russell, L. (2017). Introduction. In L. Russell & J. Reid (Eds.), *Perspectives on and from institutional ethnography* (pp. 1–28). Emerald.

Russell, D. R. (2002). *Writing in the academic disciplines: A curricular history* (2nd ed.). Southern Illinois University Press.

Rutz, C. (2016, October 18). *What can we learn about faculty development? Prizes and surprises* [Conference presentation]. Assessment Institute, Indianapolis, IN, United States.

Schneider, C. G. (2015). Foreword. In Association of American Colleges and Universities, *General education maps and markers: Designing meaningful pathways to student achievement.* Association of American Colleges and Universities.

Scott, T. & Welch, N. (2016). Introduction: Composition in the age of austerity. In N. Welch & T. Scott (Eds.). *Composition in the age of austerity.* Utah State University Press.

Seal, A. (2018, June 8). How the university became neoliberal. *The Chronicle of Higher Education.* https://www.chronicle.com/article/How-the-University-Became/243622.

Seawright, L. (2017). *Genre of power: Police report writers and readers in the justice system.* National Council of Teachers of English.

Sharer, W., Morse, T. A., Eble, M. F. & Banks, W. P. (Eds.). (2016). *Reclaiming accountability: Improving writing programs through accreditation and large-scale assessments.* Utah State University Press.

Smith, D. E. (2005). *Institutional ethnography: A sociology for people.* AltaMira.

Smith, D. E. (2006). Introduction. In D.E. Smith (Ed.). *Institutional ethnography as practice* (pp. 1–12). Rowman & Littlefield.

Smith, D. E. (2014). Discourse as social relations: Sociology theory and the dialogic of sociology. In D. Smith & S. M. Tuner (Eds.), *Incorporating texts into institutional ethnographies* (pp. 225–252). University of Toronto Press.

Smith, D. & Turner, S. M. (2014). *Incorporating texts into institutional ethnographies.* University of Toronto Press.

Smith, G. (2014). Policing the gay community: An inquiry into textually-mediated social relations. In D. Smith & S. M. Turner (Eds.), *Incorporating texts into institutional ethnographies* (pp. 17–40). University of Toronto Press.

Spady, W. G. & Marshall, K. J. (1991). Beyond traditional outcomes-based education. *Educational Leadership, 49*(2).

Strickland, D. (2011). *The managerial unconscious in the history of composition studies.* Southern Illinois University Press.

Sullivan, D. F. (2015). *The VALUE breakthrough: Getting the assessment of student learning in college right.* Association of American Colleges and Universities.

Talbot, D. (2017). The dialogic production of informant specific maps. In J. Reid & L. Russell (Eds.), *Perspectives on and from institutional ethnography* (pp. 1–28). Emerald.

Talbot, D. (2020). Institutional ethnography and the materiality of affect: Affective circuits as indicators of other possibilities. *Journal of Contemporary Ethnography, 49*(5). https://doi.org/10.1177/0891241620943276.

Thaiss, C. & Zawacki, T. (2006). *Engaged writers and dynamic disciplines: Research on the academic writing life.* Heinemann.

Trimbur, J. (1989). Consensus and difference in collaborative learning. *College English, 51*(6), 602–616. https://doi.org/10.2307/377955.

Tummons, J. (2017). Institutional ethnography, theory, methodology, and research: Some concerns and some comments. In J. Reid & L. Russell (Eds.), *Perspectives on and from institutional ethnography* (vol. 15; pp. 147–162). Emerald Group.

Turley, E. D. & Gallagher, C. W. (2008). On the "uses" of rubrics: Reframing the great rubric debate. *The English Journal, 97*(4), 87–92. https://www.jstor.org/stable/30047253.

Turner, S. M. (2006). Mapping institutions as work and texts. In D.E. Smith (Ed.), *Institutional ethnography as practice* (pp. 139–162). Rowman & Littlefield.

Turner, S. M. (2014). Reading practices in decision processes. In D. E. Smith & S. M. Turner (Eds.), *Incorporating texts into institutional ethnographies* (pp. 197–224). University of Toronto Press.

Voluntary System of Accountability. (2012). *Administration and reporting guidelines: AAC&U VALUE rubric: Demonstration project.* https://cp-files.s3.amazonaws.com/32/AAC_U_VALUE_Rubrics_Administration_Guidelines_20121210.pdf.

VSA Analytics. (n.d.). About VSA Analytics. Retrieved March 10, 2022. https://www.vsaanalytics.org/about.

Walby, K. (2007). On the social relations of research: A critical assessment of institutional ethnography. *Qualitative Inquiry, 13*(7), 1008–1030. https://doi.org/10.1177/1077800407305809.

Walker, K. (2018). *Reporting, assessment and accountability: A genre study of writing center reports* [Doctoral dissertation, Ball State University]. Cardinal Scholar.

White, E. M. (2005). The origins of the outcomes statement. In S. Harrington, K. Rhodes, R. O. Fischer & R. Malenczyk (Eds.), *The outcomes book: Debate and consensus after the WPA Outcomes Statement* (pp. 3–7). Utah State University Press.

Wood, S. (2020). Engaging in resistant genres as antiracist teacher response. *Journal of Writing Assessment, 13*(2). https://escholarship.org/uc/item/2c45c0gf.

Wiley, M. (2005). Outcomes are not mandates for standardization. In S. Harrington, K. Rhodes, R. O. Fischer & R. Malenczyk (Eds.), *The outcomes book: Debate and consensus after the WPA outcomes statement* (pp. 24–31). Utah State University Press.

Wilson, M. (2006). *Rethinking rubrics in writing assessment.* Heinemann.

Yancey, K. B. (1999). Looking back as we look forward: Historicizing writing assessment. *College Composition and Communication, 50*(3), 483–503. https://doi.org/10.2307/358862.

Yancey, K. B. (2005). Standards, outcomes, and all that jazz. In S. Harrington, K. Rhodes, R. O. Fischer & R. Malenczyk (Eds.), *The outcomes book: Debate and consensus after the WPA outcomes statement* (pp. 18–23). Utah State University Press.

Yates, J. (1989). *Control through communication: The rise of system in American management.* The Johns Hopkins University Press.

Zawacki, T. M. & Gentemann, K. M. (2009). Merging a culture of writing with a culture of assessment: Embedded, discipline-based writing assessment. In M. C. Paretti & K. Powell (Eds.), *Assessment in writing* (Vol. 4). Association of Institutional Research.

Zawacki, T.M.; Reid, E.S.; Zhou, Y. & Baker, S.E. (2009). Voices at the table: Balancing the needs and wants of program stakeholders to design a value-added writing assessment plan. *Across the Disciplines, 6.* https://doi.org/10.37514/ATD-J.2009.6.1.03

Zilvinskis, J., Nelson Laird, T.L. & Graham, P.A. (2016, Oct.). *Faculty use of rubrics: An examination across multiple institutions.* [PowerPoint slides]. 2016 Assessment Institute, Indianapolis, IN, United States. https://scholarworks.iu.edu/dspace/bitstream/handle/2022/23902/Faculty%20use%20of%20rubrics-%20An%20examination%20across%20multiple%20institutions.pdf?sequence=1&isAllowed=y.

RESEARCH PARTICIPANTS / "CAST OF CHARACTERS"

This appendix provides a quick guide to who's who at Oak and St. Rita's for easy reference while reading. The main informant at each school is listed first, and then each list is in alphabetical order. All names are pseudonyms. Only those participants mentioned in the book are included.

OAK UNIVERSITY

Kristen (main informant): A history professor who was the chair of the writing committee at Oak. Kristen was on the writing committee that developed the new writing program and is now the one in charge of developing the program assessment during my study. She attended training from the AAC&U and loves rubrics.

Amelia: A chemist who represents the sciences on the writing committee. Amelia also participated in the 2017 summer assessment workshop, which was a test run of the writing program assessment process.

Ben: A computer scientist and former Dean of First-Year Students, Ben was the first writing committee chair and instrumental in forming the new writing program. He was not on the writing committee at the time of this study but did participate in the Summer 2018 assessment. Ben was also trained by the AAC&U in using the VALUE rubrics.

Brenda: Director of the Writing Center at Oak, Brenda was involved in the field of writing studies, including SLAC-WPA (small liberal arts colleges' writing program administrators). However, Brenda was not directly involved with the writing committee or assessment of the new writing program.

Brad: An art history professor who was a member of the writing committee during the study. Brad considers himself a "critical pedagogue" and has attended many workshops on teaching writing.

Erin: Sociology professor who participated in the 2018 writing program assessment.

Eshaal: Faculty participant in the 2017 assessment workshop (not interviewed)

Jon: A political science professor who was involved in the 2018 writing program assessment. Jon had previously used the VALUE rubrics for other assessment efforts on campus and had attended training sessions with the AAC&U.

Marisella: Spanish professor who participated in the program assessment in summer 2018.

Nina: An environmental scientist, Nina served as an interdisciplinary representative on the writing committee during this study.

Phillip: The associate provost at the time of this study, Philip worked closely with the AAC&U and the grants that Oak received from them. He also personally underwent the training to use the VALUE rubrics and did scoring with the Civic Engagement VALUE rubric.

Ronnie: English department chair and ex-officio member of the writing committee.

Shawna: A religious studies professor who participated in the 2017 assessment workshop.

Shirong: History professor from Singapore who represents the humanities on the writing committee.

Wendy: Coordinator of Multilingual Learning who participated in the 2018 assessment.

ST. RITA'S

Dwayne (main informant): Originally a creative writer, Dwayne has a strong background in writing pedagogy and assessment. He was the one to introduce the VALUE rubrics to St. Rita's. He is on the general education committee where he leads the discussion about rubrics and writing. He also regularly coordinates portfolio scoring for first-year writing courses.

Andrea: Math professor and co-chair of the general education committee.

Gerald Z: Chair of the humanities department and a member of the general education committee during my site visit, although he was later removed from both positions. He has a literature background and teaches English. Gerald is the only participant to bear a last name pseudonym as his colleagues commonly refer to him by Dr. and his last initial.

Heather: Formerly part-time, now full-time faculty member in English who taught writing and coordinated the freshman learning communities.

Jeremy: English professor and co-chair of the general education committee. Jeremy also taught the remedial first-year writing courses.

Jessica: Not technically a participant in my study, Jessica is a former faculty member in English who came from rhet/comp. Dwayne still collaborates with her and mentions her several times during his interviews.

Lucinda: An English professor who was Vice President for Academic Affairs at the time of the study.

Patrice: Faculty member in the social sciences. She teaches political science, history and sociology. A member of the general education committee.

Thomas: Business professor on the general education committee (not interviewed)

APPENDIX B.
WRITTEN COMMUNICATION VALUE RUBRIC

The VALUE rubrics[13] were developed by teams of faculty experts representing colleges and universities across the United States through a process that examined many existing campus rubrics and related documents for each learning outcome and incorporated additional feedback from faculty. The rubrics articulate fundamental criteria for each learning outcome, with performance descriptors demonstrating progressively more sophisticated levels of attainment. The rubrics are intended for institutional-level use in evaluating and discussing student learning, not for grading. The core expectations articulated in all 15 of the VALUE rubrics can and should be translated into the language of individual campuses, disciplines, and even courses. The utility of the VALUE rubrics is to position learning at all undergraduate levels within a basic framework of expectations such that evidence of learning can by shared nationally through a common dialog and understanding of student success.

Definition

Written communication is the development and expression of ideas in writing. Written communication involves learning to work in many genres and styles. It can involve working with many different writing technologies, and mixing texts, data, and images. Written communication abilities develop through iterative experiences across the curriculum.

Framing Language

This writing rubric is designed for use in a wide variety of educational institutions. The most clear finding to emerge from decades of research on writing assessment is that the best writing assessments are locally determined and sensitive to local context and mission. Users of this rubric should, in the end, consider making adaptations and additions that clearly link the language of the rubric to individual campus contexts.

This rubric focuses assessment on how specific written work samples or collections of work respond to specific contexts. The central question guiding the rubric is "How well does writing respond to the needs of audience(s) for the work?" In focusing on this question the rubric does not attend to other aspects

---

13   For more information, please contact value@aacu.org.

of writing that are equally important: issues of writing process, writing strategies, writers' fluency with different modes of textual production or publication, or writer's growing engagement with writing and disciplinarity through the process of writing.

Evaluators using this rubric must have information about the assignments or purposes for writing guiding writers' work. Also recommended is including reflective work samples of collections of work that address such questions as: What decisions did the writer make about audience, purpose, and genre as s/ he compiled the work in the portfolio? How are those choices evident in the writing—in the content, organization and structure, reasoning, evidence, mechanical and surface conventions, and citational systems used in the writing? This will enable evaluators to have a clear sense of how writers understand the assignments and take it into consideration as they evaluate

The first section of this rubric addresses the context and purpose for writing. A work sample or collections of work can convey the context and purpose for the writing tasks it showcases by including the writing assignments associated with work samples. But writers may also convey the context and purpose for their writing within the texts. It is important for faculty and institutions to include directions for students about how they should represent their writing contexts and purposes.

Faculty interested in the research on writing assessment that has guided our work here can consult the National Council of Teachers of English / Council of Writing Program Administrators' White Paper on Writing Assessment (2008; www.wpacouncil.org/ whitepaper) and the Conference on College Composition and Communication's Writing Assessment: A Position Statement (2008; www. ncte.org/cc/resources/positions/123784.htm)

Glossary

The definitions that follow were developed to clarify terms and concepts used in this rubric only.

- Content Development: The ways in which the text explores and represents its topic in relation to its audience and purpose.
- Context of and purpose for writing: The context of writing is the situation surrounding a text: who is reading it? who is writing it? Under what circumstances will the text be shared or circulated? What social or political factors might affect how the text is composed or interpreted? The purpose for writing is the writer's intended effect on an audience. Writers might want to persuade or inform; they might want to report or summarize information; they might want to work through complexity or confusion; they might want to argue with other writers,

or connect with other writers; they might want to convey urgency or amuse; they might write for themselves or for an assignment or to remember.

- Disciplinary conventions: Formal and informal rules that constitute what is seen generally as appropriate within different academic fields, e.g. introductory strategies, use of passive voice or first person point of view, expectations for thesis or hypothesis, expectations for kinds of evidence and support that are appropriate to the task at hand, use of primary and secondary sources to provide evidence and support arguments and to document critical perspectives on the topic. Writers will incorporate sources according to disciplinary and genre conventions, according to the writer's purpose for the text. Through increasingly sophisticated use of sources, writers develop an ability to differentiate between their own ideas and the ideas of others, credit and build upon work already accomplished in the field or issue they are addressing, and provide meaningful examples to readers.
- Evidence: Source material that is used to extend, in purposeful ways, writers' ideas in a text.
- Genre conventions: Formal and informal rules for particular kinds of texts and/ or media that guide formatting, organization, and stylistic choices, e.g. lab reports, academic papers, poetry, webpages, or personal essays.
- Sources: Texts (written, oral, behavioral, visual, or other) that writers draw on as they work for a variety of purposes—to extend, argue with, develop, define, or shape their ideas, for example.

Written communication is the development and expression of ideas in writing. Written communication involves learning to work in many genres and styles. It can involve working with many different writing technologies, and mixing texts, data, and images. Written communication abilities develop through iterative experiences across the curriculum.

Evaluators are encouraged to assign a zero to any work sample or collection of work that does not meet benchmark (cell one) level performance.

Note: The formatting of the rubric that appears on the following pages has been modified to fit this book.

	Capstone 4	Milestones		Benchmark 1
		3	2	
Context of and Purpose for Writing *Includes considerations of audience, purpose, and the circumstances surrounding the writing task(s).*	Demonstrates a thorough understanding of context, audience, and purpose that is responsive to the assigned task(s) and focuses all elements of the work.	Demonstrates adequate consideration of context, audience, and purpose and a clear focus on the assigned task(s) (e.g., the task aligns with audience, purpose, and context).	Demonstrates awareness of context, audience, purpose, and to the assigned tasks(s) (e.g., begins to show awareness of audience's perceptions and assumptions).	Demonstrates minimal attention to context, audience, purpose, and to the assigned tasks(s) (e.g., expectation of instructor or self as audience).
Content Development	Uses appropriate, relevant, and compelling content to illustrate mastery of the subject, conveying the writer's understanding, and shaping the whole work.	Uses appropriate, relevant, and compelling content to explore ideas within the context of the discipline and shape the whole work.	Uses appropriate and relevant content to develop and explore ideas through most of the work.	Uses appropriate and relevant content to develop simple ideas in some parts of the work.
Genre and Disciplinary Conventions *Formal and informal rules inherent in the expectations for writing in particular forms and/ or academic fields (please see glossary).*	Demonstrates detailed attention to and successful execution of a wide range of conventions particular to a specific discipline and/ or writing task (s) including organization, content, presentation, formatting, and stylistic choices	Demonstrates consistent use of important conventions particular to a specific discipline and/or writing task(s), including organization, content, presentation, and stylistic choices	Follows expectations appropriate to a specific discipline and/ or writing task(s) for basic organization, content, and presentation	Attempts to use a consistent system for basic organization and presentation.

	Capstone 4	Milestones 3	Milestones 2	Benchmark 1
Sources and Evidence	Demonstrates skillful use of high-quality, credible, relevant sources to develop ideas that are appropriate for the discipline and genre of the writing	Demonstrates consistent use of credible, relevant sources to support ideas that are situated within the discipline and genre of the writing.	Demonstrates an attempt to use credible and/or relevant sources to support ideas that are appropriate for the discipline and genre of the writing.	Demonstrates an attempt to use sources to support ideas in the writing.
Control of Syntax and Mechanics	Uses graceful language that skillfully communicates meaning to readers with clarity and fluency, and is virtually error-free.	Uses straightforward language that generally conveys meaning to readers. The language in the portfolio has few errors.	Uses language that generally conveys meaning to readers with clarity, although writing may include some errors.	Uses language that sometimes impedes meaning because of errors in usage.

APPENDIX C.

"PARTS OF THE VALUE RUBRIC" FROM THE AMERICAN ASSOCIATION OF COLLEGES AND UNIVERSITIES

v∨lue RUBRICS | Learning Outcome → | **CRITICAL THINKING VALUE RUBRIC**
For more information, please contact value@aacu.org | AAC&U

The VALUE rubrics were developed by teams of faculty experts representing colleges and universities across the United States through a process that examined many existing campus rubrics and related documents for each learning outcome and incorporated additional feedback from faculty. The rubrics articulate fundamental criteria for each learning outcome, with performance descriptors demonstrating progressively more sophisticated levels of attainment. The rubrics are intended for institutional-level use in evaluating and discussing student learning, not for grading. The core expectations articulated in all 16 of the VALUE rubrics can and should be translated into the language of individual campuses, disciplines, and even courses. The utility of the VALUE rubrics is to position learning at all undergraduate levels within a basic frame[**Definition**]ons such that evidence of learning can by shared nationally through a common dialog and understanding of student success.

Definition
Critical thinking is a habit of mind characterized by the comprehensive exploration of issues, ideas, artifacts, and events before accepting or formulating an opinion or conclusion.

Framing Language
This rubric is designed to be transdisciplinary, reflecting the recognition that success in all disciplines requires habits of inquiry and analysis that share common attributes. Further, research suggests that successful critical thinkers from all disciplines increasingly need to be able to apply those habits in various and changing situations encountered in all walks of life.

This rubric is designed for use with many different types of assignments and the suggestions here are not an exhaustive list of [ ]cal thinking can be demonstrated in assignments that require students to complete analyses of text, data, or issues. Assignments [**Framing Language**] presentation mode might be especially useful in some fields. If insight into the process components of critical thinking (e.g., ho[ ] rces were evaluated regardless of whether they were included in the product) is important, assignments focused on student reflect[ ] illuminating.

Glossary
The definitions that follow were developed to clarify terms and concepts used in this rubric only.

- **Ambiguity:** Information that may be interpreted in more than one way.
- **Assumptions:** Ideas, conditions, or beliefs (often implicit or unstated) that are "taken for granted or accepted as true without proof." (Quoted from www.dictionary.reference.com/browse/assumptions)
- **Context:** The historical, ethical. political, cultural, environmental, or circumstantial settings or conditions that influence and complicate the consideration of any issues, ideas, artifacts, and events.
- **Literal meaning:** Interpretation of information exactly as stated. For example, "she was green with envy" would be interpreted to mean that her skin was green.
- **Metaphor:** Information that is (intended to be) interpreted in a non-literal way. For example, "she was green with envy" is intended to convey an intensity of emotion, not a skin color.

[**Glossary**]

Continued on the next page

Appendix C

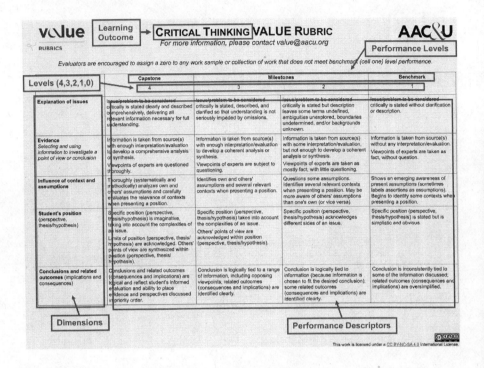

v∧lue RUBRICS — Learning Outcome → **CRITICAL THINKING VALUE RUBRIC**
For more information, please contact value@aacu.org

AAC&U

Performance Levels

Evaluators are encouraged to assign a zero to any work sample or collection of work that does not meet benchmark (cell one) level performance.

Levels (4,3,2,1,0)

Dimensions	Capstone 4	Milestones 3	Milestones 2	Benchmark 1
Explanation of issues	Issue/problem to be considered critically is stated clearly and described comprehensively, delivering all relevant information necessary for full understanding.	Issue/problem to be considered critically is stated, described, and clarified so that understanding is not seriously impeded by omissions.	Issue/problem to be considered critically is stated but description leaves some terms undefined, ambiguities unexplored, boundaries undetermined, and/or backgrounds unknown.	Issue/problem to be considered critically is stated without clarification or description.
Evidence *Selecting and using information to investigate a point of view or conclusion*	Information is taken from source(s) with enough interpretation/evaluation to develop a comprehensive analysis or synthesis. Viewpoints of experts are questioned thoroughly.	Information is taken from source(s) with enough interpretation/evaluation to develop a coherent analysis or synthesis. Viewpoints of experts are subject to questioning.	Information is taken from source(s) with some interpretation/evaluation, but not enough to develop a coherent analysis or synthesis. Viewpoints of experts are taken as mostly fact, with little questioning.	Information is taken from source(s) without any interpretation/evaluation. Viewpoints of experts are taken as fact, without question.
Influence of context and assumptions	Thoroughly (systematically and methodically) analyzes own and others' assumptions and carefully evaluates the relevance of contexts when presenting a position.	Identifies own and others' assumptions and several relevant contexts when presenting a position.	Questions some assumptions. Identifies several relevant contexts when presenting a position. May be more aware of others' assumptions than one's own (or vice versa).	Shows an emerging awareness of present assumptions (sometimes labels assertions as assumptions). Begins to identify some contexts when presenting a position.
Student's position (perspective, thesis/hypothesis)	Specific position (perspective, thesis/hypothesis) is imaginative, taking into account the complexities of an issue. Limits of position (perspective, thesis/hypothesis) are acknowledged. Others' points of view are synthesized within position (perspective, thesis/hypothesis).	Specific position (perspective, thesis/hypothesis) takes into account the complexities of an issue. Others' points of view are acknowledged within position (perspective, thesis/hypothesis).	Specific position (perspective, thesis/hypothesis) acknowledges different sides of an issue.	Specific position (perspective, thesis/hypothesis) is stated but is simplistic and obvious.
Conclusions and related outcomes (implications and consequences)	Conclusions and related outcomes (consequences and implications) are logical and reflect student's informed evaluation and ability to place evidence and perspectives discussed in priority order.	Conclusion is logically tied to a range of information, including opposing viewpoints; related outcomes (consequences and implications) are identified clearly.	Conclusion is logically tied to information (because information is chosen to fit the desired conclusion); some related outcomes (consequences and implications) are identified clearly.	Conclusion is inconsistently tied to some of the information discussed; related outcomes (consequences and implications) are oversimplified.

Dimensions

Performance Descriptors

APPENDIX D.

OAK WRITING PROGRAM ASSESSMENT RUBRIC

This rubric was gathered at the Summer 2018 assessment and is one of several versions studied.

ASSESSMENT RUBRIC

Assessment Area 1: Argument

Based on this artifact, the student's ability to craft and support a cogent argument could best be characterized as:

Weak			Developing			Stable			Mature
1	2	3	4	5	6	7	8	9	10

Assessment Area 2: Audience & Community

Based on this artifact, the student's ability to anticipate the needs of his/her audience could best be characterized as:

Weak			Developing			Stable			Mature
1	2	3	4	5	6	7	8	9	10

Assessment Area 3: Evidence

Based on this artifact, the student's ability to gather and synthesize evidence could best be characterized as:

Weak			Developing			Stable			Mature
1	2	3	4	5	6	7	8	9	10

Assessment Area 4: Process & Style

Based on this artifact, the student's ability to understand writing as a process and to apply conventions of style and grammar could best be characterized as:

Weak			Developing			Stable			Mature
1	2	3	4	5	6	7	8	9	10

GUIDING LANGUAGE

Assessment Area 1: Argument

Students should be able to craft and support a cogent argument.

- Investigate an idea, identify a compelling question, and demonstrate deep understanding of their subject.
- Formulate a clear thesis.
- Establish, support and develop an argument using evidence appropriately.
- Organize ideas effectively.

Weak	Students struggle to formulate a clear thesis. They often write about multiple, competing ideas. Their writing lacks focus and does not demonstrate an understanding of the material. They fail to incorporate relevant evidence, and their organization seems haphazard.
Developing	Students formulate a simplistic, shallow thesis. Their writing is observational rather than analytical. Their evidence is often rudimentary, consisting of lists of examples that are more or less relevant. They often fail, however, to connect their evidence directly to their claims. They employ superficial or ineffective organizational strategies.
Stable	Students formulate a clear thesis that is based on analysis, and moves beyond observation. Students accumulate and present evidence to build a case for their argument. They organize their ideas within a clear system that allows readers to follow the argument. They demonstrate an effort to guide the reader from one point to the next.
Mature	Students formulate an insightful, imaginative, compelling thesis. They engage critically with the nuances of the subject matter in ways that go beyond the obvious. Students find creative and persuasive evidence that supports a strong argument. Students employ sophisticated and effective organizational techniques; transitions between points are seamless.

Assessment Area 2: Audience & Community

Students should be able to anticipate and meet the needs of their audience.

- Provide context in their writing.
- Understand and apply discipline-specific conventions.
- See their own writing from the viewpoint of others.
- Evaluate and critique other people's writing and respond to critiques of their own writing.

Note: We recognize the difficulty of assessing the third and fourth bullet points based on a single, isolated artifact. Our guiding language for Area 2 thus focuses primarily on the first and second bullet points, but we have tried to indicate how scorers might take factors like internal consistency and students' self-awareness into account when considering this assessment area.

Weak	Students make little or no effort to consider the needs of their audience as they write, often leaving key ideas unexplained or uncontextualized. Students make little effort to employ discipline-specific conventions. The tone and mode of address often shift throughout the paper, leaving the reader confused and unable to follow the author's points. At this level, students are generally unable to convey that their writing is part of a larger conversation within a community, whether disciplinary or otherwise.
Developing	Students demonstrate an occasional but inconsistent awareness of their audience, contextualizing some ideas appropriately but not others. Their work indicates a superficial understanding of discipline-specific conventions, but they are not used regularly or well. At times the author's tone and mode of address make their ideas easy to follow, but some ideas are still vague or muddled. Students seem cognizant of the need to situate their writing within a larger conversation or community, but may not execute this task well.
Stable	Students demonstrate a consistent awareness of their audience, contextualizing their ideas appropriately. Their writing indicates a reasonable but not masterful command of discipline-specific conventions. Their tone and mode of address are consistent throughout the paper, suggesting an understanding of the community within which they're writing. Students are able to put their work in conversation with others' ideas, although they may not do this evenly throughout the paper.
Mature	Students invite their audience into their work, and consciously guide their readers throughout the entire paper. Students demonstrate a consistent mastery of discipline-specific conventions, employing them with care and nuance. Their tone and address are not only appropriate, they also draw the reader in. At this level, students can situate their work within the information landscape; they communicate their ideas as an integral part of larger conversations.

Assessment Area 3: Evidence

Students should be adept at gathering and synthesizing evidence.

- Use research tools fluently.
- Evaluate the credibility of potential research sources.
- Acknowledge the contributions of others through proper citation and engage in the ethical exchange of ideas.
- Integrate sources in rhetorically effective ways.

Note: Not all writing assignments require students to gather textual sources through traditional library research. We have framed this guiding language to try to accommodate a broad spectrum of assignments that require students to incorporate some form of evidence, while acknowledging that "evidence" may take various forms (artistic works, quantitative data, interview transcripts, primary literature, etc.) in different disciplines and genres.

Weak	Students fail to demonstrate effective engagement with their evidence. They often assert opinions without substantiating them. When students do refer to sources or data, they typically are not pertinent to the main argument or not integrated into the argument. Students do not appear to consider the credibility of their sources, and may fail to acknowledge appropriately the words and ideas of others, either by citing sources improperly or by failing to cite at all.
Developing	Students demonstrate some attempt to engage with their evidence. Their sources or data may be relevant to the argument but are not integrated in thoughtful ways. Students' analysis of their sources and/or data may be present, but is shallow or superficial, and they take the credibility of their sources for granted. At this level students often string together series of quotes or bits of information, and/or "drop" evidence into their papers without explanation; they let sources voice their ideas, rather than taking ownership of their arguments. Students cite their sources appropriately, though there may be errors or omissions in formatting.
Stable	Students demonstrate sustained engagement with their evidence. Sources or data are relevant to the argument and integrated in thoughtful ways. Students' analysis of their sources and/or data is logical and provides support for their arguments, and they make some effort to establish the credibility of their sources. Students incorporate evidence in a voice consistent with their overall writing, and demonstrate proper citation conventions as required by specific disciplines.
Mature	At this level, students carefully integrate evidence into their papers in sophisticated and compelling ways. They build their own complex arguments based, for instance, on a nuanced analysis of their data, or on the interplay of others' ideas and their own. At this level, students are able to discern which data or sources are more credible, or which are more appropriate to their arguments. Students' citation practices exemplify the ethical exchange of ideas within their discipline(s).

Assessment Area 4: Process & Style

Students should be able to understand writing as a process and to apply conventions of style and grammar:

- Incorporate the recursive process of writing including pre-writing, revising, drafting, and responding to feedback.
- Exercise control over style, mechanics, and grammar.
- Craft prose that is organized, clear, and concise.

Note: We recognize the difficulty of assessing students' understanding of writing as a process based on a single, isolated artifact. Our guiding language for Area 4 thus focuses primarily on the second and third bullet points, but we have tried to indicate how scorers might take factors like internal consistency into account when assessing the first bullet point.

Weak	At this level, students' work often appears as "early draft" work; it lacks the internal consistency that may come with revision, and the prose lacks clarity and precision. There is often little coherence within and between sentences. The weak quality of the writing frequently distracts the reader from the points the author is trying to convey. Students fail to demonstrate proper use of mechanical and grammatical conventions.
Developing	Students' work is in a more polished state, with more refinement of style and ideas. There is some effort to control tone, style, and flow from sentence to sentence, but with only partial success. Some sentences may still be distracting to the reader, but the instances of incoherence are fewer at this level. Students generally adhere to basic stylistic, mechanical, and grammatical conventions of standard written English.
Stable	Writing at this level suggests the student has revised the paper to create a more cohesive product. Style is more developed and enhances clarity. Thoughts flow logically from one sentence to the next. The prose is generally polished, but may not be elegant or sophisticated. Students adhere consistently to stylistic, mechanical, and grammatical conventions.
Mature	At this level, students' writing moves beyond mere adherence to convention. Their writing demonstrates refined control over tone, style, and flow. Sustained attention to clarity, conciseness, and cohesion creates skillful and engaging prose.

APPENDIX E.

ST. RITA'S "RUBRIC FOR WRITTEN COMMUNICATION ACROSS THE CORE CURRICULUM"

This rubric was uploaded to my 2016 survey. While I saw other drafts over the course of the study, this one remained the dominant one used with "signature assignments" at St. Rita's.

	0*	1 Insufficient	2 Developing	3 Sufficient **	4 Exemplary
Responding to assignments *(Writing appropriately for given situation)*		The purpose of the student work is not well defined and in general the work doesn't respond to the assignment or prompt.	The writer might insufficiently respond to the assignment, might be needlessly repetitive, or might frequently divert from the main purpose of the assignment.	The writer consistently and directly responds to the prompt or assignment and the central purpose of the student work is clear.	The writer engages fully with the assignment or writing prompt, and fully and directly addresses elements of the assignment in an interesting way.
Structure and Coherence *(Sequencing and structuring elements and ideas, moving from general to specific)*		Ideas are poorly sequenced or disconnected, making it difficult to follow. Introduction or conclusion distract from the work or are missing.	Ideas are presented in an order that the audience can follow with some difficulty. Portions of the text wander, digress or are seemingly unrelated.	Ideas are presented, from introduction to body to conclusion, in a logical sequence. The reader can follow with little or no difficulty, and each element of the text is in service of the whole.	Ideas are presented in a logical, engaging, entertaining sequence. The introduction and conclusion effectively serve the purpose of the work.

	0*	1 Insufficient	2 Developing	3 Sufficient **	4 Exemplary
Evidence and Analysis *(Using information and evidence and citing or referring to sources accurately when appropriate)*		Accurately lists evidence from sources or experiences without a clear focus, thesis, or controlling idea.	Accurately organizes evidence with some focus, but *without* revealing significant patterns, differences, or similarities.	Accurately organizes evidence in a way that usefully reveals significant patterns, differences, or similarities.	Accurately organizes *and* synthesizes evidence usefully in order to reveal insightful patterns, differences, or similarities.
Prose Style and Syntax *(Managing sentences, sentence variety, and grammar)*		The work is consistently or significantly distorted by a variety of sentence-level errors: run-ons, fragments, subject-verb disagreement, etc.	While frequently error free, the work consists of one sentence type and falls into slang or dialect English. Syntactical or grammatical errors distract, distort or impede understanding.	The work includes some variety of sentence types, and generally adheres grammatically to standard written English rather than spoken English. It can be read with minimal difficulty.	The work includes a variety of sentence types (simple to compound-complex), is nearly free from grammatical errors, and is easy and engaging to read.
Spelling, Word-Choice, Grammar, and Punctuation *(Typos, homonyms, "text-ese" and slang)*		The reader is consistently or significantly distracted by a variety of errors.	While a variety of errors do distract from the work, it is usually clear what the author intends to say.	The writer is generally in control of language, but the readability of the work is disrupted because the writer *makes one or a few minor errors repeatedly.*	The work is free from typographical errors, and each word seems appropriate and carefully chosen.

* A score of zero (0) should be applied to any student who fails to reach all elements in the "insufficient" column.
** Gen. Ed. Capstone Goal

INDEX